Native and Ornamental Conifers in the Pacific Northwest

Identification, Botany, and Natural History

Elizabeth A. Price

OREGON STATE UNIVERSITY PRESS

CORVALLIS

The John and Shirley Byrne Fund for Books on Nature and the Environment provides generous support that helps make publication of this and other Oregon State University Press books possible.

Cover images:
Top left: *Thujopsis dolabrata* (staghorn-cedar) foliage; top middle: *Pseudotsuga menziesii* (Douglas-fir) detail of ripening cone; top right: *Cedrus libani* (Lebanon cedar) cone; bottom: *Sequoia sempervirens* (coast redwood) bark and foliage

All photographs by the author.

Cataloging-in-publication data is available from the Library of Congress.

ISBN 978-0-87071-167-1 (paper); ISBN 978-0-87071-175-6 (ebook)

∞ This paper meets the requirements of ANSI/NISO Z39.48-1992 (Permanence of Paper).

First published in 2022 by Oregon State University Press

Printed in South Korea

Oregon State University
OSU Press

Oregon State University Press
121 The Valley Library
Corvallis OR 97331-4501
541-737-3166 • fax 541-737-3170
www.osupress.oregonstate.edu

To Michael Scheinfein
and to the Master Gardeners of the Portland-area
Tri-County MG Study Group

It is in the deep knowing of place, and in the act of observing changes over time, that allows us—even as scientists—to understand what we cannot measure.

—GREG STREVELER,
FROM *IN SEARCH OF THE CANARY TREE*
BY LAUREN E. OAKES

Contents

CHAPTER 4
TAXACEAE: THE YEW FAMILY

CHAPTER 5
SCIADOPITYACEAE: THE JAPANESE UMBRELLA-PINE FAMILY

CHAPTER 6
ARAUCARIACEAE: THE MONKEY PUZZLE FAMILY

Acknowledgments

I became an Oregon State University Master Gardener (MG) in 2008, not knowing what a grand adventure it would take me on or what an extraordinary community of people I was joining. The OSU MG program in general and the Portland-area Tri-County MG Study Group in particular led to my interest in conifers. The study group is a self-organizing bunch of brainy MGs who meet twice monthly to help slake each other's thirst for all things plants. This book would not exist without these remarkable and generous people. They encouraged and indulged me. For many years they were my sole audience, around whom the idea for this book coalesced. A sense of audience is critically important, like a subsonic tuning fork an author is always listening for. The study group MGs were my tuning fork. The many conifer workshops I led in that venue were critical in sussing out the identification processes used in this book. And the years I have spent running the study group with Margaret Bayne, Diane Cleven, Jacki Dougan, Judy Hale, and Jean Natter have been an experience of a lifetime.

Special commendation goes to the editorial SWAT team who read the manuscript, each of whom was equipped with a special skill and all of whom are, remarkably, still speaking to me. Margaret Bayne lent her discerning Master Gardener's eye. Linda Trujillo's uncanny ear for language and scrupulous editorial skills were invaluable. Gary Hembree focused his keen geologist's lens on all matters up through the Pleistocene. The book is immeasurably better as a result of their efforts. Errors, of course, are mine alone.

I would also like to thank Christian Back for tracking down and translating original German references; Tracy Lloyd for supplying details of her father's cone-picking days; and David Sandrock for fielding conifer ID questions. Special thanks to Amy Holbrook for going the distance.

Additionally, I am grateful to Aljos Farjon for answering questions of conifer morphology and taxonomy, and for personally selling me one of the two last new copies on the planet of his book *Pinaceae: Drawings and Descriptions of the Genera: Abies, Cedrus, Pseudolarix, Keteleeria, Nothotsuga, Tsuga, Cathaya, Pseudotsuga, Larix and Picea*. A remarkable feature of his taxonomic works is that an original full-page botanical drawing accompanies the technical description of each conifer species. His books, many of them tomes, have given me what certainly adds up to years of enjoyment and edification, while increasing my vocabulary considerably.

My gratitude to Oregon State University Press is enormous for taking on a book so challenging to produce. Kim Hogeland, acquisitions editor, and Micki Reaman, managing editor, were a joy to work with from the first email. Their foresight, eye for detail, and skillful shepherding of the manuscript, from book proposal to printing, were the epitome of competence and professionalism. Susan Campbell's scrupulous copyediting contributed immensely to the quality and readability of the book.

Many photographs in this book were taken at the Rock Creek Campus of Portland Community College. The grounds are a wonderful garden, a hidden gem tucked away in the far northwest corner of Portland that doubles as a teaching garden for the horticulture program. Many other photographs were taken at the Hoyt Arboretum in Portland and the Oregon Garden in Salem.

And thanks lastly to my husband, Michael Scheinfein, who valiantly read the entire manususcript countless times, in sections and as a whole. He has tolerated, encouraged, and, literally, aided and abetted my conifer obsession all these years, often manning the getaway car while I purloined plant samples and engaged in other activities unprintable lest I implicate him in minor crimes and misdemeanors.

Native and Ornamental Conifers in the Pacific Northwest

CHAPTER I

Introduction to Conifers

Why This Book Is Different

People's interest in conifers does not break cleanly into the native and ornamental, as the published literature would have one think. This book is a reference and identification (ID) guide for landscape designers, horticulturalists, arborists, Master Gardeners, and conifer enthusiasts who are confronted routinely with the task of identifying conifers in commercial and residential landscapes where the two grow side-by-side. This is considerably more difficult than identifying a native conifer in the wild and particularly challenging in the Pacific Northwest (PNW), where we are fortunate to have a great diversity of native conifers that are popular ornamentally. In-depth information on conifer plant families and genera makes this book applicable also to adjacent areas of interest, such as forestry, botany, forest ecology, and other environmental sciences, as well as to temperate regions other than the PNW where the mix of native and ornamental conifers is a bit different.

The book is organized around jargon-free charts that guide the reader to species ID. Each chart is a photographic matrix of the key features of a group of genera or species, allowing for side-by-side comparison. Each chart or set of charts is preceded by material on the characteristics, botany, and natural history of each group of conifers, all of which is supported by original photographs. Research across many disciplines is blended with direct observation and personal experience, creating a book that goes beyond ID and is both rigorous and engaging.

Many native conifers sold in the PNW for commercial and residential landscapes have been dug from the mountains and are in essence not just native plants but wild plants. These wild conifers receive special attention in this book, as do native lowland conifers, which seed down at will. A number of native PNW conifers are not included in the ID charts because they are rarely planted ornamentally, including the Jeffrey pine (*Pinus jeffreyi*), sugar pine (*P. lambertiana*), red fir (*Abies magnifica*), subalpine larch (*Larix lyallii*), and western juniper (*Juniperus occidentalis*).

Throughout the book, cultivars are highlighted as necessary to give the reader a sense of the cultivars one can expect to encounter for any given genus or species. But many cultivars go in and out of fashion. The goal is to familiarize the reader with species characteristics—foliage, cones, buds, and bark—that carry over into cultivated varieties, enabling the reader to recognize the species that a cultivated variety is derived from. Exceptions to this are species that are rare and unavailable; in these cases, the most popular cultivars are used as stand-ins for the species.

No ID book that includes ornamental conifers can account for every species. However, common as well as uncommon conifers are included, and as of this printing, this book is up to date on those that seem to be trending and becoming more available and popular.

Conifers on the Decline

In the imagination of most people, the Jurassic Period, 200 to 146 million years ago (MYA), was the reign of dinosaurs. This is an animal-centric point of view. To many botanists, it was the Golden Age of Conifers. During the Jurassic there were 20,000 species of conifers, compared with about 630 today (Farjon 2008). That's a 97 percent decline. To other botanists it was the golden age of cycads, whose numbers also peaked during the Jurassic. Conifers, cycads, and ginkgos (all gymnosperms), as well as tree ferns, were the trees of the forests. The understory was a mosaic of spore-producing ferns, horsetails, and lycopods. And mosses, the Earth's first intrepid land plants, tied it all together.

In North America, the closest experience one can have to a Jurassic forest and the Golden Age of Conifers is in the coast range of the PNW or the rainforests of the Olympic Peninsula on a warm day during the rainy season. Waist-high sword ferns are in command of the shrub layer. Fog-fresh moss gardens ascend out of the ferns on the boles of ancient conifers and disappear with them into the vertiginous canopy. A few flowering shrubs and trees lurk as they would have in the Cretaceous. Though dinosaurs are missing, they are not difficult to imagine.

Flowering plants and pollinating insects, including bees, appeared toward the close of the reign of dinosaurs, a reign that ended abruptly when an asteroid detonated on what would become the Yucatan Peninsula, ushering in the Cenozoic Era (66 MYA to present) and the reign of flowering plants. The seven conifer plant families that existed then, and still exist today, were surprisingly unperturbed by this cataclysm and survived with no loss of diversity of families or genera (Farjon 2008).

Through the middle of the Cenozoic, there was ample real estate for plant life the world over. Warm and moist at all latitudes, and without distinct seasons except at the poles, the climate on Earth was ideal for plant growth. Sea levels were much higher on this ice-free Earth than they are today, and vast swaths of many continents were flooded. Much of Central America was under the sea, as was much of Central and Southern Europe.

In the late Mesozoic and early Cenozoic, flowering plants colonized mainly disturbed sites and other niches unoccupied by conifers, moving stealthily into coniferous forests by way of the understory, muscling out the ferns and succeeding in the shade, an environment in which sun-loving

Table 1-1. Geologic History of Conifers

Mesozoic		
Golden Age of Conifers (and Cycads and Dinosaurs)		
Triassic 250 to 200 MYA*	Jurassic 200 to 146 MYA	Cretaceous 146 to 66 MYA
One conifer plant family survives a massive extinction that ushers in the Mesozoic. The first dinosaurs appear.	Conifers peak at 20,000 species.	The first flowering plants appear.
The planet is warm and wet.		

Cenozoic			
Conifers and Flowering Plants Coexist	Reign of Flowering Plants		
Paleogene	Neogene	Quaternary	
66 to 23 MYA	23 to 2.5 MYA	2.5 MYA to 12 KYA+	12 KYA to present
A massive extinction ushers in the Cenozoic. Flowering plants begin to displace conifers. Dinosaurs are extinct. At the outset the planet is warm and wet, and then cools significantly.	Flowering plants dominate the planet. Conifers decline severely. The planet cools and dries out.	Conifer species decline further during the Ice Ages of the Pleistocene Epoch.	Conifer species are reduced to 630. The planet is warming and drying out in the Holocene Epoch.

*million years ago   +thousand years ago

conifers typically do not compete well. Then flowering trees began to push conifers out of the canopy. But for a long while conifers and flowering trees coexisted, with conifers diminished but still quite prevalent.

In 35 million years, from the middle of the Cenozoic to the present, flowering plants have gone from being in the background to accounting for 90 percent of all plant species. To those of us who don't spend our professional lives with our heads in deep time, as geologists and paleobotanists do, an event that occurs over millions of years hardly seems swift, but the speed with which flowering plants diversified and came to dominate the planet so challenged Charles Darwin's belief that evolution was a gradual process, he famously called it an abominable mystery.

The onset of the ice ages (2.5 MYA) marks the beginning of the Pleistocene, but the cooling and drying of the planet was a gradual process that began in the mid-Cenozoic as a consequence of mountain building, shifting continents, and redirected ocean currents. Areas with optimum temperatures and rainfall for plant growth became more scarce. Unable to compete with flowering plants for the diminishing choice space, conifers retreated to less desirable sites like swamps, or cooler sites with poor soil, like the mountains. Initially, there were plenty of swampy areas and ice-free mountains for conifers to fall back to. The ice ages changed that.

An ice age progresses on two fronts: from the poles as continental ice sheets and from the mountains. Massive Arctic ice sheets advanced south through Canada into the northern United States, while alpine glaciers pushed down from mountain peaks into river valleys and beyond. The ice advanced and retreated many times, with more conifer species snuffed out at the close of each freeze-thaw cycle.

Around the planet, conifers and other species hid out in refugia, a beautiful word for areas out of the direct influence of the ice, where species could bide their time until conditions improved, places they sallied out from during the warm cycles and fell back to when the ice returned. In North America, the Pacific Coast was one such refugium, as was the southeastern United States, an area the ice sheets never reached, though there might have been some alpine glaciers in the southern Appalachian Mountains. In areas of Europe outside the influence of the Mediterranean, all plant species suffered great losses. They were squeezed from two sides, with Arctic ice sheets sliding south and alpine glaciers moving north from the mountains, blocking off a southerly escape route for many species (Farjon 2008). Nearly the entirety of Great Britain was beneath ice, which accounts for its paucity of native conifer species–only three. At one time non-Mediterranean continental Europe hosted all existing genera of the pine family and most of those of the cypress family. Today there are eleven conifer species, mostly pines.

No conifer plant family was spared. Worldwide, all seven families saw a significant loss of species due to extinctions, extinctions that have not been replaced with enough new species to make up for the losses. Many enduring species have tiny or limited native ranges; they are the remaining survivors of what were once vast lineages of plants. Consider the Brewer spruce (*Picea breweriana*). The rarest spruce on the planet, it is found in the farthest southwest corner of Oregon and in northwest California, and nowhere else. Two small groves are all that are left of what was once a large forest of Monterey cypresses (*Cupressus macrocarpa*), found on California's coast no farther inland than a half mile from the sea. The sinuous edge of North America from Alaska south to central California is one of the last strongholds of conifers on the planet.

Conifers are mostly sun-loving evergreen trees, with a few shrubs and some deciduous trees included. Although herbaceous and semi-succulent conifers existed during the Triassic and early Cretaceous (Farjon 2008), today all are woody long-lived species that take a number of years to set seed. All are wind-pollinated; with some notable exceptions, conifer seeds are also spread by wind. Sexual reproduction in conifers is a leisurely affair and seems downright old-fashioned compared with that of many flowering plants. From pollination to seed production requires at least six months and can take up to two and a half years.

Flowering plants have the very modern ability to reinvent themselves. Whether their wild success is due to a general talent for mutability over any one adaptation is an ongoing debate (Crepet and Niklas 2009). But the gift flowering plants have for innovation is difficult to dispute. They take every form and have adapted to every life cycle and most environments on Earth. Many flowering plants reproduce sexually and asexually. Many successful groups like grasses are wind pollinated. Many other successful groups are insect pollinated. They invented fruit. Their seed dispersal is facilitated by animals. They are sexually precocious, with many able to produce offspring in their first year of life. Many have speedy reproductive cycles. Cherry blossoms in May lead expeditiously to fruit in June. Many species have more than one generation per year. And flowering plants know an opportunity when they see it, meaning they are weedy. Disturbances, like housing and highway construction, favor weedy behavior. How much time does anyone spend pulling conifer weeds?

Certainly, conifers are not in danger of becoming extinct. Junipers and some pines have figured out how to compete with flowering plants on their terms, meaning their seeds are attractive to and spread by animals. Under certain circumstances, conifers *can* be weedy. In New Zealand, Douglas-fir (*Pseudotsuga menziesii*) and the shore pine (*Pinus contorta*) are what they call wilding conifers, a beautiful phrase for invasive conifers. And in Eastern

Oregon, with fire suppression, the western juniper (*Juniperus occidentalis*) has increased its range steadily into places it's not welcome, like grazing areas and upland forests. But conifers continue to decline and are being pushed hard in a direction they've been headed for millions of years.

Evergreen versus Deciduous

What is it about the PNW climate that allows conifers to continue to out-compete flowering trees as if it were still the late Cretaceous? To answer this question, one must consider the three main factors that determine whether an environment is more likely to support evergreen conifers, broad-leaved evergreens, or deciduous broad-leaved plants: the length of the season for photosynthesis, the timing and characteristics of the harshest season, and the soil type. The special case of deciduous conifers is discussed later in this section.

LENGTH OF PHOTOSYNTHETIC SEASON

The product of photosynthesis, glucose (sugar), is like money in the bank, which a plant spends on growth and functions. Leaves are a recurring energy expense that trees bear annually. Sturdy evergreen foliage is expensive and has lower rates of photosynthesis but has a multiyear life span. Deciduous foliage is cheaper to construct and has higher rates of photosynthesis but has a seasonal life span. However, the cost of producing all new deciduous foliage every year is a greater draw on a plant's resources than the incremental investment of replacing just a portion of the foliage each year, as evergreens do (Givnish 2002). The longer foliage remains on the tree, the more structurally sound it has to be to withstand the vagaries of winter, and it must be fortified with chemical defenses so that it is unpalatable to foraging animals. Extensive damage from herbivory, especially on young trees, can draw down a tree's resources significantly.

Evergreen foliage must make up for its increased cost to the plant with a greater photosynthetic output over its life span than does deciduous foliage. Complicating the math is that, as evergreen foliage ages, its photosynthetic output decreases 30 to 50 percent every year (Chabot and Hicks 1982). The cost of constructing foliage is balanced against how much glucose the foliage can produce over its life span, and how much glucose the foliage can produce is determined by the length of the photosynthetic season.

In an area like the PNW with a mild winter, spring, and fall, the photosynthetic season is unusually long; and the longer the photosynthetic season, the more advantageous it is to be evergreen. Evergreen conifers can begin photosynthesizing in spring before deciduous leaves have emerged and continue photosynthesizing in autumn after deciduous leaves have senesced, as well as sporadically through the winter as conditions allow. Additionally, deciduous trees must refrain from issuing leaves too early in the spring so as not to risk

10

losing an entire flush of tender foliage to a damaging frost or freeze. On the other hand, by waiting too long, a species could lose its competitive edge to another species that has better timing. Although certainly not immune to frost damage, conifers and other evergreens are afforded the luxury of waiting until later in the spring to produce new foliage. Evergreen foliage also functions as a dispersed storage system. In the spring, before the roots are active enough to support growth, resources are redistributed from older, less-productive foliage deeper in the canopy to younger more productive foliage (Chabot and Hicks 1982). And, whereas deciduous plants must extract resources from the leaves all at once in autumn, evergreen plants can pull resources incrementally, as-needed, over a period of years (Chabot and Hicks 1982).

HARSHEST SEASON

The abundant rainfall of the PNW is concentrated in fall, winter, and spring, to the point that for recording yearly precipitation the region follows what's called a water year, beginning on October 1, instead of a calendar year, which would split the rainy season in half. In much of the PNW summers are warm and droughty with low humidity and very limited rain. Some years July and August are bone-dry with zero measurable precipitation. Summer fog ameliorates this at the coast, but for PNW forests summer is often the most limiting season for growth.

The recipe for photosynthesis has three ingredients: carbon dioxide, water, and light. Carbon dioxide enters the plant through recessed apertures in the leaves called stomata. Water pulled up from the roots exits the stomata as vapor. When temperatures are moderate, stomata open at sunup and close at sundown. During hot and dry conditions (or cold), the benefits of taking in carbon dioxide for photosynthesis for the production of glucose are balanced against the loss of water. Given the choice between food or water, just like animals, plants choose water. The stomata close and photosynthesis stops. When deciduous trees shut down photosynthesis in summer, they can't compensate for the loss of productivity during the shoulder seasons, making them less competitive with evergreen conifers. In conifers, the anatomy of the xylem, which moves water from the roots to all parts of the plant, also makes them more efficient at water use than flowering plants. Some PNW plants don't even bother with summer. Consider the licorice fern (*Polypodium glycyrrhiza*), a winter-green perennial. Growing among moss in tree-trunk gardens, it produces leaves in fall and dies back in early summer when the rain stops and the fog withdraws from the forest.

In microclimates with available summer water, such as along the Columbia River, which defines most of the border between Oregon and Washington, you see a plentitude of deciduous trees, including big-leaf maple (*Acer macrophyllum*) and black cottonwood (*Populus trichocarpa*). Just upland from the river, conifers again dominate. The riparian environment provides a year-round supply of moisture to the roots, making the longer days of summer a highly productive season and giving angiosperms a competitive edge over evergreen conifers in that microclimate (Givnish 2002).

In areas with warm wet summers and long harsh winters that extend into the shoulder seasons, the cost of creating evergreen foliage is greater than what the foliage can contribute in the short photosynthetic season, and deciduous plants are more common. When soil freezes, water is no longer available to the roots, causing winter drought conditions for plants. In cold regions such as the upper Midwest and New England, late spring frosts enforce late leaf emergence, and early hard freezes shorten the life span of deciduous leaves and the photosynthetic season.

SOIL TYPE

In addition to glucose from photosynthesis, all plants need three essential nutrients—nitrogen, potassium, and phosphorous—and many other micronutrients, all of which the roots pull from the soil. Microorganisms—mainly fungi and bacteria—decompose organic matter into a mineral form that plants can take up through the roots. The less organic matter there is to decompose, the poorer the soil. This is where conifers find a niche. They are far more efficient than angiosperms at drawing nutrients out of poor soil, which is the reason conifers are often confined to mountains and high deserts and are typically displaced by angiosperms in areas with soil high in nutrients.

Additionally, in poor soil, plants must work harder to take up the nutrients they require, making the investment in longer-lasting but more expensive evergreen foliage worth the cost. Once a conifer has its full complement of multiage foliage, the amount of nutrients needed from the soil each year is significantly less than for deciduous foliage, all of which must be replaced annually. One caveat is that juvenile conifers are at a disadvantage until they are old enough to have a full complement of foliage.

The leaf litter of conifers and flowering plants both maintains the soil type that best suits them and allows them to compete better with one another. Conifer foliage is lower in nutrients and decomposes more slowly, keeping the soil poorer. The deciduous foliage of flowering plants is higher in nutrients—especially in nitrogen, the nutrient plants need most—and decomposes more rapidly, keeping the soil richer. It's not that conifers won't grow on rich soil—they flourished on all types of soil before angiosperms showed up. It's just that angiosperms are better adapted to it.

The boreal climate, also called subarctic, subpolar, or taiga, presents special challenges: long severe winters enforce an extended drought, the photosynthetic season is brief, and the light is low-angled. This poses a question many forest biologists have struggled to answer: Given these conditions, why are many boreal forests dominated by evergreen conifers and not by deciduous broad-leaved trees?

Part of the answer lies in the extraordinarily poor soils of boreal forests, due to the scarcity of organic matter and its slow decomposition in cold temperatures. Resources in boreal forests are so dear that conifers' greater efficiency in poor soils gives them a competitive advantage. Coniferous boreal forests cleared out by fires often transition temporarily to cold-adapted deciduous trees, such as birch and aspen, because of short-term enrichment of the soil from the additional organic matter (Givnish 2002).

Conifers are also better adapted to photosynthesizing at lower temperatures. The days of April and August are equally long, but those of April are much cooler, allowing conifers not just to photosynthesize in spring when deciduous trees have yet to leaf out but also to do so efficiently. In autumn, when deciduous leaves have yet to drop, the days are cooler like those of spring, but there are fewer daylight hours for photosynthesis (Sprugel 1989).

FORM AND FUNCTION

Leaf shape and tree shape go together. Typically, trees with broader crowns have fewer layers of broad foliage. This form gives wide leaves the space they need to capture sun for photosynthesis. The wider the leaves, the less light gets through to lower layers of foliage and the fewer layers of foliage the tree can support. Wide shallow canopies provide shade for picnics and other idle activities of summer. Conifers aren't typically trees you read a book under. They are strongly conical, widest at the base and tapering progressively toward the top. Narrow needles allow light to filter down into the many layers of foliage, many more than those of most deciduous trees. When wind breaks off the leading stem at the treetop, a lateral branch typically assumes dominance and reestablishes the conical form (fig. 1-1). Although a single trunk is the most common conifer form, some develop forked trunks naturally (fig. 1-2); others sometimes develop forked tops as a result of damage from insects or diseases. Old-growth trees in particular develop multiple parallel trunks in response to injury.

In summer, a single deciduous broad leaf captures more light than an individual conifer needle. But the many layers of narrow, multi-sided conifer needles make up for this by collectively having at least twice the surface area as an equivalent deciduous tree with fewer layers of

Fig. 1-1: Douglas-fir with a lateral branch assuming dominance   Fig. 1-2: Fir with a split trunk

wide two-dimensional leaves. Plus, in all-day sun, foliage can typically process only 25 to 30 percent of the light that strikes it (Sprugel 1989).

The clever geometry of needled conifers minimizes wasted light. Spruce (*Picea*) needles encircle the twig (fig. 1-3), and those of most true firs (*Abies*) fan out around the top of the twig (fig. 1-4). Each stiff needle of true firs and spruce has a set position and orientation for its entire life span. As the sun travels across the sky, each needle collects a portion of the day's light from a unique angle, lending shade to neighboring needles while doing so. This

Fig. 1-3: Needles encircling white spruce twig   Fig. 1-4: Needles fanning out around top of subalpine fir twig

strategy is particularly helpful in the low-angled light of boreal forests (Sprugel 1989). On the other hand, in low-light environments, foliage flattens and spreads out to collect more light.

DECIDUOUS CONIFERS

Most people take it as a given that conifers are evergreen, with deciduous conifers seeming peculiar because in most places they are uncommon in the wild, leading one to wonder why they exist at all. They are even more uncommon horticulturally. Of the fifteen deciduous conifer species across five genera, three are rare and endemic to China, including the dawn redwood (*Metasequoia glyptostroboides*), thought to be extinct until 1944 when a population was identified. Ten of the other twelve are larches (*Larix*), and two are baldcypresses (*Taxodium*).

Boreal Forests and the Larch Paradox

Scientists puzzle over something often called the larch paradox—how, in boreal forests, certain deciduous larch species perform as well as or outperform evergreen conifers—because, as discussed above, when the environment is tough, the soil is poor, and resources are scarce, being an evergreen conifer is typically the winning strategy. But as you travel far north, north of the Arctic Circle, at the very limit of where trees can survive, resources become that much more scarce, and the equation that every plant must balance—taking in more than it puts out—becomes even more tricky. The more parsimonious a tree is in its use of both soil nutrients and food (glucose), the greater its chances of surviving. In Siberia, two larches (*L. gmelinii* and *L. sibirica*) essentially redraw the boreal tree line by growing at higher latitudes than any other trees, north of where evergreen conifers can survive.

Larch needles have a number of adaptations that help them get the most out of the shorter time they remain on the tree. Plants are natural recyclers, but just like people, some are better at it than others; when it comes to trees, larch recycle best. All plants move resources from aging soon-to-drop foliage, either down into the roots for storage or into other plant parts. (Roots are literally a plant's root cellar.) Evergreen conifers and deciduous broad-leaved trees are equally efficient at this task, retrieving about 50 percent of all nutrients held in the leaves. Larch do quite a bit better, withdrawing 20 percent more nutrients (Gower and Richards 1990).

Studies show that, by weight, same-age deciduous larch needles have two to three times the surface area and photosynthesize at twice the rate of evergreen needles of staggered ages (Gower and Richards 1990). Short-lived larch needles can manage without a thick epidermis or cuticle, both of which evergreens in harsh environments require in their defense against winter desiccation and herbivory. By investing in lightweight foliage that, pound-for-pound, is less of a draw on the tree's food bank, larch opt for cheap disposable needles over more expensive high-functioning ones (Gower and Richards 1990). A word of caution when planting larch in the landscape: the lack of a cuticle makes them especially susceptible to herbicide damage.

The Canadian Arctic Archipelago

For the first twenty million years of the Cenozoic, the planet was warm year-round all the way to the poles, and there was essentially no boreal tree line, no latitude north of which trees did not grow. Not even in winter did the Arctic experience a hard frost, and at 67°F/19°C, the Arctic Ocean was warm enough for a non-hypothermic swim. The Antarctic continent was also temperate and forested.

When I first read this, I had to pause to process the thought, so linked in my mind were the words "Arctic" and "polar" to year-round cold and permanent ice. The planet experienced hothouse or greenhouse conditions—the entire world was mild and moist year-round. Unlike today, the climates of the Arctic and the equator weren't drastically different. One could've packed a light suitcase to travel from one to the other. The only places on the planet with tree lines, snow, and ice were high elevations on mountains.

Where the northernmost part of Canada breaks apart into dozens of ragged islands, an area called the Canadian Arctic Archipelago, the fossil remains of forests are considered by many to be representative of the flora throughout the Arctic during this time of greenhouse conditions (Basinger et al. 1994). The composition of the paleo-forests of two of the northernmost islands, Axel Heiberg and Ellesmere, have been the subject of much study and reconstructed by paleobotanists from fossils. At approximately 75 to 85 degrees N latitude, these islands are 10 to 20 degrees north of the Arctic Circle, places one would have to mount an expedition to visit today.

In the extensive swampy forests that typified this area during the early Cenozoic, when the islands of the Canadian Arctic Archipelago were a connected landmass and part of the North American continent, deciduous conifers were not only common, they were dominant (Basinger et al. 1994). Spectacularly preserved leaf, cone, and tree stump fossils tell the story of these forests. Though species from all five currently existing deciduous coni-fer genera are present in the fossil record, the litter layers are often almost entirely composed of dawn redwood (*Metasequoia occidentalis*) needles. And the number and size of fossilized tree stumps, up to three feet wide, tell not of a stunted or sparse forest struggling to make a go of it, as one might expect, but of a vigorous and highly productive forest with trees of all sizes and ages (fig. 1-5). Though today's extant dawn redwood (*M. glyptostroboides*) has been given a different species name than that of the extinct dawn redwood (*M. occidentalis*) botanists have observed that their characteristics are virtually indis-tinguishable and that the two are most likely the same species (LePage et al. 2005). Larch species were also common, whereas baldcypresses and pseudo-larch were uncommon. Though many evergreen conifer genera were in the mix, they were far less common than dawn redwood, as were deciduous flowering trees found on drier upland sites (Basinger et al. 1994). It should be noted that plant species adapted to swamps and other wet anaerobic envi-ronments are preferentially preserved in the fossil record.

No equivalent forest exists on the planet today to help one imagine this strange combination of trees, climate, and lighting—a thriving old-growth deciduous coniferous forest adapted to three months of unin-terrupted summer light and three months of unequivocal winter darkness among which the ances-tors of today's alligators slithered. However, if one had to make an analogy, the closest example in North America is the warm and swampy alligator-rich forests of the southeastern United States, where today deciduous baldcypresses are common.

These paleo-Arctic forests test one's assumptions about why plants are deciduous. In broad-leaved plants, deciduousness is generally considered an adaptation to the drought conditions of cold win-ters. In the frost-free paleo-Arctic,

Fig. 1-5: Dawn redwood in fall

seasonal leaves were an adaptation to extended winter darkness. On the flip side, the constant sun of the Arctic summer seems like it would be a boon to plant growth, but it also required adaptations, posing challenges for some species and presenting opportunities for others.

Chloroplasts, found in cells of the leaves, are a plant's microscopic food factories, where photosynthesis takes place and glucose is produced. But chloroplasts can become saturated with light much in the way roots can become saturated with water—they can take in and process only so much. When the food factories receive more light than they can handle, the system breaks down, chloroplasts deteriorate, and photosynthesis plummets.

When scientists conduct experiments on an extinct plant species, they often use what's called the "nearest living relative" as a stand-in, a species alive today that is the closest genetically to the extinct species. When exposed to continuous light, the dawn redwood—a stand-in for *Metasequoia* of the paleo-Arctic—photosynthesizes almost as efficiently as it does under fluctuating light conditions. The eastern larch (*L. laricina*) and the baldcypress (*Taxodium distichum*), two more stand-ins, saw markedly lower photosynthetic rates. *Metasequoia* were able to take advantage of the opportunity that a nonstop supply of light afforded, giving them an enormous competitive advantage over other deciduous conifers (Equiza et al. 2005). As seen in the ample growth rings of the fossilized tree stumps, this fueled vigorous growth and was instrumental in *Metasequoia*'s dominance in swampy deciduous forests of the paleo-Arctic.

Cold Adaptations

The pine family (Pinaceae) is the most cold-tolerant of the seven conifer plant families and includes the most cold-hardy trees on the planet: the buds of some larch, spruce, true fir, and pines can survive temperatures as low as −94°F/−70°C. The eastern white-cedar (*Thuja occidentalis*) is an outlier, being the only conifer in the cypress family (Cupressaceae) tolerant of temperatures as low as the most cold-hardy conifers in the pine family, but its foliage desiccates in winter (Sakai and Larcher 1987), a limitation that can be seen even in the mild winters of the PNW. Many junipers are also very cold hardy, but none to the degree of the most hardy of the pine family species. The pine and cypress families are restricted almost entirely to the Northern Hemisphere. Oddly, conifer families of the Southern Hemisphere have not achieved anywhere near the hardiness of those in the Northern Hemisphere but make up for it by being far more prevalent in the tropics and subtropics, where Northern Hemisphere conifers are poorly represented. Many flowering boreal trees, such as birch, are as cold hardy as boreal conifers, but the most cold-hardy trees on Earth are two larches, the Dahurian larch (*Larix gmelinii*) and the Siberian larch (*L. sibirica*). Both are native to Siberia, with ranges that extend north of the Arctic Circle.

Most plants suffer the greatest cold damage during late spring or early fall, not in winter, as one might expect. Plant cells must ready themselves for winter in much the same way that people in cold climates winterize their homes. It's a gradual process, set in motion by environmental signals. Plants or plant parts that would, in a typical year, be fully winterized and ready for subzero temperatures and biting wind by the end of December can easily perish in a freak mid-October cold snap. (Or during late cold weather in spring, after they have de-winterized.)

But it's not cold that damages or kills plants—it's ice. Water is essentially the only liquid on Earth that becomes less dense when it freezes, expanding and taking up more space. Other fluids become more dense and shrink when they freeze. This fact changes everything. It's why ice floats in a cocktail instead of sinking to the bottom; it's why you can skate on a frozen lake and why fish in the lake survive winter beneath the insulating ice. If water shrank as it froze, it would form on the lake surface and sink, repeatedly, layer by layer. Ice would accumulate in the lake from the bottom up, resulting in fewer fish and no ice-skating.

Trees and other woody plants are 60 percent water. (Herbaceous plants are over 90 percent water.) The beauty of liquid water is that it takes the shape of whatever contains it. In plants that container is the cell. But as water begins to freeze, extra space is needed for expansion, and even more space is needed for ice to grow into intricate crystals. Ice crystals are lethal to the cell, slicing into cell parts, including the cell membrane. Cells can survive the formation of extremely small ice crystals, as long as the crystals melt before reaching a destructive size.

Plants have adapted to deal with ice. Adaptations differ from species to species and from one part of the plant to another, but no matter what the species or plant part, the methods used—extracellular freezing, extraorgan freezing, supercooling, and deep supercooling, either alone or in combination—all share the goal of preventing ice crystals from forming inside the cell.

The most common adaptation to freezing in all plants, woody and herbaceous, is extracellular freezing. As winter approaches, most plant parts export water out of the cells, where ice crystals can form without inflicting harm. This increases the concentration of sugars and other dissolved substances inside the cell, which, just like salt tossed on ice, lowers the freezing temperature. The more water withdrawn, the higher the sugar concentration, the lower the freezing temperature, and the more cold the cell can endure. This adaptation is often described as a plant having antifreeze, but that's not quite accurate. Antifreeze is added to water to lower the freezing temperature; with extracellular freezing, water is removed, the cell dehydrates, and the cell wall collapses. A plant's degree of hardiness (the lowest temperature it can survive) is in large part a measure of how tolerant the cells are to dehydration.

Terminal buds form at the end of the growing season, become dormant as the weather changes, and then overwinter. Buds are an unassuming bit of plant anatomy but, inside the bud, an astonishing amount is going on, and there is a lot at stake. The majority of a bud has one function, to protect the precious area at the core—called the bud primordium—which contains cells at their earliest stage of development destined to be next season's leaves, shoots, and apical meristems, in other words, the future of the tree.

The buds of certain boreal larch, spruce, and true fir species have an additional method of sequestering ice: an extra bit of anatomy, a relatively large chamber or freezer, if you will, whose sole function is ice storage. Called the crown, this specially adapted organ lies just beneath the primordial cells. As temperatures drop, water migrates out of the tender thin-walled primordial cells into the tough thick-walled cells below the crown and then freezes where it can do no harm. This process reverses as temperatures warm (Kuprian et al. 2017). Extracellular freezing occurs on the cellular level. In contrast, extraorgan freezing is an adaptation of the bud as a whole and is considered unique to certain boreal tree species.

The bud is also protected on the outer, visible side. To prevent winter desiccation, buds of many true firs and pines are coated with sticky pitch. Below the pitch, buds dress in layers to stay warm, just like people. Layers of overlapping scales protect and insulate the bud. The colder the environment, the more layers of scales a bud has. Larch buds have about forty layers; buds of species in the cypress and yew (Taxaceae) families have far fewer, and species in warmer climates have just a few. If the bud scales are injured or removed, ice forms, and the primordial cells die (Kuprian et al. 2017).

The thick and rigid secondary cell walls of living xylem cells of most trees present a barrier through which water, either in liquid or solid form, cannot pass. This means extracellular freezing and extraorgan freezing are not possible, as in both cases water must pass through the cell wall (Endoh et al. 2009). This makes xylem cells the least cold-hardy part of most trees, requiring a different adaptation for preventing ice from forming there.

In winter, water inside xylem cells becomes supercooled, meaning it remains in a liquid state even when temperatures fall below freezing, to as low as −40°F/−40°C. The cells remain fully hydrated and at full volume. A peculiarity of the physics of ice crystal growth makes supercooling possible. All crystals need something to get started, some kind of particle to grow on, like pearls in oysters or the crystallized sugar on a stick used for dissolving into hot beverages. The stick isn't just a clever sugar-delivery system; it provides the substrate for the sugar crystals to grow on, what's called a nucleation site. Once an ice crystal forms, it provides its own nucleation sites—called a seed crystal or a crystal embryo. The larger the crystal, the more sites it has and the faster it grows. Ice doesn't form inside xylem cells because the cells harbor no nucleation sites. Other cells besides xylem supercool, but for xylem it is typically the sole mechanism of preventing freezing.

There are two types of nucleation sites: heterogeneous and homogeneous. Down to −40°F/−40°C, water requires nucleation sites to form ice crystals (heterogeneous) but once the temperature drops below that threshold, ice crystals will form without nucleation sites (homogeneous). This is why the cold hardiness of xylem cells in most trees is no lower than the heterogeneous freezing point of water (−40°F/−40°C), and why you find fewer and fewer species hardy to below this temperature as you travel farther north.

The xylem cells of boreal conifer and hardwood tree species have an additional trick. Deep supercooling sounds like some kind of advanced meditation technique, but it refers to how living xylem cells resist freezing well below −40°F/−40°C for long periods of time, to temperatures as low as −94°F/−70°C. This is an active area of research, and it is still not completely understood how xylem cells accomplish this, but pressure inside the cell and an increased concentration of solutes during winterization when the cells convert starch to sugar lowers the freezing temperature further. Also, it appears that the xylem cells of the most cold-hardy boreal trees are somehow capable of a modicum of extracellular freezing.

Plants also have adaptations for contending with ice after it has formed. Ice-binding proteins, known for decades to exist in Antarctic fish and insects, have also been discovered in plants. Proteins occupy the nucleation sites on an ice crystal when the crystal is still too small to damage the cell, arresting the growth of the crystal and preventing it from increasing to a destructively large size. Most research on this topic has been in agricultural crops, but ice-binding proteins have also been identified in conifers, specifically the needles of Norway spruce (*Picea abies*) and Colorado spruce (*P. pungens*) (Jarzabek et al. 2009).

Ice-binding proteins sometimes assume a second role in preventing freezing injury and combating pathogens. Certain cunning bacteria mimic ice crystals by being armed with nucleation sites. These bacteria are able to penetrate the plant surface and raise the freezing temperature in supercooled cells. In the ongoing weapons race between pathogen and host, ice-binding proteins in plants occupy the ice-nucleating sites on the bacteria, preventing the growth of ice crystals and the spread of the bacteria (Bredow and Walker 2017). These bacteria have yet to be discovered on conifers, but to date most research has been on cash crops.

Conifer Reproduction

Large groups of plants are differentiated by their reproductive structures. Conifers are distinguished by their male and female cones. The small male pollen cone is soft at maturity and composed of scales that hold pollen and attach to a central axis. The larger female seed cone is usually woody at maturity and composed of scales (and bracts) that hold the seeds and attach to a central axis. (Refer to the pine and cypress family introductions for specifics on cone evolution and anatomy.)

Even though conifers are the oldest surviving seed plants, pre-dating angiosperms by nearly 200 million years, the reproductive parts of flowering plants are the standard against which conifers are typically compared. Many books even refer to conifer cones as male and female flowers, a practice as strange as referring to roses or orchids as female seed cones.

Sexual reproduction in all plants requires transportation. In conifers, pollen must first complete a relatively long journey from the male pollen cone to the female cone. Then nonflagellated sperm must make a journey, very short in distance but long in time, to the ovule (egg). The resulting seeds (offspring) must distance themselves from the parent plant. In conifers these processes are largely wind-powered, although a brief water voyage is also often involved.

Pollen released by the male cones is the first visible part of the conifer reproductive cycle (table 1-2). Prodigious amounts of pollen are produced

Fig. 1-6: Male pollen cones releasing pollen

Fig. 1-7: Young (½ inch) female ponderosa pine cone with specks of pollen

23

(fig. 1-6), such that when wind blows the pollen in all directions, there is a high probability a portion of it will land on female cones of its own species, which flex open their scales to receive it (fig. 1-7). However, the vast majority of pollen just falls to the ground. Pines (*Pinus* spp.) in particular set massive numbers of pollen cones. In areas with high concentrations of pines, plague-like storms of sulfur-colored pollen blow ominously in spring.

The ovules in the female cones of most genera exude small sticky drops for capturing pollen. In a number of genera, including the pine genus, the ovule and the drop face downward. Each pollen grain is equipped with a pair of buoyant water wings, called sacci, that floats the pollen up through the drop against gravity (Leslie et al. 2015) (fig. 1-8). In other genera, nonbuoyant pollen without water wings sinks down through an upward-facing pollen drop. Yet others have a system intermediate between these two, with ovules positioned at varying angles and with different strategies for securing pollen. In the pine genus, pollination is nocturnal. Each ovule issues its pollen drop after dusk; if by dawn the drop hasn't captured pollen of its own species, it retracts, reappearing for several consecutive nights, except when it's raining. Within minutes of capturing pollen of its own species, the drop withdraws into the ovule, taking the pollen with it. The drop hydrates the pollen and moves it to the proper place for germination (Williams 2009).

The pollen grain swells and bursts its coat. A tube that delivers nonflag-ellated sperm from the pollen grain to the ovule begins to grow toward its destination and then pauses. The cone scales shut tight, and the cone goes dormant until the following spring, when the pollen tube reinitiates growth

Fig. 1-8: Vast quantities of buoyant pine pollen washing onto a lakeshore

and the sperm finally reaches and fertilizes the ovule. In species with cones that develop over one growing season, the time between pollination and fertilization is shorter (table 1-3). After fertilization, the seeds and female cone grow in earnest. By late summer or early fall, the cone has dried out and releases seeds equipped with one or two wings for aerial flight. Exceptions to this are species with seeds dispersed by animals; seeds of those species are wingless or have vestigial or reduced wings.

This process reveals the two conflicting roles of the female cone: the scales must open to allow pollen access to the ovules and then close to protect the developing seeds (Tomlinson and Takaso 2002). Translated literally from Greek, gymnosperm means naked seed (as in exposed and unprotected), but in most conifer genera the seeds are in fact very well protected; it is the unfertilized ovules that are exposed. However, early in the cone's evolutionary history this was not the case; the female cone had a much looser open structure with a lot more space between the scales. Clearly conifers have made adaptations in this regard, with one botanist suggesting that gymno-ovule rather than gymnosperm might be a more appropriate term (Tomlinson and Takaso 2002).

CONIFER SEEDLING DEVELOPMENT

Every seed contains a plant embryo with miniature leaves, stem, and root, as well as food stored in the cotyledons to fuel growth until the plant can begin to photosynthesize. Since conifers are never grown from seed in the residential or commercial landscape, few are familiar with how they germinate aboveground. The elongating stem and cotyledons push the seed up through the soil, and before it is shed, the seed coat sits atop the seedling like punctuation, pinching the cotyledons together (fig. 1-9a, b). Once you know what to look for, in spring you notice these aspiring conifers everywhere. This is epicotyl germination, as opposed to hypocotyl germination in flowering plants, in which the seed germinates and (in most cases) the seed coat remains belowground.

In contrast to flowering plants, which are defined by having either one (monocots) or two (dicots) cotyledons, the number of cotyledons varies from species to species in conifers, and even within a species (fig. 1-9c, d). This is particularly true of the pine family. Douglas-firs (*Pseudotsuga menziesii*) have five to eight cotyledons and ponderosa pines (*Pinus ponderosa*) six to twelve. The rare Martinez pine (*P. maximartinezii*), native to Mexico, has the most, with eighteen to twenty-four. Most species in the cypress family have two cotyledons, as do all species in the yew family. Other characteristics to note are cotyledon length, shape, and orientation to the stem. Stem color and length also vary from species to species.

Before the cotyledons shrivel, the seedling develops juvenile foliage, which is prickly and awl-shaped in the cypress family and linear in the pine family (fig. 1-9e, f). By summer's end, adult foliage usually appears and, except for most species in the cypress family, the conifer's first terminal bud is visible, often revealing or confirming its identity (fig. 1-10).

Fig. 1-9: Conifer Seedling Development

	Seed coat and cotyledons	Cotyledons and juvenile foliage	Juvenile foliage and adult foliage
Cypress Family	Port-Orford-cedar (a)	Incense-cedar with two cotyledons (c)	Incense-cedar (e)
Pine Family	Deodar cedar (b)	Douglas-fir with eight cotyledons (d)	Shore pine (f)

VEGETATIVE REPRODUCTION

A number of species also reproduce vegetatively by layering, but this occurs mostly in the mountains where snow pins lower branches against the ground long enough for them to develop roots, making the trees appear to have skirts. These species include mountain hemlock (*Tsuga mertensiana*), subalpine fir (*Abies lasiocarpa*), and Alaska-cedar (*Chamaecyparis nootkatensis*).

Fig. 1-10: Grand fir seedling with its first small red pitchy terminal bud

CONIFER POLLEN YEAR

The conifer pollen year begins in autumn when the true cedars (*Cedrus*) release pollen, continues unabated through spring, and then pauses for the summer, the least windy time of year. (table 1-2)

Conifer Allergies

The pollen of species in the pine family causes allergies far less frequently than those in the cypress family. Species in the cypress family known to cause the most allergies include the Japanese-cedar (*Cryptomeria japonica*), Hinoki-cypress (*Chamaecyparis obtusa*), Italian cypress (*Cupressus sempervirens*), and western juniper (*Juniperus occidentalis*). Moisture in the nose or mouth hydrates the pollen grain and the pollen grain germinates just as it would if it had been captured by an ovule. The pollen grain swells, bursts through its coat, and begins to grow a pollen tube into the tissue, all of which trigger allergic reactions (Williams 2009).

Table 1-2. Conifer Pollen Calendar

Autumn			Winter		
Early	**Mid**	**Late**	**Early**	**Mid**	**Late**
				Araucaria	
		Calocedrus			
Cedrus					
				Cephalotaxus	
					Chamaecyparis
			Cryptomeria		
				Cupressus	
				Juniperus	
	Metasequoia: Pollen cones set in fall, release pollen in spring				
					Platycladus
			Sequoia		
			Sequoiadendron		
					Taxus
					Thuja
					Thujopsis
					Torreya

Note: This pollen calendar applies to the PNW and only to species in this book. Also note that spring and summer occur later in the mountains, after snowmelt.

Spring			Summer		
Early	Mid	Late	Early	Mid	Late
	Abies				
Larix					
	Picea				
	Pinus				
	Pseudotsuga				
Taxodium					
	Tsuga				

Table 1–3. Number of Growing Seasons
for Seed Cone Development

One	Two	Three
Pinaceae—Pine Family		
Abies	*Pinus* (almost all non-tropical species)	*Cedrus*
Larix		*Pinus pinea*
Picea		
Pseudotsuga		
Tsuga		
Cupressaceae—Cypress Family		
Calocedrus	*Chamaecyparis nootkatensis*	
Chamaecyparis spp.	*Juniperus*	
Cryptomeria	*Cupressus*	
× *Cupressocyparis*	*Sequoiadendron*	
Metasequoia	*Thujopsis*	
Platycladus		
Sequoia		
Taxodium		
Thuja		
Taxaceae—Yew Family		
Taxus	*Cephalotaxus* *Torreya*	
Sciadopityaceae—Japanese Umbrella-Pine Family		
	Sciadopitys	
Araucariaceae—Monkey Puzzle Family		
	Araucaria	

Cultivars

Perhaps it's too obvious to put in writing that native plants are as they appear in the wild, without human intervention, and that cultivars have been selected by humans for desirable traits, propagated, and raised under controlled conditions. When differentiating between a native plant and a cultivar of that plant, the former is referred to as "the species," a practice followed throughout this book. For the ornamental market, native plants are dug from the wild or raised from seed. In the PNW, the national forests issue commercial and personal-use permits for digging plants. Commercial permits are issued to money-making enterprises like native plant nurseries; personal-use permits are like hunting or fishing permits. In certain locations and under a set of prescribed conditions, one can dig and take a limited number of plant species for free, including most native conifer species. Such a permit also allows you to collect cuttings and seeds.

Because every seed is a unique combination of genes, native plants display much greater variability in traits than cultivars. Cultivated plants are typically propagated from cuttings—genetically identical clones—making individual plants of many cultivars largely the same from specimen to specimen. One sees fields of them growing in tidy rows, each one a reliable copy of the original. The traits conifer cultivars are selected for can be aesthetic or practical, and fall into a number of categories—size, form, foliage characteristics, unique cones, and resistance to pests—with many cultivars possessing traits from many categories and often more than one foliage characteristic.

SOURCES OF CULTIVARS

Some cultivars originate from discoveries of conifers in the wild that have genetic mutations that differentiate the entire plant from what is typical for the species, like yellow foliage, a condition caused by insufficient chlorophyll. New specimens are grown from cuttings of the wild conifer. Many dwarf conifers are discovered as witches'-brooms, a growth deformity of congested and stunted twigs growing on a single branch of an otherwise normal tree (figs. 1-11, 1-12). Most often, a witches'-broom is due to a virus, fungus, bacterium, or parasitic plant (mistletoe). If more than one broom is found in a tree or in neighboring trees of the same species, a pathogen is likely the culprit. But sometimes a witches'-broom is the result of a genetic mutation in a single bud. Enterprising conifer growers keep an eye out for these as sources of new cultivars and actively search for them. Broom-seekers typically harvest the entire witches'-broom, often risking personal safety in doing so. Once

Fig. 1-11: Witches'-broom

you become sensitized to their existence, you start noticing them regularly as dark bunchy areas in trees. Plants propagated from broom cuttings are observed for many years to ensure the traits remain fixed, as they often revert to what's typical for the species. If the traits hold true and the characteristics are different enough from what's already on the market, the conifer grower names and registers the conifer as a new cultivar.

One very popular cultivar that has been around for a hundred years, the dwarf Alberta spruce (*Picea glauca* 'Conica'), is notorious for not holding true and for reverting back to the species. This juxtaposition of cultivar and reversion is very odd-looking, in many ways a curiosity on its own, particularly if the reverting part hasn't been pruned away promptly (fig. 1-13). It's also instructive, allowing one to examine differences between the species and the deviant cultivar conveniently in one plant. In the wild, viable seed deposited in the forest by cone-producing witches'-brooms can be the source of naturally occurring abnormal specimens, which is what the dwarf Alberta spruce was thought to be when discovered in western Canada by a plant collector from the Arnold Arboretum in the early 1900s.

The tendency to produce genetic mutations seems to be an inherited trait and responsible for second- and third-generation cultivars. For example, the 'Skylands' Oriental spruce (*P. orientalis*), a smaller yellow version of the species but still an upright tree, generated a witches'-broom that was the source of 'Tom Thumb', a mounding yellow miniature.

CULTIVARS WITH JUVENILE FOLIAGE: CYPRESS FAMILY

Species in certain genera in the cypress family, particularly *Chamaecyparis*, *Thuja*, and *Cryptomeria*, are known for producing seedlings with genetic mutations that trigger plants to retain juvenile awl-like foliage throughout their life cycle. Conifer growers keep an eye out for these oddities in the wild and in their seedbeds as a source of potentially new cultivars. Those that make it into the nurseries as named cultivars often have other characteristics considered desirable, such as dwarfism or variegated or dense foliage.

The foliage and form of these plants bear zero resemblance to the species. You cannot work your way back to the species they're derived from

Fig. 1-12: Enormous witches'-broom in the crown of a western juniper

Fig. 1-13: Dwarf Alberta spruce (bottom) that reverted many years ago

by examining their characteristics. Many are so common that you become familiar with them, but even then, you can get tripped up. And there are literally hundreds of these popular landscape plants.

Horticulturalists and botanists have been dealing with these naturally occurring mutations for a long time. In the past, these cypress family forms with juvenile foliage were placed in *Retinospora*, a catch-all genus into which these misfit conifers across a number of genera were shunted (Sax 1958). For example, *Chamaecyparis pisifera* 'Filifera', the popular threadleaf Sawara-cypress, was *Retinospora pisifera* 'Filifera'. For obvious reasons, this practice and genus are now obsolete, but it was pragmatic in a way appealing to my sense of order. These abnormal juvenile forms look far more like each other than they do their parents. A genus of misfits to toss them into would be very handy.

Many people outside horticulture consider these forms to be abominations, insipid perversions of magnificent trees. They have a point. Comparing the 'Treasure Island' cultivar (fig. 1-14) of the Port-Orford-cedar (*Chamaecyparis lawsoniana*) or the 'Goldcrest' cultivar of the Monterey cypress (*Cupressus macrocarpa*) to the species is an act of futility. In *A Natural History of Western*

Trees, Donald Culross Peattie, master of the perfectly turned phrase, likens these forms to "garden pets."

During the holidays, these forms often go from garden pet to house pet when sold as tabletop trees. In an extreme example, an enterprising nursery in California noted that the 'Goldcrest' cultivar of the Monterey cypress and The Grinch in *How the Grinch Stole Christmas* are the same anemic chartreuse color. The nursery binds the small tree tightly in thick red ribbon so it bends whimsically to the side like a stocking cap and markets it as a "Whoo-Ville Tree" (fig. 1-15). I felt so sorry for these trees sold in the floral section of a grocery store, I had to buy the

Fig. 1-14: Port-Orford-cedar 'Treasure Island'

one that looked the most humiliated and bring it home, like a plant rescue. (A number of tutorials online demonstrate how to make your own Grinch Tree.)

But these pets have their uses in the landscape. The mounding cultivars typically hold their shape over time and pull their weight in the garden, but the popular multistemmed pillar-shaped forms often do not. Their spindly branches often give way under the strain of wind, snow, or ice. Space opens up between the weak limbs, compromising the form, while the outer branches often flop to the side. It's not long before they look like they're having a bad hair day. It's best to accept their limitations up front, or else they eventually disappoint you. I wouldn't go so far as to say they are disposable, but they are best placed in pots or other locations where you don't expect them to stand the test of

Fig. 1-15: Monterey cypress 'Goldcrest'

Fig. 1-16: Old cultivar with juvenile foliage

time. For instance, they can be used to plug a hole in a planting area until younger more valued conifers fill in the space—a plant you won't feel too bad about yanking out. (Rocks also work well for filling spaces.)

Of course, there are exceptions. Sometimes one sees old specimens that have maintained a tight form and that time has endowed with gravitas. Each is so odd-looking, at first it's difficult to comprehend what manner of plant you're looking at. You find them in older parts of town that have escaped redevelopment and that, frankly, have been a little neglected, as these dwarf conifers have often grossly outgrown the spots in which they were planted. The conifer in figure 1-16 was tiny in the nursery pot when planted many decades ago but now is almost as tall as the house and nearly half as wide and even looks as if at some point it was sheared across the top. In a larger space with a little tidying up it would be stunning, but ironically, this dwarf conifer has in effect miniaturized the house. Plants are like some fish—they continue to grow throughout their lives, so even a dwarf or miniature culti-var will get large given enough time.

Other exceptions are cultivars with juvenile foliage that have a strong central stem and with time grow into proper-looking trees, such as the *Chamaecyparis pisifera* 'Boulevard'. These can become quite tall and are often limbed up, as they often outgrow their allotted space.

JUVENILE FOLIAGE: PINE FAMILY

Juvenile foliage in all species in the pine family is similar to the adult foliage; it is linear but typically shorter and thinner. Even species in the pine, true fir, and larch genera, which have adult foliage that is bundled, bear juvenile foliage of individual needles. Cultivars with juvenile foliage are less common in the pine family. However, the Italian stone pine (*Pinus pinea*) is known for its long-lasting juvenile foliage, which persists for three to ten years. Over the holidays, young specimens with all juvenile foliage are sold in decorative pots as tabletop trees and look nothing like a pine (fig. 1-17).

Fig. 1-17: Italian stone pine with all juvenile foliage

Conifer Plant Families in Brief

The seven or eight conifer plant families worldwide is a paltry number compared with the more than four hundred flowering plant families. With six conifer plant families, given its size Japan is particularly diverse at this taxonomic level; for comparison, North America has three plant families.

NATIVE PLANT FAMILIES

When identifying a conifer in the PNW, one can typically assume it is from one of three families:

- In the pine family (Pinaceae), many native and nonnative species across seven genera are popular horticulturally.

- In the cypress family (Cupressaceae), many native and nonnative species across twelve genera (plus one hybrid genus) are popular horticulturally.

- In the yew family (Taxaceae), one native species and a few nonnative species across three genera are popular horticulturally. Cephalotaxaceae, the plum yew family, is considered a genus (*Cephalotaxus*) of the yew family by many botanists and is treated as such in this book.

NONNATIVE PLANT FAMILIES WITH LIMITED HORTICULTURAL PRESENCE

One species in each of the two following nonnative plant families is found in the landscape in the PNW. The foliage of both is unique enough that confusing them with other conifers is highly unlikely.

- The Japanese umbrella-pine family (Sciadopityaceae) is monotypic, with one genus and one species, the Japanese umbrella-pine (*Sciadopitys verticillata*), cultivars of which are becoming more commonly available.

- Species of the monkey puzzle family (Araucariaceae) are largely confined to the Southern Hemisphere. One novelty species is somewhat uncommon in the PNW landscape, the monkey puzzle tree (*Araucaria araucana*).

NONNATIVE PLANT FAMILIES NOT SEEN IN THE PNW

Two nonnative plant families will not be discussed beyond this paragraph, as they are very rare horticulturally. Their foliage resembles the leaves of flowering plants more than the needles, scales, and awls of Northern Hemisphere conifers.

- The podocarp family (Podocarpaceae) is a large family of mostly tropical and subtropical species found throughout the Southern Hemisphere, as well as in Central America, China, India, and Japan.
- The celery-pine family (Phyllocladaceae) has one genus and four species and is placed in the podocarp family by some botanists. Species are native to New Zealand, Tasmania, and neighboring island nations. The foliage is formed from flattened branches.

Conifer Identification Process

The conifer identification process in this book is organized around ID charts. The Diagram of ID Charts is a visual representation of all the charts in the book; it shows how to navigate from one to the other by characteristics visible with the naked eye or a 10× hand lens.

The Foliage Types and Pine Family Genera ID charts are master charts, in that they lead to other charts on the way to species ID. The approaches to species ID in the pine and cypress families reflect inherent differences in the foliage between the two families. Pine family foliage sorts neatly by genus in that the foliage of each has features unique to that genus. Accordingly, there is one ID chart (or set of charts) for each genus in the pine family. This is not the case in the cypress family: many species across several genera have similar foliage that is difficult to tell apart; for example, six genera have flattened scales. Accordingly, nearly all ID charts for the cypress family contain multiple genera.

After absorbing the content in this book, you should be able to move fluidly from one chart to another in identifying a species. And once you become familiar with the characteristics of the plant families and genera, you should be able to skip the master charts and go directly to the species ID charts.

RANGE INFORMATION IN THE ID CHARTS FOR PNW CONIFERS

In this book, the PNW region is defined, from south to north, as Northern California, Oregon, Washington, northern Idaho, western Montana, southern British Columbia, southwestern Alberta and Southeast Alaska. In the ID charts, each species native to this region is indicated as a "PNW native." PNW native conifers with ranges that extend beyond this defined region are indicated with an asterisk.

BOLDED TEXT IN THE ID CHARTS

In the ID charts, bolded text is meant to draw your attention to the differentiating characteristics of each species or genus.

USDA HARDINESS ZONES IN THE ID CHARTS

In the ID charts, the lowest USDA hardiness zone for each species is the last information given at the bottom of the column and is abbreviated; for example, a conifer hardy to USDA zone 4 is shown as Z4.

Diagram of ID Charts

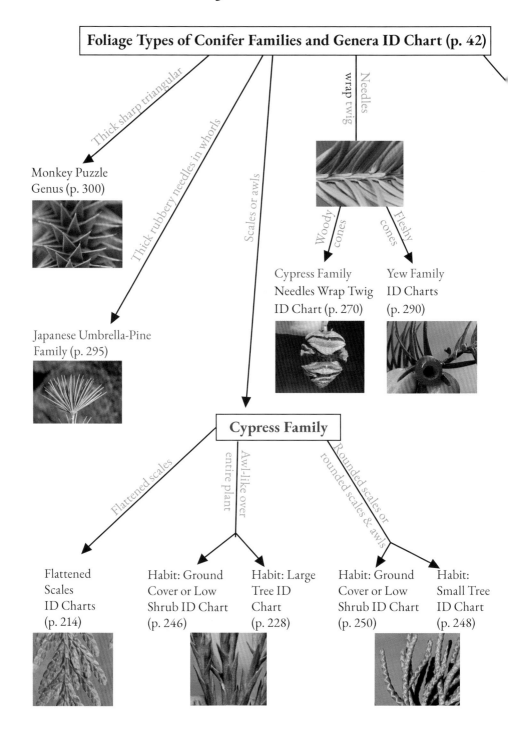

Foliage Types of Conifer Families and Genera ID Chart (p. 42)

Thick sharp triangular

Monkey Puzzle
Genus (p. 300)

Thick rubbery needles in whorls

Scales or awls

Needles wrap twig

Woody cones

Fleshy cones

Cypress Family
Needles Wrap Twig
ID Chart (p. 270)

Yew Family
ID Charts
(p. 290)

Japanese Umbrella-Pine
Family (p. 295)

Cypress Family

Flattened scales

Awl-like over entire plant

Rounded scales or rounded scales & awls

Flattened
Scales
ID Charts
(p. 214)

Habit: Ground
Cover or Low
Shrub ID Chart
(p. 246)

Habit: Large
Tree ID
Chart
(p. 228)

Habit: Ground
Cover or Low
Shrub ID Chart
(p. 250)

Habit:
Small Tree
ID Chart
(p. 248)

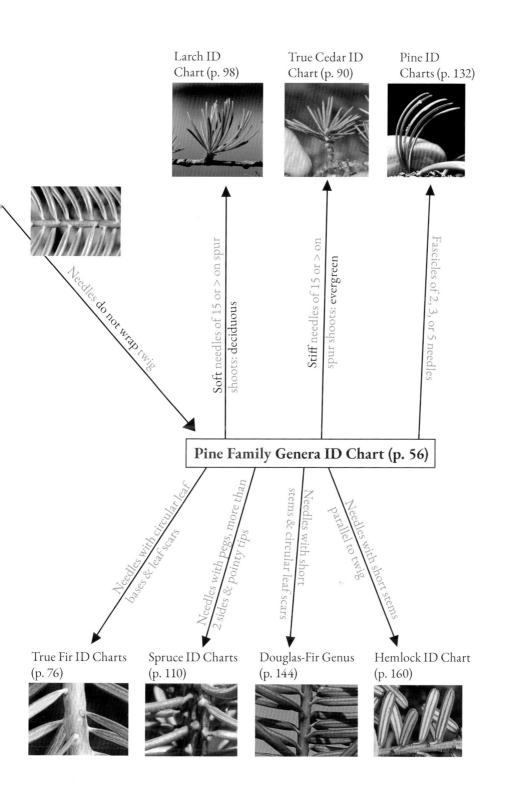

Larch ID Chart (p. 98)

True Cedar ID Chart (p. 90)

Pine ID Charts (p. 132)

Needles do not wrap twig

Soft needles of 15 or > on spur shoots: deciduous

Stiff needles of 15 or > on spur shoots: evergreen

Fascicles of 2, 3, or 5 needles

Pine Family Genera ID Chart (p. 56)

Needles with circular leaf bases & leaf scars

Needles with pegs, more than 2 sides & pointy tips

Needles with short stems & circular leaf scars

Needles with short stems parallel to twig

True Fir ID Charts (p. 76)

Spruce ID Charts (p. 110)

Douglas-Fir Genus (p. 144)

Hemlock ID Chart (p. 160)

Foliage Types of Conifer Families and Genera

	Pinaceae Pine family		Cupressaceae Cypress family		
Family					
Foliage	1 type of foliage Needles do not wrap twig: bundled or individual		4 types of foliage		
	Bundled needles of 2 or more	Needles attach to stem individually	Flattened scales	Awl-like over entire plant	
Genera	*Cedrus* True cedar *Larix* Larch *Pinus* Pine	*Abies* True fir *Picea* Spruce *Pseudotsuga* Douglas-fir *Tsuga* Hemlock	*Calocedrus* Incense-cedar *Chamaecyparis* False-cypress × *Cupressocyparis* Leyland-cypress *Platycladus* Oriental arborvitae *Thuja* True arborvitae *Thujopsis* Staghorn-cedar	*Cryptomeria* Japanese-cedar *Juniperus* Juniper *Sequoiadendron* Giant sequoia	
Charts	Go to Pine Family Genera ID chart (p. 56).		Go to Cypress Family: Flattened Scales ID charts (p. 214).	Go to Cypress Family: Awl-Like Foliage ID charts (p. 228 if large tree; p. 246 if ground cover or low shrub).	
Other	All species in the larch genus are deciduous.		Cultivars of a number of species with flattened scales have juvenile foliage, which is all awl-like and often prickly. These novelty plants can be difficult to identify.		

		Taxaceae Yew family	Sciadopityaceae Japanese umbrella- pine family	Araucariaceae Monkey puzzle family
		1 type of foliage	1 type of foliage	1 type of foliage (in PNW)
Rounded scales or rounded scales and awls	Needles wrap twig	Needles wrap twig	Thick rubbery needles in whorls	Thick sharp triangular leaves
Cupressus Cypress *Juniperus* Juniper	Deciduous: *Metasequoia* Dawn redwood *Taxodium* Baldcypress Evergreen: *Sequoia* Coast redwood	*Cephalotaxus* Plum yew *Taxus* Yew *Torreya* Stinking-cedar	*Sciadopitys* Japanese umbrella-pine	*Araucaria* Monkey puzzle
Go to Cypress Family: Rounded Scales or Rounded Scales and Awls Foliage ID charts (p. 248).	If cones are woody, go to Cypress Family: Needles Wrap Twig ID chart (p. 270).	If cones are fleshy, go to Yew Family ID charts (p. 290).	Go to Japanese Umbrella-Pine Family (p. 295).	Go to Monkey Puzzle Genus (p. 300).
Some junipers bear 2 foliage types on same plant: rounded scales and awls.	The foliage of species in the cypress family with single needles is very similar to species in the yew family. Differentiate plants in question by form, cones, and growth rate.		The unique foliage of these species looks like nothing else in the PNW.	

TRUE AND FALSE IN COMMON NAMES

Some conifer genera have the word "true" in their common names, as in the true fir genus (*Abies*) or the true cedar genus (*Cedrus*). This differentiates them from species with "fir" or "cedar" in their common names that are not in *Abies* or *Cedrus*, such as Douglas-fir, which is in *Pseudotsuga,* or western redcedar, which is in *Thuja*. Only species in *Abies* are firs; only species in *Cedrus* are cedars. Common names are ungoverned and often regional. Like many species, Douglas-fir has many aliases, including Douglastree, Oregonpine, Douglas-spruce, and so on, but every species has only one botanical (scientific) name, in this case, *P. menziesii*. The same is true for the western redcedar (*T. plicata*), also known as canoe cedar, shinglewood, and giant arborvitae. When the common and botanical names of a species are out of sync, it is customary to compound or hyphenate the common name, as an indicator, as in Douglas-fir or western redcedar, a practice followed throughout this book.

In each section, on first mention the botanical name of a genus or species is given in parentheses after the common name, and thereafter just the common name is used, in most cases. However, the common names of a number of genera in the cypress family are cumbersome; for instance, the common name of *Thuja* is the true arborvitae genus. In these sections, the botanical names are used throughout for the sake of ease and brevity.

HAND LENS

The conifer ID process in this book assumes the reader has a 10× magnification hand lens, or loupe. This inexpensive tool improves one's ID skills instantly, opening up a world of characteristics essential in conifer ID that one would otherwise be blind to. Make sure to hold the lens very close to your eye and to hold the plant sample very close to the lens, minutely adjusting the distance of the sample from the lens until the sample comes into focus.

CHAPTER 2

Pinaceae: The Pine Family

Introduction to the Pine Family

The pine family comprises approximately 225 species across eleven genera, not including subspecies and naturally occurring varieties. Almost all are in the Northern Hemisphere. Fifty-one species across seven genera are included in the ID charts in this book. Table 2-1 shows the number of species in each genus worldwide, compared with how many are included in the ID charts and how many of those are native to the PNW. Keep in mind that the number of species recognized in each genus varies depending on the source.

Four native PNW species in the pine family not included in the ID charts (or in table 2-1), because they are uncommon ornamentally, are the Jeffrey pine (*Pinus jeffreyi*), sugar pine (*P. lambertiana*), red fir (*Abies magnifica*), and subalpine larch (*Larix lyallii*).

The four other genera in the pine family, all native to Asia, count just six species among them:

Cathaya: one rare species (China)

Keteleeria: three species (China, Laos, Vietnam)

Nothotsuga: bristlecone hemlock, one rare species (China)

Pseudolarix: golden larch, one rare species (China)

Table 2-1. Pine Family Genera and Species Numbers

Native Genera	Worldwide	Book	PNW
Pinus Pine	110	20	6
Abies True fir	46	10	5
Picea Spruce	34	8	3
Larix Larch	10	4	1
Tsuga Hemlock	9	4	2
Pseudotsuga Douglas-fir	4	1	1
Nonnative Genus			
Cedrus True cedar	4	4	0

FOLIAGE

All species in the pine family have needle-like foliage that is clearly delineated from the branch. Aside from vascular tissue, the anatomy of the needle stops where it attaches to the twig. This is in contrast to all species in the yew family and a few species in the cypress family, which have linear foliage that continues down along and wraps the twig, a characteristic called decurrent. Compared to those two families, twigs in the

Fig. 2-1: Pine family: naked twig

pine family look naked (fig. 2-1). This fact alone tells you that you are in the pine family and allows you to move on to the next step, genus ID.

THREE TYPES OF SHOOTS

Once you've established that your specimen is in the pine family, look to see whether the needles attach to the branch individually or are bundled together.

Long Shoot: Individual Needles

All species in the true fir, spruce, hemlock, and Douglas-fir genera have long shoots only, which we recognize simply as branches and twigs (fig. 2-2), with needles that attach to the branch individually.

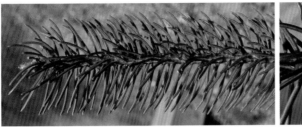

Fig. 2-2: Long shoot: individual needles

Short Shoot: Bundled Needles

In addition to long shoots, larch and true cedar species have short spur shoots (fig. 2-3). Each spur shoot holds fifteen or more needles in a focused whorl above the long shoot and grows a small increment each year. This phenomenon of having branches that grow at two vastly different rates is known as shoot dimorphism.

Fig. 2-3: Short shoot: bundled needles

Dwarf Shoot/Fascicle: Bundled Needles

In addition to long shoots, species in the pine genus have dwarf shoots, more commonly known as fascicles (fig. 2-4). Depending on the species, each fascicle has two to five needles bundled together. Fascicles attach directly to the branch (or long shoot). Once they fully emerge in their first season, barring injury, fascicles never change, never grow any longer, never add or drop any needles. This is shoot dimorphism in the extreme.

Fig. 2-4: Dwarf shoot or fascicle: bundled needles

STOMATAL BLOOM ON NEEDLES

Water pulled up from the roots travels throughout the plant via the xylem and exits as vapor through openings in the foliage called stomata. The stomata themselves are too small to see with the naked eye or a hand lens, but the white waxy coating around the openings is visible. This coating, called stomatal bloom, reduces water loss by reflecting light and lowering the temperature. The number, density, and pattern of the stomata vary from species to species, but on linear foliage stomata most often forms in bands (fig. 2-5). With a hand lens, in some species one can see clear separation between the bands; in other species the bands are densely packed and barely distinguishable from one another.

Light reflected by the stomatal bloom affects needle color and is responsible for blue-green and blue foliage. Needles with a few scattered stomata remain green (fig. 2-2), whereas blue-green foliage typically has a few lines of stomata on one or two surfaces. Conifers adapted to environments with intense light often display stomata on all sides of the needles, making the

Fig. 2-5: Close-up of stomatal bands

foliage blue (fig. 2-3). And when one surface is densely covered with stomata and another surface much less densely, a distinct contrast in color is evident between the two (fig. 2-4). You will notice that foliage farther back on the branch has darkened with age, due to the bloom abrading off, but at this point the needles are typically shaded.

FEMALE SEED CONES

Cone Anatomy

Nearly all female seed cones in the pine family are longer than they are wide and have the same basic anatomy, with two or four parts, depending on how you think about it. Picking up a dry open cone off the ground after it has released seeds is how most of us experience cones (fig. 2-6).

In the two-part version, many woody scales and the central spike that the scales attach to hold the whole cone together. In all genera, the scales overlap one another like shingles, leaving only a portion of the scale exposed. The scale narrows where it attaches to the axis. In some species the central spike extends beyond the top of the cone, where it

Fig. 2-6: Pine family cone

functions as a stalk. The cones of other species have no stalk, a characteristic called sessile. It can be a helpful thing to note in species ID.

But each scale has three integrated components: the scale itself, two ovules that mature into seeds after successful pollination and fertilization, and a bract. In most species, each seed has a thin, lightweight, aerodynamic wing. Winged seeds have evolved to rotate in the wind, which helps slow their descent and maximize flight time. Also, most cones are typically found high in trees, which also creates a longer flight path, with the goal of putting as much distance as possible between parent and offspring (Stevenson et al. 2015). On each flexed scale of a mature cone, you can see two light imprints where the seeds and their wings rested on the concave side before they were released (fig. 2-6). The seeds were tucked away at the innermost part of the scale, right before it attaches to the cone. In a number of species in the pine genus, seeds have evolved to be dispersed by birds; these have much larger seeds and vestigial wings or no wings at all.

Fig. 2-7: Ponderosa pine seed and wing, 1¼ inches long

Conifer seeds and their wings typically go unnoticed. In urban and suburban areas, you often see them blown into small windbreaks, such as street curbs, where they pile up ignominiously, only to be hoovered up by street cleaners. But in conifer seeds, as with so many of the small things in nature one slows down to observe carefully, one can find startling beauty. Conifer cones are a common sight on my desk, where they disgorge seeds as the scales dry out and open. For years I brushed them away into the wastebasket when cleaning up. Only after I started saving seeds to germinate did I notice how exquisite they are.

Fig. 2-8: Grand fir seed and wing, ¾ inch long

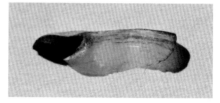

Fig. 2-9: Lodgepole pine seed and wing, ½ inch long

Winged pine seeds are the shape of tadpoles or small wrasses, with piles of them looking like schooling fish (figs. 2-7, 2-9). The pistachio-colored seed and speckled pink wing of the grand fir (*A. grandis*) look like a sail billowed with wind (fig. 2-8). Except for wingless seeds, one can anticipate the shape of a seed and seed wing for any species in the pine family from the shape of the scale. Because there are two seeds per scale, a seed and its wing are always a bit less than half the size of the scale, with the wing curved in the shape of the dry scale it detached from.

In addition to scales and seeds, a third papery structure called a bract is obvious in the mature cones of some species (fig. 2-10) but small and hidden inside the mature cones of most species (fig. 2-11). Early in their development, however, when cones are still quite small and not usually noticed, the bracts are the largest part of the cone (fig. 2-12). Only after successful fertilization of the ovules does the conifer invest in building the scales whose job it is to cradle and protect the developing seeds from predation and harsh weather. After fertilization, the scales increase in size rapidly and quickly overgrow the bracts.

When the bracts are visible in mature cones, they are said to be exserted (fig. 2-13). This less common trait is a key feature that in some cases takes you directly to species ID. Some larches, some true firs, and all Douglas-fir species have exserted bracts.

Fig. 2-10: Scale with exserted bract

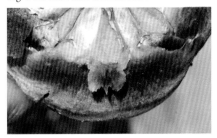

Fig. 2-11: Scale with non-exserted bract

Cone Evolution

The fact that the scale is fused to the bract at the base and not the other way around hints at the evolutionary history of the cone. Although today the bract seems decorative at best, like it doesn't have a real job to do, it is a remnant of what was once a long leaf. A second fertile leaf with ovules raised up on stalks grew out of the axil of this long leaf. (The more you learn about the evolution of plants, the more you realize that almost all of their reproductive parts evolved from leaves.) Over time the long leaf became smaller, thinner,

Fig. 2-12: Bracts on a young spring cone

and less significant, transforming into today's bract, while the fertile leaf became more woody and compact, transforming into today's scale. Along the way the ovules hunkered down and lost their stalks. But, then as now, the scale was fused to the bract and the bract was split at the end that is not attached to the axis (fig. 2-13).

INTACT, DISINTEGRATING, AND DISASSEMBLED CONES

In most genera in the pine family, the scales remain attached to the central axis for the life of the cone (fig. 2-6). However, in the true cedar and true fir genera, the cones disintegrate at seed release. The scales drop to the ground, while the axis remains on the branch. Interestingly, cones in both of these genera also grow erect on the branch tops. In the image of a Korean fir cone (*A. koreana*) (fig. 2-14), you can see that the axis is no longer holding the scales tightly together. One bump and this cone falls to pieces.

The seeds of many species of cones in the pine family are an important source of food for squirrels and chipmunks, among other animals. Cones that have been disassembled scale by scale are a common sight (fig. 2-15). In figure 2-16, in the partly intact ponderosa pine cone you can see just how deeply the scales overlap and that a rodent took six to ten bites to remove each scale precisely where the seeds are tucked in at the end closest to the spike. The dark hollows beneath the chewed areas are where the seeds were. More typically, no seeds are left uneaten, and you find cones that have been gnawed to the core with what looks like a drumstick left behind.

Fig. 2-13: Ripening Korean fir cone with exserted bracts

Fig. 2-14: Mature Korean fir cone about to collapse

Fig. 2-15: Ponderosa pine cone chewed down to a drumstick

Fig. 2-16: Ponderosa pine cone: partially chewed with bite marks

BRANCHING

One of the first questions posed in identifying a flowering tree or shrub is whether the branching is alternate or opposite. This is not a relevant question in conifer ID. In most genera in the pine family—larch, pine, spruce, and true fir—branches grow in whorls, setting one major whorl per growing season (fig. 2-17), though a smaller secondary whorl or two often grows between the main whorls. As a tree ages, the whorls are less apparent as branches are shed and the structure becomes more complex. Although hemlock branches also form whorls, this feature is not typically distinct. Douglas-fir branches form whorls, but not always reliably enough to be a useful ID characteristic. True cedars have random branching.

So, dead conifer trees do tell tales. If the branches of a dead tree are in whorls, then you can probably assume it was in the pine family (fig. 2-18). The visible bumpy pegs on the twigs of the dead tree in figure 2-18 identify it as a spruce. Its location in a natural area of the Columbia River Gorge means it was an Engelmann spruce (*P. engelmannii*), as that is the only native spruce found in that area.

Fig. 2-17: Whorled branch pattern on Japanese white pine

Fig. 2-18: Whorled branch pattern on a dead Engelmann spruce

HOW TO USE THE PINE FAMILY GENERA ID CHART

The Pine Family Genera ID chart is a photographic matrix of the key features of the pine family genera included in this book. As indicated by the headings, these seven genera are split into two groups: those with bundled needles (three genera) and those with needles that attach to the twig individually (four genera). Once you determine the genus of the conifer you are trying to identify, move on to the proper ID chart for that genus, as indicated at the bottom of each column.

Lebanon cedar cone

Pine Family Genera

	Foliage: Needles do not wrap twig			
	Genera with needles that attach to branch in bundles			
	Cedrus True cedar	*Larix* Larch DECIDUOUS	*Pinus* Pine	
Needles and Twigs	 Stiff needles of 15 or more on **spur shoots**	 Soft needles of 15 or more on **spur shoots**	 2, 3, or 5 needles per bundle	
	 Short side shoots give tree layered look	 Deciduous; winter twig above	 **Fascicle** unique to pine genus	
Buds	Very small buds not useful for ID	Very small buds hidden inside spur shoots not useful for ID	 Many bud types useful for species ID	
Cones	 **Erect oval seed cones** disintegrate in place	 Upright to 1½" (l), held indefinitely	 Woody cones, some with stalks	
Bark	 Vertical fissures	Vertical fissures; bark varies by species	Smooth young bark with resin blisters; mature bark often useful in species ID	
Charts	Go to True Cedar ID chart (p. 90).	Go to Larch ID chart (p. 98).	Go to Pine ID charts (p. 132).	

Genera with needles that attach to branch individually			
Abies True fir	*Picea* Spruce	*Pseudotsuga menziesii* Douglas-fir	*Tsuga* Hemlock
2-sided, blunt; often grooved or notched	Often sharp, stiff, 4-sided, not always square	Rounded, slightly pointed tips	Shorter, soft needles; blunt tips
Circular attachment; circular leaf scar	**Attach by peg**; grooved; encircle twig	Short stems and small circular leaf scars	**Short stems parallel to twig**
Close together; often but not always pitchy	Often rusty colored and rosebud-like	**Pointy, hard, and red**	Mostly tiny
Erect seed cones disintegrate in place	At branch tips, scales papery (l) or stiff (r)	**Mouse-tail cones** to 3" (l)	Papery cones
			Vertical fissures; bark varies by species
Smooth young bark with resin blisters	Flaky bark sloughs off	Smooth young bark with resin blisters; rutted mature bark	
Go to True Fir ID charts (p. 76).	Go to Spruce ID charts (p. 110).	Go to Douglas-Fir genus (p. 144).	Go to Hemlock ID chart (p. 160).

Abies: The True Fir Genus
Pinaceae: Pine Family
NEEDLES WITH CIRCULAR LEAF BASES AND LEAF SCARS

More than half of the forty-six or so species of true firs (*Abies*) worldwide are native to Asia. Six of the nine native to the United States are in the PNW, including the white fir (*A. concolor*) (fig. 2-19), making the region particularly rich in true fir species. The rest are scattered across the Northern Hemisphere. True firs are largely trees of the mountains. The PNW native grand fir (*A. grandis*) and a few boreal species, such as the balsam fir (*A. balsamea*), are exceptions. Many widely available ornamental European and Asian firs have highly restricted native ranges, places they retreated to during the ice ages of the Pleistocene and where a warming and drying climate has shrunk their ranges even further. Many European conifers were pushed into southern

Fig. 2-19: White fir with a double crown

58

Spain and northern Africa, where the endangered Spanish fir (*A. pinsapo*) inhabits a restricted number of alpine areas on either side of the Strait of Gibraltar. The endangered Korean fir (*A. koreana*) is scattered in small, isolated stands on or near mountaintops in North and South Korea, while the Nordmann fir (*A. nordmanniana*) adheres to the southern and eastern coasts of the Black Sea. Though many native PNW firs are suffering the effects of warmer and dryer conditions, thankfully none is endangered.

The native ranges of two of the most beautiful true firs in the world—the subalpine fir (*A. lasiocarpa*) and the noble fir (*A. procera*)—overlap in the PNW. The noble fir is restricted to Western Oregon and western Washington, and far northwest California, whereas the subalpine fir stretches across the entirety of western North America, with an immense latitudinal range from 64 degrees N in the Yukon to 32 degrees S in Southern Arizona. In the most southerly part of the subalpine fir's range, in mountainous areas of Arizona, New Mexico, and southern Colorado, one encounters the corkbark fir (*A. lasiocarpa* var. *arizonica*), a naturally occurring variety with corky bark and bluer foliage than the subalpine fir. In southwest Oregon and northwest California, the noble fir hybridizes with the very similar red fir (*A. magnifica*). Red and noble firs are most easily differentiated by their female cones: red fir cones lack the bright yellow exserted bracts of the noble fir.

True fir is the most difficult genus in the pine family to identify. Often one arrives at the conclusion something's a fir by the process of elimination: it's not a spruce, not a hemlock, not a Douglas-fir; therefore it must be a true fir. Actually, this can be an effective approach. If you are in doubt as to what genus you're looking at, start by ascertaining what you know it isn't and see what you're left with.

Identifying a species of true fir is that much more difficult. As Donald Culross Peattie says in his classic book, *A Natural History of Western Trees*, "There are so many Firs in the West that it takes an expert, sometimes, to tell them apart and even he is not always prepared to identify a specimen at first glance." And Peattie was writing about native firs only; ornamental firs weren't thrown into the mix.

Peattie devotes a loving essay to each native western tree species, but he is at his most eloquent when writing on certain conifers, particularly the redwoods and true firs of the American West, parts of which read as if he were recollecting a dream. These essays are best enjoyed one at a time, like a delicacy, with space in between to contemplate the beautiful prose and to let the tree materialize in your imagination. One has the feeling of having actually encountered the tree, right down to the aromas his words stir up out of memory. Peattie's essays are the best substitute I know for a walk in a coniferous forest. Not a book to be rifled through in search of facts, but a book one lives with and picks up when feeling calm and receptive.

FOLIAGE CHARACTERISTICS OF ALL TRUE FIRS

To determine whether a specimen is in the fir genus, examine how the needles attach to the twig. The defining characteristic of true fir needles is that they narrow just before widening into circles at the base where they affix to the twig, like miniature suction cups (fig. 2-20a). When the needles drop, well-defined circular leaf scars mark the spot. In some species with large needles, like the white fir, this feature is easily seen. White fir is what I call a large-print species. All the features are readily observed with the naked eye,

Fig. 2-20a: Circular needle bases, circular leaf scars, and smooth twigs

Fig. 2-20b: Two-sided needles

Fig. 2-20c: Two stomatal bands on lower side

making ID easy. Of course, there are also small-print species, ones for which you'll probably need to reach for a loupe to see the features well enough to be satisfied you've made a proper ID. Also note that fir twigs are smooth, as opposed to spruce twigs, which are grooved.

All fir needles are flat, with two sides (fig. 2-20b). They do not roll back and forth in your fingers like spruce needles. All have two stomatal bands on the underside, separated by a midrib (fig. 2-20c). The denser the stomata, the whiter and more striking the stomatal bands will be (true for all conifers). Some species have one or two additional bands on the topside; it is these stomatal bands, such as on noble fir, that give some firs a blueish hue.

OTHER FOLIAGE CHARACTERISTICS TO LOOK FOR

In some fir species, the needle tips are notched (fig. 2-21a), or the needle is grooved along the length on the upper side (fig. 2-21b). For true fir species ID, you'll also need to take a close look at how the needles are oriented to the twig. In the spruce genus, the needles of most species encircle the twig. In true firs, how needles attach to the twig varies from species to species and is an important clue in ID. Look at the twig from all angles, from the top looking down, from the side, and on end. It helps to think of what you see in terms of hairdos. In some species the needles look combed forward, concealing the twig (fig. 2-21c); in others the needles expose the twig like hair parted down the middle (fig. 2-21d); and in yet others the needles encircle the twig like an afro (fig. 2-21e) or point sharply skyward in an updo (fig. 2-21f).

For certain species, you must also be conscious of variations. For example, grand firs are shade-tolerant trees that can grow in the understory, in partial sun, or sometimes even in full sun. Foliage in the shade grows quite flat, as if it has done time in a plant press (fig. 2-21d), an adaptation that maximizes surface area and allows needles to harvest as much light as possible in low-light conditions. However, grand fir needles in the sun will arch up, softening the sun's angle and protecting foliage from intense light. If you walk around a grand fir, from full shade to partial shade to full sun, you'll see the needles arching up at increasing angles to the twig in a gradient, like nature's perfectly engineered solar panels. Without knowing anything else about the conifer, you could infer from the orientation of the needles of white fir (an updo) (fig. 2-21f) that it is a species adapted to full sun. The blue color corroborates this, as it is an adaptation for reflecting ultraviolet light from the needle surface. The botanical name of the white fir, *A. concolor*, means one color, referring to the even hazy blue of both surfaces of the needles.

Other Foliage Characteristics to Look For

Fig. 2-21a: Notched tips

Fig. 2-21b: Grooves on the upper surface

Fig. 2-21c: Combed forward on silver fir

Fig. 2-21d: Parted down the middle on grand fir

Fig. 2-21e: Encircling on Spanish fir

Fig. 2-21f: Upswept on white fir

FEMALE SEED CONES

True fir seed cones mature in one growing season on one-year-old twigs. They stand erect on the branch tops, like sentinels. The cones of a number of species ooze prodigious amounts of pitch that looks like hardened candle wax when cold and melted sugar when warm. Fir cones do not drop intact like spruce or pine cones. They disintegrate in place; the scales break away from the cone axis, which is left unoccupied on the branch, like a spindle, for a year or two (figs. 2-22a–f).

The scale narrows to little more than a point at the end where it joins the axis. On an individual fallen cone scale, this narrow point can at first glance look like an exserted bract; however, it's important to remember the anatomy of the scale, from the pine family introduction. The bract and scale join at the narrow end where they attach to the stalk and are separate from each other along the rest of their lengths.

With a couple of exceptions, most true fir species set cones only after many years, when the trees are already quite tall. This, in addition to the fact that they are typically confined to the treetops, well out of arm's reach, and break apart rather than drop whole, makes the cones of most species difficult to observe or collect. This is most annoying. You might get lucky and stumble on a fertile blown-down branch. But beware, the needles of cone-bearing branches of some species tend to be short, curved, pointy, and thick, regardless of the needle characteristics on other parts of the tree, which can throw you off. Sometimes a young, and therefore short, highly stressed tree close to death will do the cone-seeker a favor and divert all remaining resources to seed production and set a few reachable cones.

Another way to get close to true fir cones of certain native species is to hike or drive near tree line, where specimens both diminutive and mature enough to set cones can be found. These timberline specimens, pruned into natural dwarfs by harsh alpine conditions, are called *krummholz,* a German word meaning crooked wood. Timberline is a zone populated mainly by low shrubs and krummholzed trees. Any plant part that dares jut into the wind, like the main leader of a conifer, is sheared away and with it the apical bud and apical dominance, or the apical buds perish in the desiccating wind. Growth is redirected down into those lateral buds that survive because they are low enough in winter to lie beneath the sheltering snow. This stunting, often seen in combination with a windward growth pattern, makes some krummholz specimens appear to be cowering (which in effect they are).

Female Seed Cones

Fig. 2-22a: Young noble fir cone

Fig. 2-22b: Mature noble fir cone

Fig. 2-22c: Disintegrating noble fir cone

Fig. 2-22d: Spikes of disintegrated cones left on tree

Fig. 2-22e: Close-up of exserted bracts of noble fir cone

Fig. 2-22f: Interior of grand fir cone

Another source of cones is cliffside (fig. 2-22g). If you're walking on a trail with a steep drop-off and the top of a 40-foot subalpine fir growing up from below is heavy with pitchy cones, you might be able to lasso one with the

Fig. 2-22g: Pitchy cones high in a subalpine fir, cliffside

Fig. 2-22h: Potpourri of grand fir cone scales and seed wings

Fig. 2-22i: Cone bound like a ham

ABIES BRACTEATA Hook & Arn

Fig. 2-22j: Bristlecone fir: The exception with long bracts and sharp needles

loop of your hiking pole and yank it toward you. (Note that it is illegal to remove plant material from some federal lands, like national parks.) And it's a happy day when you discover a whole or partial cone lying on the ground like a gift, one that a squirrel or chipmunk has gnawed off the tree and forgotten about or that you have gotten to first. More typically, you happen upon the remains of a rodent's recent meal. A dismantled grand fir cone is a surprisingly beautiful mess, a potpourri of creamy bright-green scales and seed wings one is amazed to discover are the deep pink and purple hues of the closing moments of a sunset (fig. 2-22h).

Once you do take possession of an intact cone you are loath to see it disintegrate—you never know when you might get another. In older horticultural books you see images of true fir cones bound up tightly in thick cord like a holiday ham, an effect I have re-created (fig. 2-22i), or wrapped in heavy-gauge wire in attempts to hold the whole thing together for posterity. While these tortured specimens transmit the idea of true fir cones, they look insipid and sad in captivity.

You may be able to see that an older tree is in the true fir genus by spotting upright cones at the treetop and noting their general color, or, with binoculars or a telephoto lens, you may also be able to see if the cones have exserted bracts—but suffice it to say you will probably be making a genus and species ID without the aid of a cone, one of the main difficulties of true fir ID.

As a consolation, with mature trees you can often find individual cone scales on the ground. In freshly fallen scales that have yet to age to brown, the edge tells you the color of the intact cone. In the image of the grand fir potpourri (fig. 2-22h), the widest edge is bright green, the color of the cone before it was dismantled. In all species, when the cone is young the bracts are longer than the seed scales, but as the cone matures, the seed scales usually overtake the bracts and obscure them. However, in some species, the bracts of mature cones are longer than the scales and are an identifying characteristic, such as with noble (fig. 2-22e) and Korean firs.

One of the many delights Korean and Spanish firs bring to the garden is that they set cones at a young age, where you can admire them at eye level, often even when they are still in pots at the nursery. In some species, like subalpine and Korean firs, the cones often crowd together at different angles as if jostling for space (fig. 2-22g). In others like the noble fir, the cones typically stand apart from one another, which seems fitting for a species that sets the largest cones in the genus, up to nine inches tall and four inches wide, as if cones so grand demand plenty of personal space.

The most difficult true fir cone to procure is from the exceedingly rare bristlecone fir (*A. bracteata*), endemic to the Santa Lucia Mountains of California. Even photographs are uncommon. The species is in fact named for its bizarre cones, which have comically long exserted bracts, making it the porcupine of cones (fig. 2-22j). It also has the distinction of being the only true fir species in North America with sharp-tipped needles.

MALE POLLEN CONES

True fir male pollen cones begin to develop in late winter, typically high in the tree along the underside of last season's growth (fig. 2-23a). Unique to the true fir genus, the cones leave small persistent cups behind after they drop (fig. 2-23b), which could be mistaken for pathogenic galls. Depending on the species and stage of development, the pollen cones are red, purple, yellow, or green. In most cases one sees pollen cones on blown-down branches, but on dwarf cultivars, where they are low enough to be visible, pollen cones provide a surprising decorative element.

Fig. 2-23a: Bright red pollen cones

Fig. 2-23b: Last season's pollen cone cups and developing pollen cones

BUDS

The terminal buds of true firs usually come in sets of three or more. Most species' buds are rounded and sticky, with insulating pitch such that the bud scales are obscured. The look of the pitch is temperature-dependent: when cold, it hardens into white crystals (fig. 2-24a); when warm, it is clear and glossy (fig. 2-24b), giving the buds a polished look. Non-pitchy buds can be a useful clue in species ID (fig. 2-24c). In some species, needles at the twig tip curl protectively around the buds like fingers, and you must pull back or remove a few needles to get a look at the buds (fig. 2-24d).

BARK

The bark of young fir trees is smooth, a smoothness interrupted by bulgy resin blisters (fig. 2-25a). You can pierce open a blister easily with a thumbnail to experience the resin (fig. 2-25b). But beware, while you might enjoy the heady aroma, it is very sticky and difficult to remove from skin and clothing, and whatever you do, don't touch your hair. Though some species retain smooth bark and resin blisters for decades, with enough age true fir

Buds

Fig. 2-24a: Cold and pitchy buds on Korean fir   Fig. 2-24b: Warm and pitchy buds on Korean fir

Fig. 2-24c: No pitch on noble fir buds   Fig. 2-24d: Shy buds of Pacific silver fir

bark becomes vertically fissured, especially at the lower part of the tree (fig. 2-25c). One exception is the subalpine fir, whose bark often remains thin and blistery for its entire life span. Young Douglas-fir (*Pseudotsuga menziesii*) bark also has resin blisters, which can throw one off when trying to identify a Douglas-fir specimen that hasn't yet developed the distinctive thick, rutted bark the species is known for.

FORM AND ADELGIDS

True firs have perfect posture, with single trunks straight as flagpoles and regularly spaced whorls of branches, which they add at the rate of one whorl per year (figs. 2-26a–e). On occasion they develop multiple leaders as a result of damage. In the image of the subalpine firs in the wild (fig. 2-26b), the tree to the left has the steeple-like form the species often adopts in its native environment; the specimen to its right is likely a victim of the balsam woolly

Bark

Fig. 2-25a: Smooth young bark with resin blisters on noble fir

Fig. 2-25b: Pierced resin blister on bark of noble fir

Fig. 2-25c: Mature fissured bark of grand fir

adelgid (*Adelges piceae*), as evidenced by its misshapen crown and thin lateral growth, giving it a bit of an upside-down look. Healthy subalpine firs are striking when they thrive in the residential or commercial landscape (fig. 2-26a); unfortunately, ailing specimens that sometimes look beheaded are far more common (fig. 2-26c).

The forms of wild and domesticated noble firs are similar, though the latter never live as long as the former and, like subalpine firs, are often unhealthy, often for the same reasons (fig. 2-26d). But fortunate are the landscapes graced with vigorous decades-old noble firs (fig. 2-26e); their blue foliage, small footprint, and great height—they are the tallest firs in the world—are a spectacular combination.

Adelgids are tiny insects, too small to see with the naked eye or a loupe, whose anatomy is similar to that of aphids. The mouthparts of both are adapted to accessing and consuming their entirely liquid diets. Part bayonet,

Form and Adelgids

Fig. 2-26a: Healthy subalpine fir in the landscape

Fig. 2-26b: Subalpine firs in the wild. Healthy-ish specimen (left) Unhealthy specimen (right)

Fig. 2-26c: Unhealthy subalpine fir in the landscape

Fig. 2-26d: Unhealthy noble fir in the landscape

Fig. 2-26e: Healthy noble fir in the landscape

part two-way straw, it is a multipurpose tool with which the adelgid pierces the tree to reach and draw up the sweet phloem and to inject toxic saliva down into the host. When the bayonet is not in use, it is tucked along the underside of the adelgid's body.

The balsam woolly adelgid feeds on the buds, nodes, and bark of true firs. The buds and nodes become swollen and arthritic looking (fig. 2-26f), with the damage often concentrated in the crown, where there is plenty of succulent new growth, but damage can be found throughout the tree (fig. 2-26d). (If the tree is heavily infested, it can be difficult to find healthy buds for species ID.) Early in the 1900s when these symptoms were first noticed

 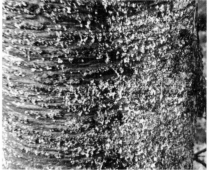

Fig. 2-26f: Subalpine fir branch with adelgid damage

Fig. 2-26g: Subalpine fir with adelgid infestation on the trunk (white specks)

on firs in the eastern United States, the problem wasn't well understood, and plant pathologists called it "the gout disease" or "dropsy," an old-fashioned term for swelling caused by pooling of fluids (Balch 1932). Firs with stem and crown infestations typically fail incrementally over many years, often surviving in a diminished state for decades.

However, a longer-term problem for subalpine, grand, and Pacific silver firs—the most susceptible native species in the PNW—is that the adelgids' preference for feeding in the crown, right where firs set all their cones, has led to a drastic reduction in cone production and an impoverished seed bank in the wild. This is especially true for subalpine firs at mid to high elevations and for the grand and Pacific silver firs at low elevations, where attrition is taking out old trees without enough young ones taking their place (Mitchell and Buffam 2001). Also hard hit are certain disturbed sites—avalanched areas, old lava flows, and meadows—settings where subalpine firs have been serving as a pioneer species, with no other species apparently able to step in to fill the void (Mitchell and Buffman 2001). As bad as this sounds, infestations of the main trunk are even more serious (fig. 2-26g), often causing a speedy decline over just a few years. The woolly part of the adelgid's name refers to the white waxy coating the adult insect exudes to protect herself and her eggs.

The adelgid's common name reflects the host these pests were first discovered on, the balsam fir, a species native to New England, Canada, the upper Midwest, and as far south as Virginia. However, the pest is now found on true firs up and down the East and West Coasts of the United States and Canada. Noble, white, and red firs seem to be resistant in the wild but less so in other settings, such as the residential landscape or arboreta. This woolly adelgid is native to Europe, and, as such, European fir species like the Spanish fir and European silver fir (*A. alba*) are asymptomatic, showing no swelling at the feeding sites. For fir species native to Asia, such as the Korean fir, resistance to the adelgid falls somewhere in between, with some tolerating the pest and others not (Ragenovich and Mitchell 2006). So, if an ornamental true fir shows adelgid damage, you can be sure that it's not an Old World species. And before purchasing a New World true fir, whether wild or cultivated, be sure to examine it carefully for adelgid damage.

WILD NATIVE FIRS IN THE LANDSCAPE

Both subalpine and noble firs sold as landscape trees have often been dug from the wild, a difficult transition many don't survive. Because of the high mortality rate, some landscape companies plant dug-up firs in customers' gardens only after the trees have survived for a few years off the mountain. This is a very good strategy I wish I had known about before selecting and buying half a dozen subalpine and noble firs from a native plant nursery just as they were unloaded from the truck on the very day they'd been dug up and transported off the mountain. I had assumed freshly dug specimens were a better choice than those languishing on the lot, mainly because I was sure they would do better if under my personal care from day one—and I felt lucky to be getting first pick.

Unlike specimens in Christmas tree farms, which are typically sheared into perfect little pyramids, dug-up noble and subalpine firs often have unique forms from which you can infer details of their history. Two noble firs I chose were growing like identical twins and had been dug as a matching set. Counting the whorls told me they had germinated together twelve seasons earlier, and the distinct complementary curves at the same location in their otherwise straight trunks told of some shared experience in their third year; one subalpine fir had a pronounced lean that suggested something pinned it down early in life, diverting it from the straight form the species is known for. Sadly, nary a one survived. Some died right away the first season; others perished after a few years. One that seemed like it was going to buck the odds and be the lone survivor called it quits after seven years. The higher up in elevation you go and the closer to the mountains you get, the better subalpine and noble firs fare in residential and commercial landscapes.

GRAND FIR SEEDLINGS IN THE LANDSCAPE

Aside from boreal species, the grand fir is the only fir to grow below 1,500 feet elevation in the wild (although it is also found as high as 6,500 feet). It is one of the conifers of the PNW lowland native forest. So, it happily seeds down among us, typically in the shade and in places you'd never plant a tree that could become more than 200 feet tall. These seedlings tend to go unnoticed (fig. 2-27), often maintaining a stealth presence in the landscape until they're several years old, when you finally spot them and wonder where in the world the little fir tree came from. When you see grand firs growing in odd places, like right out of the center of a three-by-five-foot shrub that was most certainly there first, you can bet that the grand fir chose the location. The Nordmann fir will also occasionally seed down.

Fig. 2-27: Grand fir seedling with six long cotyledons

ADVANCED *ABIES* ID: GRAND FIR OR WHITE FIR?

In the wild, white fir and grand fir hybridize in Central and southwest Oregon, where their natural ranges overlap. I was happily perplexed the first time I encountered one of these hybrids in the wild (figs. 2-28a,b). My initial thought was that it was a grand fir with foliage that had adapted to full-sun conditions—I was convinced by the small pitchy buds, notched needle tips, and green cones. However, white firs also have green cones, and this specimen also had upswept needles with stomata on both upper and lower surfaces, which is typical of white fir. And it was growing in full sun on top of what's called Little Crater overlooking Paulina Lake in Central Oregon.

Most likely the correct ID is that the specimen is some of both, a beautiful natural hybrid (a white grand fir or a grand white fir). The white fir DNA allows the grand fir to come out of the shadows into areas of intense light, while the grand fir DNA maybe nudges the white fir's range a little bit to the north. And it turns out that an isolated population of white firs resides in the Lake Paulina area (Little 1971). Though this specimen is a fairly obvious hybrid, many are more subtle, with often just a few lines of stomata on the upper surface of the needles indicating that the DNA is not pure grand fir or pure white fir. Keep an eye out for volunteers of these hybrids in ornamental gardens where white and grand firs grow in close proximity.

Fig. 2-28b: Hybrid foliage

Fig. 2-28a: Hybrid form

CULTIVARS

Many dwarf true fir cultivars allow you to have what is in essence a miniature version of these lovely trees. A close examination of the buds and needles should lead you to species ID. 'Rick's Foxtail' is an outstanding dwarf cultivar of the noble fir that I have had better luck with than the difficult-to-grow species. 'Glauca Compacta', a cultivar of the corkbark fir with vivid blue foliage and a tight form, fares better in ornamental gardens than specimens dug from the wild.

Foliage: Needles with circular leaf bases and leaf scars   Cones: Upright

	A. alba European silver fir Native to Europe		*A. amabilis* Pacific silver fir PNW NATIVE	
Needles and Twigs	To 1¼" (l); 2 bands below	Brush forward	¾"–1¼" (l); 2 bands below	**Brush forward and conceal twig**
		Notched tips; grooves on upper surface		Grooves along the length of the needles; notched tips
Buds		Dark red, pointy **non-pitchy buds**		Very small round resinous buds tightly enclosed by needles
Cones and Form	Green to brown; exserted bracts	Columnar, straight tree	Dark purple	Straight form
Bark		Fissured scaly bark		Silver bark flaky and fissured
Other	Nordmann fir very similar; Z4		Shade tolerant; a few cultivars; uncommon ornamentally; Z5	

A. balsamea 'Nana' Balsam fir 'Nana' Native to US and Canada		*A. concolor* White fir PNW NATIVE*		*A. grandis* Grand fir PNW NATIVE*	
½" (l); usually encircle twig	Two stomatal bands below	1½"–2½" (l); blue all over; **U-shaped**	View from the side; twig yellow green	To 2" (l); glossy; **twig exposed**	Two distinct bands below
	Rounded tips; often 1 scattered stomatal band in center of upper surface	**Rounded tips; no grooves** NOTE: Needles sometimes more green than blue			Notched, grooved, short and long needles; twigs light green to red-brown; **needles flat in shade, arched in sun**
	Pitchy dark red buds		Bud scales with slight projections		Very small red pitchy buds usually concealed by needles
Mostly small cultivars that do not normally set cones		Green cones age to brown	Conical, low branching	Green, to 4" (l), occ. purply	Conical, low branching
Bark concealed by foliage on small cultivars			Brownish-gray fissured older bark		Brown and gray bark fissured with age
Very similar to *A. fraseri*/Fraser fir (not included); Z3		Hybridizes with grand fir where ranges overlap; Z3		Hybridizes with white fir where ranges overlap; Z4	

	Foliage: Needles with circular leaf bases and leaf scars Cones: Upright				
	A. koreana Korean fir 'Silberlocke' Native to Korea		*A. lasiocarpa* Subalpine fir PNW NATIVE*		*A. nordmanniana* Nordmann fir
Needles and Twigs	½" (l); wider tip; shallow groove	**Two dense silver bands**	¾"–1½" (l); **star-like viewed on end**	Two stomatal bands below	To 1¼" (l), glossy; may obscure twig
		Slight notch; base can be yellow; needles curve sharply in this and some other cultivars, exposing bands		**Usually one wide central stomatal band on top**; tips rounded or slightly notched; blue cast to foliage	
Buds		Rounded red pitchy buds		Dark red pitchy buds look fused	
Cones and Form	Exserted bracts; sets cones young	Small tree to 7' in 10 years	Dark purple and pitchy	Narrow pyramid when healthy	Exserted bracts; lighter colored
Bark		Young bark with resin blisters in image		**Thin blistery bark throughout most of life**	
Other	Many bun-like cultivars: 'Ice Breaker' same foliage as 'Silberlocke'; Z5		Subalpine tree; hard to grow in lowlands; Z4		Low spreading and yellow cultivars; Z4

Native to Turkey and W. Caucasus	*A. pinsapo* Spanish fir Native to Spain and Morocco		*A. procera* Noble fir PNW NATIVE	
Dark green above and silver below	To ¾" (l); encircle twig	Bottlebrush look	1"–1½" (l); **blue above and below**	Twig usually rusty
Tips rounded, notched and grooved; dense stomatal bands below; **needles directed forward and arched**		Rounded tips; short, stiff and **plastic-like**; 2 dim stomatal bands above and below		Two stomatal bands above; **needles form J at twig**; tips rounded w/occ. notch; slight groove
Deep red pointed buds **not pitchy**		Reddish-brown buds not pitchy		Needles enclose pink **non-pitchy buds**
Conical, up-curved branches	Pointed tip; sets cones young	Conical	To 9" (l), yellow exserted bracts	Narrow column
Grayish-brown smooth-ish bark		Older bark brown, rough, and scaly		Brown, fissured bark
	Many smaller and blue cultivars; Z6–7		Tallest fir; hard to grow in lowlands; Z5	

Cedrus: The True Cedar Genus
Pinaceae: Pine Family
Stiff Needles of Fifteen or More on Spur Shoots: Evergreen

Worldwide, there are four species in the true cedar genus (*Cedrus*), though some taxonomists believe all four represent disjunct populations of one or two species. At one time the three species native to mountains of the Mediterranean may have had a continuous range: the Atlas cedar (*C. atlantica*) in Algeria and Morocco; the Lebanon cedar (*C. libani*) in Lebanon, Syria, and Turkey; and the Cyprus cedar on the island of Cyprus (*C. brevifolia*). The deodar cedar (*C. deodara*) (fig. 2-29) is native to a continuous stretch of the Himalayas in Tibet, India, Pakistan, and Afghanistan. Under the pressure of a warming and drying climate, the already limited range of the endangered Atlas cedar is contracting further as it moves higher up the mountains in search of suitable conditions (Cheddadi et al. 2017). And though the Lebanon cedar's fate is more secure, its timber has been exploited for thousands of years, and it is endangered in its namesake country.

True cedars are popular landscape trees but bear little resemblance to the conifers called cedars in the PNW. The fragrance of a number of New World conifers so reminded European settlers of cedars from the Old World that many have cedar in their common names. However, only trees in *Cedrus* are true cedars; all species in Pinaceae have needles

Fig. 2-29: Deodar cedar

Foliage

Fig. 2-30a: True cedar foliage: most needles on short spur shoots

Fig. 2-30b: False-cedar foliage: scale-like

Fig. 2-30c: Individual needles concentrated at ends of leading branches

Fig. 2-30d: Individual needles grow sparsely along leading branches

(fig. 2-30a). Western redcedar (*Thuja plicata*), incense-cedar (*Calocedrus decurrens*), Alaska-cedar (*Chamaecyparis nootkatensis*), and Port-Orford-cedar (*C. lawsoniana*) are in the cypress family and have flattened scale-like foliage (fig. 2-30b).

It can be strangely difficult to accept that trees one feels such affection for aren't real cedars, so inextricably linked is one's sense of them to the word. But this type of mismatching of names occurs often with common names, and not just by nonspecialists. Botanists understandably placed unfamiliar plants they encountered in the New World in genera already known to them from the Old World, in time realizing that some represented new genera. Both true cedars and the false cedars of the PNW experience wet winters and droughty sunny summers in their native environments, and it is not uncommon to see them keeping company and thriving side-by-side in the landscape.

FOLIAGE

True cedars exhibit something called shoot dimorphism: they produce short spur shoots that grow as little as one-fifth of an inch per year (fig. 2-30a), as well as long leading branches that grow several inches a year (fig. 2-30c). The arrangement of needles (phyllotaxy) is different as well. Most of the tree's foliage is borne by the short spur shoots, with each spur raising fifteen to forty needles (depending on the species) above the branch in focused tuft-like whorls. The older the shorter shoot is, the more raised up the needle cluster will be. A much smaller portion of the needles attach individually to the long leading branches, with most of these concentrated at the branch ends, but some are also found growing sparsely along the length (fig. 2-30d). Needles remain on the tree for three to six years, with each year's fresh needles adding to the total number in the cluster or replenishing fallen needles.

One might confuse true cedars with larches (*Larix*), as larches also have needles elevated on spur shoots, but the similarities end there; larch needles are soft and deciduous, and the much smaller cones remain intact.

Tip Blight

True cedars are susceptible to a fungus that turns the tips pink (fig. 2-30e). In wet humid springs the problem can be severe, affecting a large percentage of the plant, giving it a distinct pink cast. Cedars typically tolerate the fungus well. In small cultivars, it's possible to prune away infected tips to control the problem, but this is impractical in large trees.

Fig. 2-30e: Blue Atlas cedar with tip blight

FEMALE SEED CONES

Each female true cedar cone is nature's minor work of art and, as such, it is fitting that each sits prominently atop a spur shoot, which doubles as a pedestal, raising the cone up for display (figs. 2-31a–d). The broad thin smooth cone scales overlap tightly in an undulating pattern reminiscent of wave-rippled sand (fig. 2-31e). The cones themselves are three to six inches long and, like Humpty Dumpty, fatter at the middle, with a base that's more plump than the top. It is a pleasing shape that conforms naturally to the palm of one's hand. The densely packed scales make the cone hefty for its size, to the point that the spur shoot sometimes appears to compress beneath the weight. Plus, true cedars usually set at least a few cones low on the tree, allowing one to appreciate them at eye level.

Unfortunately, these exquisite cones do not remain intact but disassemble scale-by-scale while still atop the branch and, like Humpty Dumpty, cannot be put back together again. Furthermore, there's nothing you can do to prevent the cones from breaking apart. Take it from experience—dousing intact cones with hairspray or dipping them in polyurethane or any other such foolishness will not stop them from slouching into a heap of scales on your desk. The cone must and will disassemble, leaving the cone axis behind on the tree, which can persist for some time. The cone scales litter the ground in heavy-cone-set years, crunching audibly underfoot when dry. The wide cone scales narrow to little more than points where they attach to the axis (fig. 2-31f).

Though the highly prized Lebanon cedar was introduced to Britain in the late 1630s, nearly a hundred years had passed before anyone was able to coax one into producing cones. This was accomplished by the country's leading horticulturalist, Philip Miller of the Chelsea Physic Garden, London's oldest

Female Seed Cones

Fig. 2-31a: Spring year 1   Fig. 2-31b: Summer year 1   Fig. 2-31c: Summer year 2   Fig. 2-31d: Winter cone axis

Fig. 2-31e: Overlapping cone scales reminiscent of wave-rippled sand

Fig. 2-31f: Individual cone scales

Fig. 2-31g: Deodar cedar seedling with nine cotyledons and shorter juvenile leaves

botanical garden, founded for the study of medicinal plants. (In this context "Physic" means the science of healing.) Trees that were planted in 1683 were graced with cones for the first time in 1732. How thrilled Miller must have been when he first spotted nascent cones atop the spur shoots, perhaps having seen them only in drawings and in his own imagination. What patience he must've had while observing the slow-moving drama of true cedar cone development, which takes up to two years to play out.

Oddly enough, the drama doesn't begin in spring as it does with every other genus in the pine family. Unique to *Cedrus*, pollen cones form and release pollen in the fall, after which the female cones, not yet visible, enter their first winter rest period. Growth restarts in earnest the following spring and summer, when the cones swell into their egg-shaped form, only to go through a second winter rest, becoming mature enough to release seeds the second spring, summer, or fall. This makes it rather common to see two generations of maturing cones on the tree at the same time, though some years very few or no cones are set.

Clearly Miller's first Lebanon cedar cones were precious, but they were also important and treated a bit like celebrities. The owner of the garden, Sir Hans Sloane, pruned off branches bearing nine prized cones to present to the Fellows of the Royal Society (Wulf 2010). Only those who love conifers can perhaps appreciate how truly exciting this landmark horticultural event must have been. Even today, mature cedar cones create a stir when those unfamiliar with them experience them for the first time. In Miller's day, long before Instagram or express mail, the cones must have created quite a commotion. Imagine how disappointed Miller must have been when the cones didn't stay intact. Perhaps he found consolation when those first cones produced viable seed that he was able to germinate and grow into seedlings. Deodar cedars old enough to produce cones seed down readily (fig. 2-31g), so you're likely to find seedlings under and just beyond the canopy. The longer cotyledons arch up and surround the shorter juvenile leaves.

MALE POLLEN CONES

In all species in the pine family, male and female cones appear on the same tree. Male pollen cones of most conifers are small (½-inch to ¾-inch long, ⅛-inch wide) and, though large in number, usually go unnoticed. However, the male pollen cones of true cedars are very large, up to three inches long, the largest in the pine family, and grab your attention (figs. 2-32a,b). They also stand erect on the branch tops but drop intact in autumn after releasing pollen, often in numbers great enough to blanket the ground around the tree (fig. 2-32c).

Male Pollen Cones

Fig. 2-32a: Young pollen cones   Fig. 2-32b: Mature pollen cones   Fig. 2-32c: Intact pollen cones on ground

BUDS

The center of the spur shoot is a region of great activity, out of which grows either a bud (fig. 2-33a), a female seed cone, or a male pollen cone. Buds that bear individual needles are found on the long leading branches (fig. 2-33b). But true cedar buds are very small, indistinct, and not useful for species ID, becoming noticeable only after bud swell. However, the bud scales are noteworthy: after they have finished protecting and insulating the bud through the winter, the scales are incorporated into the spur shoot, each year adding another ring to the shoot and marking the yearly growth (fig. 2-33c), allowing

Fig. 2-33a: Emerging buds of spur shoots   Fig. 2-33b: Emerging branch bud   Fig. 2-33c: Bud scales

you to determine the age of a short shoot by counting the bud scale rings. The tawny new bud scales curl back decoratively, forming a ribbon-like collar.

BARK

Young true cedar bark is thin and smooth (fig. 2-34a), with age splitting it into two-toned narrow furrows of silver ridges and reddish-brown corky ruts (fig. 2-34b).

Fig. 2-34a: Smooth bark of a young tree   Fig. 2-34b: Two-toned furrowed bark of older tree

FORM

The differential growth rates of the long leading branches and the short spur shoots are responsible for true cedars' distinctive layered look, with one often able to see sky between the layers in old specimens. The longer branches in essence provide scaffolding for the short whorls. The species with the shortest and stiffest needles and the most horizontal branches display the most pronounced layering. The deodar cedar, with the longest and thinnest needles of all four species, is the only cedar species that drapes, a characteristic that tends to obscure the layers (fig. 2-29).

True cedars are dramatic large trees in the wild, reaching up to 200 feet high and 25 feet wide given enough time, in some areas forming pure open forests. They are understandably popular landscape trees but are rarely given the room necessary to achieve beautiful form. One often sees them topped or otherwise thoughtlessly pruned to make way for utility wires, pedestrians, and cars. Sometimes the cedar is one of many in a crowded planting of trees that all need just as much room. They also tend to hold on to their lower branches; being the widest part of the tree, these are often the first limbs pruned away when the tree outgrows its space. Given enough age, some specimens develop multiple trunks, taking an intricate candelabra-like form (fig. 2-35).

Fig. 2-35: Candelabra-like branching

CULTIVARS

The foliage of true cedar cultivars typically looks the same as the species, though the needles are often shorter. Many lovely dwarf cultivars fit nicely into a garden with restricted space. But beware, not all cultivars—so cute in the pot—remain small. The blue Atlas cedar 'Pendula', probably the most popular, is a case in point. It has the same impulse as the species to achieve a large size, growing nearly as vigorously horizontally as the species does vertically. It takes an irregular shape that tends to be longer than wide but can grow in unpredictable directions. The shape, direction, and size can be controlled with yearly pruning, though the trunk can become nearly as thick as that of the species. The spectacular specimen in figure 2-36a is forty or more years old; at about 30 feet long, it has outgrown the generous spot allotted to it and requires pruning and training to stay contained.

When the 'Pendula' cultivar does set cones, it shows that true cedar cones don't typically need to know where up is, because the branches of the species are never pendulous. In the picture of the specimen in a pot (figs. 2-36b,c), you can see that the cones are horizontal to the ground, growing in the same direction they would if the branch were horizontal. Compare this to the larch genus, which also has cones that sit atop spur shoots; however, draping branches are common in species in that genus, and the spur shoots hook to whatever angle necessary to ensure the cones point skyward.

Fig. 2-36a: Blue Atlas cedar 'Pendula' (note lamppost for scale)

Fig. 2-36b: Blue Atlas cedar 'Pendula' in a pot

Fig. 2-36c: Horizontal cone on a pendulous branch

Cedrus   True Cedar Genus

	Foliage: Stiff evergreen needles of 15 or more on spur shoots		
	C. atlantica (Glauca Group) Blue Atlas cedar Native to mts of Morocco and Algeria	*C. brevifolia* Cyprus cedar Native to Cyprus	
Foliage and Branches	20–35 stiff pointy **silvery blue needles** ¾"–1½" (l) on each spur shoot; stomatal bands on both sides of needles Branch with spur shoots	Looks like a cross of blue Atlas and Lebanon cedars; blue-green foliage in whorls of 15–20 up to ¾" (l); stomatal bands on both sides; **shortest foliage of the 4 species**	
Cones and Form	 Year 2 female cone of 'Pendula'	 Branches arch up; retains branches to the ground	 **Very layered**	
Bark		Mature bark tends to be more silver than the other species		
Other	'Pendula' most popular of the many cultivars, becomes large; Z6		Species **uncommon**; Z6	

Cones: Upright and barrel-shaped

C. deodara	*C. libani*
Deodar cedar	Lebanon cedar
Native to the Himalayan Mountains	Native to Lebanon, Syria, and Turkey

 20–30 pointy needles 1"–2" (l) on each spur shoot; thinner and less stiff than needles of other true cedar species

 20–35 stiff ¾"–1½" (l) needles per spur shoot

Branch with spur shoots

Branch with spur shoots

3"–6" (l); rounded apex; year 2 female cone

Longer needles give **draping look**

Flattened apex; year 2 female cone

Layered open branches

 Older bark silvery brown

 Furrowed bark

Many lovely small cultivars; species Z6–7; some cultivars Z5–6

Many lovely smaller cultivars; 'Green Prince' is low spreading and becomes large without pruning; Z5–6

Larix: The Larch Genus
Pinaceae: Pine Family
Soft Needles of Fifteen or More on Spur Shoots: Deciduous

Larch (*Larix*) is a small genus of ten or so species with deciduous foliage (fig. 2-37). All are adapted to cold, very cold, or frigid environments. In many cases larch redraw the alpine and boreal tree lines by inhabiting areas higher in elevation and north of which no other tree can survive, including evergreen conifers, areas that would otherwise be treeless tundra. (Refer to the section titled Cold Adaptations for more on this topic.) During the warm intervals of the ice ages of the Pleistocene, larches followed closely behind retreating alpine glaciers and continental ice sheets, and when the glaciers and ice sheets changed course, they were the first trees to get pushed back.

Fig. 2-37: Larch foliage in autumn

Three boreal larch species scrape out existences north of the Arctic Circle, where there are twenty-four hours of darkness on the winter solstice. All have surprisingly wide latitudinal ranges. The eastern larch (*L. laricina*), also known as tamarack, sprawls from as far south in the eastern United States as Pennsylvania, New Jersey, and parts of Maryland to the northern limit of trees across Canada, with a disjunct population in the interior of Alaska, an area that was glacier-free during the ice ages and where the eastern larch is thought to have persisted in small refugia and to have had a larger range then than it does today (Napier et al. 2020). When ocean levels were low during the ice ages, Alaska and Siberia formed an uninterrupted stretch of land that blocked Pacific Ocean currents and moisture from reaching the lowland interior, such that the snow that fell was never enough to form glaciers. The two other boreal larches, the Siberian larch (*L. sibirica*) and Dahurian larch (*L. gmelinii*), essentially split Siberia between them and hybridize in the middle where they meet. All are adapted to swampy, peaty soils.

The more southerly larches are found higher in the mountains. Two of these, the European larch (*L. decidua*) and the Japanese larch (*L. kaempferi*), are the most popular in cultivation. The western larch (*L. occidentalis*) is relatively abundant east of the Cascades from Central Oregon north into southern British Columbia, as well as throughout northern Idaho and western Montana. It is a pioneering species adapted to survive fires and to move in quickly after. Thick bark insulates the vascular cambium from heat, and once a blaze has swept through and cleared out the competition, western larches seed down rapidly and grow quickly; when other species eventually fill the spaces in between, western larches are high above with their crowns in the sun. However, they do eventually become shaded out by competing species, especially when fires are suppressed. Western larch benefits, as do so many species in the American West, from regular low-intensity blazes. Western larches also shed their lower branches, making it more difficult for fire to walk up the trees to the crowns.

A different type of pioneer species, the much less common subalpine larch (*L. lyallii*), is found from subalpine areas to tree line in the North Cascades and in the Rocky Mountains of northern Idaho, in western Montana, and in southern British Columbia and Alberta. Its current fragmented range is thought to comprise remnants of a once continuous distribution, from a time when suitable timberline habitat was more abundant. Though rare to nonexistent in cultivation, and not included in the larch ID chart, its pluckiness in the wild and unique adaptations are too interesting to go unmentioned. The subalpine larch colonizes areas recently vacated and scraped bare by glaciers. The trees anchor themselves in the poorest soil imaginable, if you can call the jumble of rocks and sand discharged at the edge of a disappearing glacier soil, soil that has never before been touched by roots. Being partially winter-green helps young subalpine larches get by in a barren substrate. The tree grows slowly for the first twenty to twenty-five years, during which time the lower branches hold on to their foliage for two summers instead of one, when the tree is still small enough for the foliage to be insulated beneath winter snow. During this time, the subalpine larch devotes much of its resources to developing deep roots for strong anchorage in high mountain winds (Arno 1990). The subalpine larch and western larch are known to hybridize where their ranges overlap. The other mostly rare larch species are native to the mountains of China.

Fig. 2-38a: Fresh needles emerging in spring: fairy whisk brooms

FOLIAGE

Larch exhibit shoot dimorphism: they have long shoots that grow several inches a year and short spur shoots that grow just a small amount. Fresh whorls of fifteen or more needles rise each spring from the shoots (fig. 2-38a). Single needles are found at the ends of established and newly forming long shoots. New long lateral shoots often issue from the center of short spur shoots (fig. 2-38b). Being deciduous, larch needles are soft, as they don't need the same kind of strength and protection as overwintering foliage.

Fig. 2-38b: Short spur shoot giving rise to a new long lateral shoot

In autumn larch foliage turns a lovely coppery yellow. The needles of some cultivars, such as the Japanese larch 'Wolterdingen', exhibit a gradation of hues from aqua green to gold, adding a hypnotic display of color to the fall garden (fig. 2-38c).

Fig. 2-38c: Japanese larch 'Wolterdingen' in autumn

FEMALE SEED CONES

Larch seed cones mature in one growing season and issue from the tops of spur shoots, where even on pendulous branches they remain upright, as the cone stalks curve to whatever angle necessary to keep them pointing up (fig. 2-39a). On a horizontal branch, the cone

Fig. 2-39a: Developing female cones from spring through summer

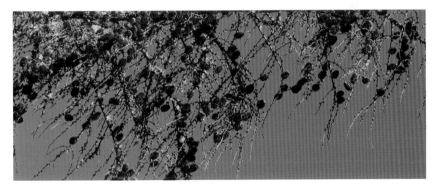

Fig. 2-39b: Branch in winter dark with cones

stalk is perpendicular to the branch; on a pendulous twig, the stalk makes a 90-degree hairpin turn. When young, all larch cones have long exserted bracts. In some species, like the western larch, the bracts are still evident when the cone is full size; in others, like the Japanese larch, the scales grow over and conceal the bracts as the cone matures.

Cones remain attached to the tree indefinitely and typically drop with the twig when it is shed. In winter, the combination of no foliage and a full load of dark mature cones has the effect of making the tree look quite dead (fig. 2-39b).

MALE POLLEN CONES

Larch pollen cones emerge from the tops of spur shoots, which angle themselves to whatever degree necessary to keep the pollen cones upright (fig. 2-40). However, they're not much to look at; even for pollen cones they're small and dull looking, showing little of the striking, though brief, magenta colors of pollen cones of some of the other genera in the pine family.

BUDS

Larch buds are rounded, reddish-brown and woody, and not useful for species ID.

Fig. 2-40: Male pollen cones

BARK

The thick bark of landscape-aged western larches is typically grayish-brown with pink undertones, but in the wild, where western larch can live well beyond five hundred years, the bark of old trees—more than a foot thick—takes on vibrant red colors that can mislead you into thinking it's a ponderosa pine. The bark of other ornamental larch species, which are mostly small cultivars, is typically obscured by foliage and not helpful in species ID.

FORM

Larch form straight trunks that are thin for their height compared with evergreen conifers, as larch don't need as much mechanical strength to withstand the greater ice, snow, and wind loads borne by evergreen foliage in winter (figs. 2-41a,b). This gives larches a lanky look, especially in winter when the trunks aren't concealed by foliage. However, the deep and extensive roots of larch species native to mountainous areas are an adaptation that keeps their tall and slender trunks upright under harsh winter conditions that would beat other species into krummholz.

Fig. 2-41a: Larch in autumn   Fig. 2-41b: Larch in winter

CULTIVARS

Larch are interesting and beautiful plants that are underused in the land-scape. But it is important to remember that the larch genus is the most intol-erant of shade of any conifer genus; many of their adaptations help ensure they receive sun. In even partial shade they can deteriorate rather quickly. As long as they have sun, larches are fairly easy plants to care for.

The foliage of larch cultivars is very similar to the species, though a few have twisted or variegated needles. Many of the dwarf forms are also weeping.

Larix Larch Genus

Foliage: Soft deciduous needles of 15 or more on spur shoots		Cones: Upright	
L. decidua European larch Native to Europe		*L. kaempferi* Japanese larch Native to Japan	

Foliage and Branches

30–40 per shoot	Winter stem, 'Pendula'	20–35 per shoot	Stem at bud swell
Branch with spur shoots		Branch with spur shoots	

Cones and Form

		1" (l) cones; bracts **slightly exserted on lower scales**	To more than 100' in wild
3 seasons of 'Pendula'	To 100'; cones to 1½" (l)		

Bark

	Nondescript brown-gray bark	Smooth young bark, pinkish-gray older bark

Other

Species rare; 'Pendula' most common of the **many weeping cultivars**; Z2	Species rare; 'Wolterdingen' one of the smaller common cultivars; Z4

L. laricina		*L. occidentalis*	
Eastern larch, tamarack Native to eastern US, Canada, and Alaska		Western larch PNW NATIVE	
15–25 per shoot	Winter stem	20–35 per shoot	Stem in winter
Branch with spur shoots		Branch with spur shoots	
Cones yellow and red to ½"–¾" (l); **bracts not exserted**	More than 100′ in wild	Cones to 1¾" (l); **exserted bracts**	To more than 200′ in wild
	Smooth young bark, reddish-brown older flaky bark		Bark thick and fire-resistant with age
Species uncommon; Z1		Pioneer species that moves in after fire and grows quickly; tallest of all larches; Z4	

Picea: The Spruce Genus
Pinaceae: Pine Family
Needles with Pegs, More Than Two Sides, and Pointy Tips

The vast majority of the thirty-four or so species in the spruce genus (*Picea*) are native to Asia, including Japan. Of the seven native to North America, three are in the PNW. Spruce are typically very cold hardy, some to USDA zone 2. Certain species, like the white spruce (*P. glauca*) (fig. 2-42) and Norway spruce (*P. abies*), the two most popular in cultivation, moved in quickly and successfully after the ice ages of the Pleistocene to dominate boreal forests and cover vast areas. The range of white spruce spans nearly the entirety of Canada, stopping short before reaching the Pacific, where it encounters the Coast Mountains. It extends as far north as Alaska

Fig. 2-42: White spruce 'Pendula' (center) at Iseli Nursery

and as far south as Montana, the upper Midwest, and the US Northeast.

The Engelmann spruce (*P. engelmannii*) and Colorado spruce (*P. pungens*), adapted to the long cold winters and short warm summers of interior mountains, have thick needles with waxy coatings and thick cuticles for limiting water loss through the stomata (Farjon 1990). These characteristics are particularly true of the Colorado spruce, the most drought-tolerant of all species in the genus. Both are native to the Four Corners states, as well as Idaho and Wyoming, but the Engelmann spruce alone sprawls north into the Rocky Mountains of Montana and Canada, where it meets and hybridizes readily with the white spruce. It is also common in the Cascades of Oregon and Washington.

Species neither boreal nor montane, such as the Sitka spruce (*P. sitchensis*), Brewer spruce (*P. breweriana*), and Serbian spruce (*P. omorika*), are maritime. The Sitka spruce, with a long thin range from Alaska into Northern California, rarely strays more than fifty miles from the water's edge. The wood's unique combination of strength and light weight allows it to withstand the relentless Pacific storms that line up offshore in winter as if waiting in turn. The Sitka spruce's straight trunk, a delight to the lumber industry, belies this; only the foliage seems to register the severity and direction of wind. Prior to the ice ages of the Pleistocene, the Brewer spruce was plentiful, found across four western states, but today is confined to a small mountainous area on either side of the Oregon and California border that is a botanical and geological ark. Now the rarest spruce in the world, the Brewer spruce is one of 280 endemic plant species in this limited area, while the rock formations date back to the Mesozoic and Paleozoic, having escaped the glaciers, volcanism, and oceanic submergence of everything around them (Ledig et al. 2005). An isolated population of Engelmann spruce in this area allows one to see all three native PNW spruces within a few miles of one another.

Common throughout Europe before the ice ages, the Serbian spruce is becoming more popular ornamentally and losing the obscurity afforded by its tiny present-day range in the mountains of Serbia and Bosnia and Herzegovina, where it is scattered in a few dozen isolated stands. A strikingly slender tree—a characteristic emphasized in a number of cultivars—it has the distinction of being the sole spruce with two-sided needles. Long popular horticulturally, the Oriental spruce (*P. orientalis*) is native to the eastern shore of the Black Sea. Its unusual needles look like they've had a manicure: short, tidy, and buffed—glossy all around, with softened square edges and eased tips that are not painful to the touch, a quality few spruce can boast of.

FOLIAGE AND TWIGS

Picea means peg. All spruce needles, without exception, attach to the twig by short pegs called pulvini (singular, pulvinus) (fig. 2-43a). In some species these pegs are visible with the naked eye; in others a loupe is necessary to see them clearly. When still-living needles are pulled from the twig, the peg will generally pull off with it; when dead needles are pulled, or drop, the peg remains attached to the twig. Twigs from which all the needles have fallen are

Foliage and Twigs

 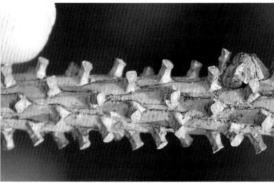

Fig. 2-43a: Needles on short pegs Fig. 2-43b: Twig with pegs after needle drop

Fig. 2-43c: Four-sided needles, often square

Fig. 2-43d: Tips often pointy and sharp

Fig. 2-43e: Stiff encircling needles

Fig. 2-43f: Grooved twigs often rusty colored

Fig. 2-43g: Tip blight damage

bumpy with pegs along the entire length (fig. 2-43b). (Hemlock needles also attach to the twig by pegs, but the pegs are very short.)

With some notable exceptions, spruce needles are four-sided and roll in your fingers (fig. 2-43c). Some needles are square, with four sides of equal length; these usually have stomatal bands on all four sides, with typically more lines of stomata on the sides facing up. In some species, two of the four sides are somewhat flattened; these needles usually have stomatal bands on the two lower sides only.

Spruce needles are usually pointy and in some cases very sharp to the touch (fig. 2-43d). If you involuntarily say "ouch" when examining single-needle conifer foliage, you can be assured it's a spruce. The botanical term for needles sharp enough to inflict pain is pungent, as in *P. pungens*, which has the sharpest needles of all the spruces. Spruce needles encircle the twig and are almost always stiff (fig. 2-43e), sometimes to the point of feeling like vinyl. They are also typically all the same length at the same spot on the branch, in contrast to some true firs and hemlocks, which often have needles of varying lengths. Young twigs are typically grooved and yellow to orange in color but gray with age (fig. 2-43f).

Tip Blight

Spruce tip blight is a fungus (*Sirococcus conigenus*) that infects emerging needles in spring, altering needle color and twig shape (fig. 2-43g). As the twig lengthens, the needles brown and the twig may die back to the initial point of infection, assuming a distinctive hooked shape. Most trees tolerate the infection well. However, if the blight is on a younger tree where the tips can be reached easily, you can just prune away the infected areas. This fungus also affects some true cedars, pines, and hemlock.

FEMALE SEED CONES

Spruce seed cones ripen in one growing season, with pollination occurring in spring and seeds released in autumn. Spruce cones issue from the branch tips of the current season's growth, making them look like extensions of the branches. The scales come in two forms: thick and woody (fig. 2-44a) or thin and papery (fig. 2-44b). If you have a cone from a spruce you're trying to identify, this scale form is the first characteristic you want to determine; it will narrow down your choices considerably. (A word of caution: woody scales that are soaking wet may not feel sufficiently stiff to make you think they're woody. If in doubt, bring the cone inside and let it dry out.) Depending on the species, the edges of the cone scales are jagged (fig. 2- 44d) or smooth (fig. 2-44e). Woody cones tend to have smooth scale edges; papery cones tend to have jagged edges.

Many species are prodigious cone setters, and though there is a concentration of cones high in the tree, many are also set lower down within arm's

Female Seed Cones

Fig. 2-44a: Cone with woody scales

Fig. 2-44b: Cone with papery scales

Fig. 2-44c: Adelgid gall: cone lookalike

Fig. 2-44d: Jagged-edged scales

Fig. 2-44e: Smooth-edged scales

Fig. 2-44f: Norway spruce 'Pusch' cones

Fig. 2-44g: Norway spruce cones from spring through seed release

reach. The cones of many species are a striking magenta color when immature (fig. 2-44f) but age to yellow and then brown (fig. 2-44g).

Spruce Cone Look-Alike

The Cooley spruce adelgid (*Adelges cooleyi*) is a tiny gall-making insect. Young adelgids (nymphs) pierce the bases of developing spruce needles and siphon out the contents. Hormones in their saliva signal the tree to construct a gall around them, a seasonal home with a private chamber for each nymph. The succulent, sheltering gall is both food source and protection from predators and insecticides. The gall dries and contracts as it ages over the summer, creating exits for the now-mature winged adults. The galls not only resemble cones, they also often form at branch ends where one expects to see spruce cones (fig. 2-44c). The galls are most noticeable when vacant and have aged from green and purple to brown, often remaining on the tree in this state for many years. This adelgid's life cycle usually requires Douglas-fir (*Pseudotsuga menziesii*) as an alternate host, but the adelgids do not trigger a gall-making response on Douglas-fir.

MALE POLLEN CONES

Spruce pollen cones appear in spring on the previous year's growth. They are typically a vibrant deep red while maturing, turning yellow at pollen release. Those of some species tend to be plump and wider at the base, making them look a bit like wild strawberries (fig. 2-45), lending an unexpected decorative element in spring. Look for them in particular on Norway and Oriental spruces, as on these species they form low enough on the tree to admire.

Fig. 2-45: Male pollen cones on Norway spruce: wild strawberries

BUDS

Spruce buds are most often yellowish to rusty-colored and sometimes reddish (figs. 2-46a,b). The bud scales of some species curl back under certain conditions. In contrast to the buds of many true fir species, spruce buds are usually not covered in protective pitch and often deepen in color when wet. There are a couple of exceptions, however: Sitka spruce and Serbian spruce buds sometimes have some resin.

Fig. 2-46a: Recurved bud scales   Fig. 2-46b: Non-recurved bud scales

BARK

Young spruce bark is smooth, with age becoming flaky and typically not splitting into fissures or furrows (fig. 2-47a). The flaky pieces eventually slough off (fig. 2-47b), exposing a lighter-color younger bark, often giving the trunk a multitoned, mottled look. In coastal Northwest forests, Sitka spruce deposit so much bark onto the forest floor that the trees appear to be self-mulching. The constant exfoliating maintains a thin bark, which is why spruce are not fire-tolerant.

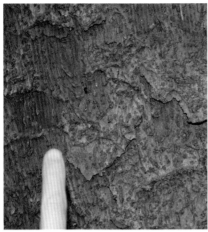

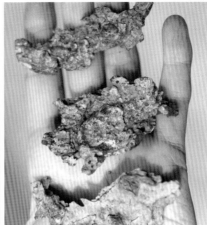

Fig. 2-47a: Flaky two-toned bark   Fig. 2-47b: Bark flakes

FORM

Spruce are tall, single-trunked straight trees known for pendulous branchlets, helpful for shedding snow, which on many species hang straight down from the main branch. Brewer spruce is one that exhibits this characteristic to an extreme, as both the branches and the twigs droop dramatically (fig. 2-48).

Fig. 2-48: Extreme drooping branches of a Brewer spruce

CULTIVARS

The most popular cultivated spruce is the one most prevalent in Europe, the Norway spruce, of which there are countless cultivars in every shape and size. The species and many of its cultivars readily set female cones, including the mounding 'Pusch', which has been selected for its especially deep pink cones (fig. 2-44f). The Oriental spruce is prone to throwing yellow cultivars (fig. 2-49a). Many require sun to maintain their pale color, but too much sun can be fatal; careful placement is paramount.

Many white spruce cultivars are distinctively dense and lumpy looking. 'Conica' is the most common, but many others with more interesting foliage look equally gnome-like in silhouette (fig. 2-49b). I've seen these cultivars used creatively in mass plantings of twenty or more, where they look like a gathering of huddled gnomes. Many other white spruce cultivars are bun-shaped. 'Pendula' is a supreme choice when one wants a tall conifer with a small footprint (fig. 2-42). Though there are far fewer cultivars of the native PNW spruces (Sitka, Brewer, and Engelmann), one of the bun-shaped Sitka spruce cultivars is a wise choice over the species, which is very wide and too large for most settings.

Fig. 2-49a: Oriental spruce 'Tom Thumb'

Fig. 2-49b: White spruce 'Alberta Blue'

HOW TO USE THE SPRUCE ID CHARTS

The spruce ID charts are organized by cone type and needle shape, as indicated by the headings. First determine whether the cone of the species in question has woody or papery scales: five of the eight species in the charts have woody scales and three have papery scales. Of the five species with woody scales, three have square needles and two don't. Of the three species with papery scales, two have square needles and one doesn't. These two characteristics alone swiftly narrow your choices.

	Foliage: Needles with pegs, more than 2 sides, and pointy tips			
	Cones: Thick woody scales			
	Needles square			
	P. abies Norway spruce Native to Eurasia		*P. glauca* White spruce Native to US and Canada	
Needles and Twigs	 	Light to dark green square needles to 1″ (l) with faint stomatal lines on all sides; **stiff and plastic-like;** twigs and distinct pegs rusty color	 	Powdery green to bluish-green square needles, **pointy but not usually sharp,** ½″– ¾″ (l), with stomatal bands on all sides; twigs rusty
Buds		Scales of rusty-colored buds sometimes curl back		Buds rounded and light brown to rusty-colored
Cones and Form	 **4″–6″ (l),** sessile	 Pendulous branches	 1¼″–2½″ (l), sessile	 Lower branches droop
Bark		Nondescript brown bark		Bark reddish- to gray-brown
Other	'Pendula' and 'Bird's Nest' two of the most common of the many cultivars; Z2		Hybridizes with Engelmann spruce; many small cultivars; 'Pendula' tall narrow form; Z2	

		Needles not square	
P. orientalis Oriental spruce Native to Turkey, Georgia, and Russia		*P. breweriana* Brewer spruce PNW NATIVE—endemic	
	Short, stiff, emer-ald-green, glossy, square needles with eased edges to ⅓"–½" (l) **feel like plastic** and point forward; small pegs; shortest needles in genus		1¼" (l) **pointy but not sharp** needles brush forward; 2 bright stomatal bands below; **tri-angular with one rounded side**; twigs hang straight down
	Buds pointy and rusty-colored		Small buds light brown to rusty-colored
	Woody cones 4"–6" (l) with smooth scale edges		
2"–4" (l), sessile	Branches to ground		**Branches weep**
	Younger bark reddish-brown, older bark gray-brown		New bark pink, old bark pinkish-gray
Many cultivars, especially yellow forms; Z4		Rarest spruce in wild; **dramatically drooping**; Z6	

	Foliage: Needles with pegs, more than 2 sides, and pointy tips			
	Cones: Thick woody scales		**Cones: Thin papery scales**	
	Needles flat, 2-sided		**Needles square**	
	P. omorika Serbian spruce Native to Serbia and Bosnia–Herzegovina		*P. engelmannii* Engelmann spruce PNW NATIVE*	
Needles and Twigs		Very small pegs; only spruce with **2-sided needles**; green above, 2 stomatal bands below; 1″ (l)		Green to blue-gray-green needles to 1″ (l) point forward; **sharp tips** and thin stomatal bands on all sides
Buds		Red-brown pointy buds; some with some resin at base		Rounded apex; rusty to brown; scales sometimes curl back
Cones and Form	 2″, purple then tawny	Narrow form	 1″–2½″, sessile	Columnar
Bark		Bark reddish-gray-brown		Old flaky bark gray-brown, new bark red-purple
Other	Species uncommon; common cultivars 'Pendula' and 'Pimoko'; Z4		Grows in shade; hybridizes with white spruce; uncommon; Z2	

		Needles not square	
P. pungens var. *glauca* Colorado blue spruce Native to western US		*P. sitchensis* Sitka spruce PNW NATIVE*	
	Colorless tips; pegs and stems tan to rusty colored; very sharp thick square needles 1½" (l); blue needles from waxy coating but not all so blue		Sharp, to 1" (l), 3-sided; 2 partial stomatal bands on upper surface, 2 dense bands on lower; pegs 90 degrees to stem
	Buds tan to rusty-colored with recurved scales		Reddish buds occasionally pitchy toward base
To 4", usu. sessile	Branches to ground	2½"–4", usually sessile	Branch ends upturn
	Bark flaky and silvery-brown, more silver in sun		Younger bark purplish-brown, older bark more silvery-brown
Most drought-tolerant of all spruces; many cultivars; Z2–3		Largest spruce in world; a few small mounding cultivars; Z7	

Pinus: The Pine Genus
Pinaceae: Pine Family
Fascicles of Two, Three, or Five Needles

The pine genus (*Pinus*) first appeared in the early Cretaceous about 130 MYA; from then to the mid-Cenozoic, the distribution of pines expanded and contracted with changing planetary conditions. About 35 MYA, toward the middle of the Cenozoic, when the number of species in other conifer genera was declining rapidly, the pine genus began to diversify. Though there are exceptions, as a group, pines generally do not do well enough in warm and humid conditions to compete with flowering trees. As the planet cooled and dried out, pines—particularly well-adapted to stressful environments of poor soil and aridity, as well as cold— spread from refugia they had retreated to when the Earth

Fig. 2-50: Ponderosa pine

was very warm and humid into areas that better suited them (Millar 1998). Many genera in both the pine and cypress families barely made it out of the ice ages alive, but remarkably, every North American pine species, including the ponderosa pine (*P. ponderosa*) (fig. 2-50), survived the Pleistocene (Millar 1998).

With approximately 110 species—nearly half of the pine family—*Pinus* is the sole genus to have added species since the end of the Pleistocene 12,000 years ago. These 110 species are divided into two subgenera, *Pinus* and *Strobus*. Though the defining feature—whether the needles have one vascular bundle (*Strobus*) or two (*Pinus*)—cannot be seen with the naked eye or a loupe, many other features that differentiate these two subgenera are readily observable, highlighted throughout this section and summarized in table 2-2.

SYMBIOSIS AND SUCCESS OF THE PINES

One reason for pines' success is that the seeds of a number of species, nearly all in the subgenus *Strobus*, have evolved to be nutritious enough to attract and be dispersed by birds, something uncommon in conifers. In a well-known example from the American and Canadian West, the life cycles of the white-bark pine (*P. albicaulis*) and the Clark's nutcracker (*Nucifraga columbiana*) are so interwoven that both species would be imperiled if either were at risk. The whitebark pine depends almost entirely on the bird for seed dispersal, and the bird depends almost entirely on the pine for food for its hatchlings. As the two species coevolved, whitebark pine seeds became larger and more nutritious, and the seeds lost their wings and the ability to be dispersed by wind; the cone adapted by remaining largely closed at maturity (fig. 2-51a), holding onto the wingless seeds for the Clark's nutcracker to dig out with its beak specially designed for the task. The bird cracks some seeds open to eat on the spot and stores up to eighty more in a specialized expandable pouch below its tongue. The bird then caches up to fifteen seeds at a time in the ground, at the ideal planting depth of one inch, some distance away from the parent trees (Lanner 1996).

Laying eggs as early as late February, the Clark's nutcracker is one of the earliest breeders; when the hatchlings appear about two and a half weeks later, while the mountains still slumber deep in snow, their diet consists largely of whitebark pine seeds retrieved from caches shrewdly placed the previous fall in spots the wind blows clear of snow, allowing year-round access to food reserves (Lanner 1996). The portion of seeds the birds fail to retrieve remain in the ground, where they can germinate and perhaps grow into trees (fig. 2-51b). All of the approximately twenty so-called bird pines throughout the Northern Hemisphere with this type of symbiosis with corvids (birds in the crow family) are native to dry exposed habitats where cached seeds, sheltered from desiccating sun and wind, are more advantageous than wind-dispersed seeds that would settle on a parched soil surface (Lanner 1996).

Look for the whitebark pine (fig. 2-51c) and the Clark's nutcracker (fig. 2-51d) near tree line in mountains throughout the western United States and

Symbiosis and Success of the Pines

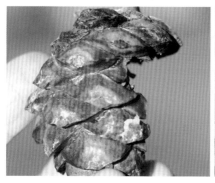

Fig. 2-51a: Excavated whitebark pine cone

Fig. 2-51b: Cluster of whitebark pines grown from a cache

Fig. 2-51c: Dwarfed, windswept whitebark pine at tree line

Fig. 2-51d: Three views of a Clark's nutcracker

Canada. The tree can take almost any form. Upright when sheltered, under the full abuse of wind at tree line it hunkers down and grows at a low angle to the ground. You're likely to hear the Clark's nutcracker before you see it—be attentive to its distinctive caw, which sounds similar to that of the American crow, only not as loud or insistent, and higher pitched. Nutcrackers can be gregarious, often gadding about in small flocks—the more there are, the more talkative they seem to become—and appear to be as curious about us as we are about them, often making eye contact and seeming to pose for the camera.

The whitebark pine is uncommon ornamentally, but the few dwarf cultivars available at specialty nurseries are worth seeking out. Two of the seven other pines with bird-dispersed seeds included in this book are native to the western United States and Canada: the limber pine (*P. flexilis*) and Rocky Mountain bristlecone pine (*P. aristata*), both subalpine species. The other five are native to Europe and Asia: the Italian stone pine (*P. pinea*), Swiss stone pine (*P. cembra*), Japanese white pine (*P. parviflora*), Korean pine (*P. koraiensis*), and lacebark pine (*P. bungeana*). To learn more about the bird pines of the world, refer to Ronald Lanner's wonderful book, *Made for Each Other: A Symbiosis of Birds and Pines* (1996).

FOLIAGE IN FASCICLES

Pine foliage is bundled together into fascicles, a characteristic unique to pines. No other genus of conifers has this anatomy. Each pine species has either two, three, or five needles per bundle (figs. 2-52a–c). The single-leaf pinyon pine (*P. monophylla*), native to the southwestern United States and Mexico, is an exception, and the only one-needle pine in the world; a genetic mutation suppresses the development of a second needle (Lanner 1981). The number of needles is the first feature you ascertain when identifying a pine to species. Two-needle pines are most common in the *Pinus* subgenus; five-needle pines are most common in the *Strobus* subgenus.

Fascicles are considered dwarf shoots. They never get any longer, and new needles are never added to the fascicle no matter how many years it remains on the tree. Barring injury, the number of needles per fascicle is constant. The bundle is shed as a unit when the tree drops its oldest foliage. This is in contrast to the whorled needles of true cedar and larch, which sit atop a short spur shoot. Unlike fascicles, spur shoots gain a small amount in length each season; in the case of true cedars, a few new needles are added and a few old needles are dropped each year. Larch are deciduous.

Foliage in Fascicles

Fig. 2-52a: Two-needle: mugo pine

Fig. 2-52b: Three-needle: lacebark pine

Fig. 2-52c: Five-needle: Japanese white pine

Fig. 2-52d: Two-needle pine

Fig. 2-52e: Three-needle pine

Fig. 2-52f: Five-needle pine

Fig. 2-52g: Persistent basal sheaths

Fig. 2-52h: Deciduous basal sheaths

The more stressful the environment, the longer a pine species keeps its needles. The fascicles of the Great Basin bristlecone pine (*P. longaeva*), held for thirty or more years, obscure the branches and give the tree a densely clothed look. A species like the Japanese red pine (*P. densiflora*), native to a more accommodating coastal mountain climate, sheds its needles after two years, making the tree open and airy.

Needles Compose a Cylinder

If you pinch the pine needles in one bundle together between the tips of your fingers, you can feel that, taken as a whole, they compose a cylinder (figs. 2-52d–f). This makes each needle in a two-needle pine a half-moon. In five-needle pines, each needle is one-fifth of a circle, in the shape of a piece of pie.

Basal Sheath

A papery sheath composed of the remnants of bud scales wraps the base of each bundle of needles. In the subgenus *Pinus,* the sheaths are persistent for the life of the fascicle (fig. 2-52g) but are deciduous in the subgenus *Strobus* (fig. 2 52h). The length and color of the persistent sheaths can be useful in species ID, as some are short and brown whereas others are long and white.

Color, Length, and Width

Needle color distinguishes some pines. The blue-green foliage of the Scots pine (*P. sylvestris*) looks like no other pine in the PNW. Ponderosa pine needles are notable for being exceptionally long (up to ten inches). Thick, short, and stiff needles are typical of subalpine species, like the whitebark pine, Rocky Mountain bristlecone pine, and Japanese white pine.

FEMALE SEED CONES

It takes less time to make a human baby than it does for pines to make cones. The woody female seed cones require two growing seasons to develop (figs. 2-53a–d), with the Italian stone pine requiring three growing seasons. In the images of the shore pine cones (*P. contorta*), the small reddish bristly conelets that are evident at the branch end form in spring of year one. The bristles are the bracts, and the scales—which at this point are open to accept pollen— are smaller than the bracts. After pollination, the scales shut tight; the cone grows slowly through the first summer and becomes inactive fall through winter.

Female Seed Cones

Fig. 2-53a: Spring year 1

Fig. 2-53b: Summer year 1

Fig. 2-53c: Spring year 2

Fig. 2-53d: Fall year 2

 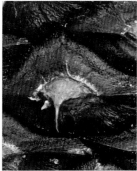 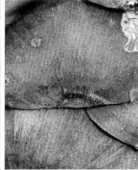

Fig. 2-53e: Flat central umbo without prickle

Fig. 2-53f: Raised central umbo armed with prickle

Fig. 2-53g: Umbo at edge without prickle

Fig. 2-53h: Short stalk and tight angle on Scots pine

Fig. 2-53i: No stalk and 90-degree angle on Japanese white pine

A year elapses between pollination and fertilization of the eggs in the spring of year two. After fertilization, the seeds mature and enlarge, and the cone grows rapidly, turning green and pitchy. By summer's end or fall, the cone dries out, opens its scales, and releases the seeds. Exceptions to this are serotinous cones, whose scales open in response to fire, such as the extraordinarily hard cones of the knobcone pine (*P. attenuata*), native to southwest Oregon and California, and cones of the bird pines. Lodgepole pines hedge their bet: some cones are serotinous and some release seeds at the end of the second growing season. Interestingly, cones of subtropical pine species mature in less time, as there is no winter rest period (Farjon 2005b).

Cone Scales and Umbos

In pines, the umbo is an artifact of the extended time pine cones require to mature. The umbo is the part of the cone scale that was exposed to the elements during the first growing season, after pollination and before fertilization, when the cone was still small, and is evident in the second growing season after the cone has begun to enlarge. The umbo of species in the subgenus *Pinus* is in the middle of the scale and looks a bit like a belly button. And, like a belly button, it can be raised, flat, or sunken (figs. 2-53e,f). Thought to be an adaptation that guards the seeds against animal predation (Coffey et al. 1999), the umbos of some species are armed with prickles, or prickles that eventually slough off—a helpful detail to note for species ID. But for a few exceptions, including the bristlecone pines, umbos of species in the subgenus *Strobus* are at the scale edge rather than at the center, are less defined, and lack a prickle (fig. 2-53g). The double umbos of Italian stone pine cones are evidence that the cones endure two winters on the tree, with the umbo from the second winter encircling the umbo from the first.

Cone Orientation and Stalk

In pines, the angle at which the cone attaches to the branch and the length of the stalk are also telling. The shorter stalk of the Scots pine cone curves to such a tight angle that the cone is nearly parallel to the branch (fig. 2-53h). The cones of bird pines tend to be perpendicular to the branch and sessile, adaptations that hold the cones firmly in place, making it easier for birds to access the seeds (fig. 2-53i). Cones with long flexible stalks, such as the Himalayan white pine (*P. wallichiana*), sway, creating moving targets and unstable places for birds to perch (Lanner 1996).

Look to the pine cone! No other conifer genus has such variation in cones from species to species. Each is unique enough that the cone alone is often sufficient for identifying the species.

Table 2-2. *Pinus* Subgenera

Pinus subgenus **Hard Pines Diploxylon** Two-thirds of species	*Strobus* subgenus **Soft Pines Haploxylon** One-third of species
Two vascular bundles per needle	One vascular bundle per needle
Mostly 2-needle pines	Mostly 5-needle pines
A few 5-needle pines	A few 2-needle pines
A few 3-needle pines	A few 3-needle pines
Central umbos usually with prickles	Umbos at scale edge and without prickles, with a few exceptions
Persistent basal sheaths	Deciduous basal sheaths
Includes fire-adapted pines	Includes the bristlecone pines
Almost all species with winged seeds	Includes the pinyon pines*
	Includes the stone pines*
	Includes the white pines+

*Wingless or nearly wingless seeds
+Some with wingless or nearly wingless seeds

MALE POLLEN CONES

Unique to pines, the buds of pollen cones are contained within the apical buds, making the apical buds that produce pollen cones compound structures. In the image of the Japanese black pine (*P. thunbergii*), the male pollen cones rise directly from the elongating apical bud (fig. 2-54a), showing that the pollen cones emerge before the needles. The image of the shore pine shows two structures, pollen cones and needles, emerging from the same compound bud (fig.

2-54b). As in all conifers, pollen cone maturation and pollen release are timed to occur when the female conelets are receptive and have opened their scales.

Though pollen cones can be quite beautiful, with striking colors before pollen release, they are seldom used in identification, because of their fleeting presence on the plant. Shortly after releasing pollen, their job done, the cones drop to the ground and shrivel into what look like brown legless grubs. What they lack in size they make up for in numbers, and they can often be seen blanketing the ground.

Fig. 2-54a: Pollen cones of Japanese black pine   Fig. 2-54b: Pollen cones of shore pine

BUDS

Pine buds are the most unique buds of all conifers and a key feature in ID from late summer when they set until bud break in spring (figs. 2-55a–c). Those of some species are sticky with pitch, while others are distinctly shaped or colored. The similar Austrian black pine (*P. nigra*) and Japanese black pine are quickly differentiated by their buds; the domed tawny buds of the former bear no resemblance to the straight long white buds of the latter. And though buds can't be observed year-round, they are in place from the first year of the pine's life, long before cones show up. A sunny fall or winter day is a great time to practice pine ID by restricting yourself to the buds alone.

Each pine bud contains, in microscopic form, all the needles that will develop on next year's shoot. As such, in a drought year pine buds set fewer needles, resulting in decreased shoot growth the following year. Alternatively, a good water year results in more needles and vigorous shoot growth the next growing season (Lanner 2007). The long-lived bristlecone pines form about half of all shoots from buds found inside the fascicles, giving even the most aged trees the ability to regenerate their crowns. This trait differentiates them from all other pines and is at least partly responsible for their longevity. In other pines, this type of bud is activated solely by injury.

Buds

Fig. 2-55a: Domed fibrous bud of Austrian black pine

Fig. 2-55b: Narrow, white bud of Japanese black pine

Fig. 2-55c: Pitchy bud of shore pine

BARK

Though the mature bark of many pine species is drab and nondescript, the bark of a few provides a valuable clue in species ID. For example, the bark of both the Japanese red pine and Scots pine is red and flaky, though as the trees age, you must look into the upper younger parts of the tree to observe

Fig. 2-56a: Desert camo bark of lacebark pine

Fig. 2-56b: Bark transitioning from young to mature

it. Bark is distinctive enough in some pines, such as the lacebark pine, to take you directly to species ID—its thin smooth bark peels away in thin cumulus-cloud-shaped pieces, leaving the trunk as a whole looking as if dressed in desert camo. The newly exfoliated lighter-colored areas darken over time to a sandy brown (fig. 2-56a). However, like true firs, except for resin blisters, the bark of young pines is typically smooth before transitioning into whatever is typical for that species (fig. 2-56b).

Ponderosa Pine Bark

One could dedicate an entire book to the endlessly fascinating bark of the ponderosa pine (fig. 2-50). The thick red bark conveys, perhaps more than any other conifer, that You Are in the Dry West, with every western state and province (except for Alberta) part of its range, as well as areas of Nebraska and the Dakotas.

The bark cleaves vertically and horizontally into irregular chunks, with the vertical fissures often deepening and widening into dark mini-canyons you can sink your fingers into. A close inspection reveals the surface of the chunks themselves to be multitoned and a bit flaky, looking like 3D topographical maps. The tree's habit of shedding lower branches, as a way of depriving fire access to the crown, makes the bark easy to spot, like a blaze among other drab-barked conifers; a pure stand of ponderosa pines with sun on it looks like fire that has organized itself into a forest. The tall vertical trunks of old trees disappear into the sky, keeping the crowns high above the frequent ground fires the species is adapted to. Though in most areas of the West the bark alone is enough to identify this species, the intensity of the red color varies significantly from tree to tree and the bark of young ponderosas is darker.

Another pleasure of ponderosa pine bark is its aroma—warm caramel with a dash of vanilla—that contributes significantly to the unique scent of the dry interior West in areas where these trees dominate. On summer mornings, when breezes stir colder air that has settled overnight, the candy shop aroma is unmistakable, a bracing tonic to the sinuses and lungs. In southwest Oregon, California, and Nevada, the ponderosa pine's range overlaps with the Jeffrey pine (*P. jeffreyi*), another three-needle pine with red aromatic bark; however, the Jeffrey pine has much larger cones with curved prickles and is not typically seen in the landscape. These two species are known to hybridize where their ranges overlap.

Form

Fig. 2-57a: Leading shoot and whorl on Scots pine

Fig. 2-57b: Longest bud leading shoot and shorter buds whorl on Japanese black pine

Fig. 2-57c: Sierra lodgepole pine growing in a circle in an exposed site

Fig. 2-57d: Needles emerging from candle

Fig. 2-57e: Candled bud

FORM

No single form is common to all pines. However, all pine branches grow in distinct whorls, as do those of spruce, true fir, and larch, setting one main whorl per year; sometimes in a favorable season a second flush of growth forms a secondary smaller false whorl. Whorls are easiest to see on a young tree with a simple structure (fig. 2-57a). Out of the cluster of pine buds, the longest central bud becomes the main leading shoot; the smaller buds become the whorl of shorter lateral shoots (fig. 2-57b). One can determine the tree's age by counting the main whorls, including any lower whorls that the tree might have shed, evident from branch scars. The space between whorls is called the internode.

Many conifers assume a shrub-like form when exposed at tree line but are otherwise upright trees. The only two species in the pine family that are truly multistemmed shrubs are in the pine genus. Both are subalpine species, an environment that guarantees a low-growing shrub will receive full sun. One of these, the mugo pine (*P. mugo*), is extremely popular horticulturally, with countless cultivars; it is native to the mountains of Central and Eastern Europe, where it often forms dense thickets. The slow-growing Bosnian pine (*P. heldreichii*), native to mountains of the Balkan Peninsula, is known for maintaining a flame-shaped form as it ages; a few dwarf cultivars that grow even more slowly are superior selections for tight spaces.

The Shore Pine versus the Lodgepole Pines

When you look at a USDA hardiness zone map for the middle of the United States and Canada, with no mountains to confuse the issue, zones transition predictably from south to north in a well-sorted palette of colors, from warm reds to temperate greens to cool blues and cold purples. These colors and the zones they represent take a decisive 90-degree turn when encountering the mountains of the western states and provinces. If there is any semblance of orderly transition of zones in Oregon, Washington, Northern California, and southern British Columbia, it is from east to west, owing to the Cascades, which break the region into maritime and desert climates. Longitude more than latitude dictates climate and hardiness zones in the PNW.

P. contorta and its subspecies are an expression of this, with the shore pine (var. *contorta*, zone 7) ranging more than 1,300 miles latitudinally along the coast from Glacier Bay, Alaska, to Eureka, California, while one need travel just over a hundred miles east latitudinally from the Oregon or Northern California shore before encountering the Sierra lodgepole pine (var. *murrayana*, zone 3). The Rocky Mountain lodgepole pine (var. *latifolia*) is a second inland form found in the mountains of Washington and Idaho, as well as in many other western states, and its range extends far north into the Yukon.

Onshore winds enhance the shore pine's somewhat naturally irregular form, but on the leeward side of the coast range, where it is popular ornamentally and sometimes seeds down, it takes a far less contorted shape. Out of the wind it starts to resemble the two inland subspecies known for their ramrod-straight trunks. Conversely, in exposed sites higher in the mountains, wind often twists the flexible trunks of young lodgepole pines into tortuous shapes: loops (fig. 2-57c), U-turns, and other inexplicable configurations, with some branches even tied into knots. The pliant trunks of young pines of many species allow them to adapt to the environments they find themselves in.

Pine Candles and Restricting Growth

Pine buds elongate dramatically in the spring, something no other conifer buds do, forming what are called candles, because of their obvious resemblance to tapered candles (fig. 2-57d). A common practice at Japanese gardens and in bonsai is to break off a portion of these soft candles as a means of limiting growth and shaping the plant (fig. 2-57e). The more of the candle you remove, the more restricted the growth will be for that season.

Candling is best done when the needles are about halfway emerged, when you can see what the maximum length of the candle will be for the season. This can be done on any sized pine, but is best practiced on small or dwarf specimens when candles can be easily reached and aren't so vast in number as to require a paid staff.

CULTIVARS

Though the shore pine is hardy to USDA zone 7, a few noteworthy cultivars hardy to zone 5 are good choices for gardens higher

Fig. 2-58a: Shore pine 'Chief Joseph'

Fig. 2-58b: Japanese red pine
'Oculus Draconis' foliage

Fig. 2-58c: Japanese red pine 'Umbraculifera'

in elevation and east of the Cascades. The pricey 'Chief Joseph', a smaller yellow form, shows up nicely against a gray or blue sky (fig. 2-58a); 'Spaan's Dwarf' grows slowly into an open bonsai-like shrub.

Cultivars of a number of pine species are notable for their green-and-yellow-banded needles (fig. 2-58b). These cultivars can be confounding when you first lay eyes on them, but remember to go back to the basics. First ascertaining the number of needles and then examining the buds, cones, and bark should lead to species ID. 'Umbraculifera', aka Tanyosho pine, is a stellar Japanese red pine cultivar with low branching that maintains a perfect dense form as it ages (fig. 2-58c).

HOW TO USE THE PINE ID CHARTS

The pine ID charts are organized by the number of needles in each bundle, as indicated by the headings. There are two charts for two-needle pines, one for three-needle pines, and three for five-needle pines. The five-needle charts are not organized alphabetically; each chart groups pines with the most similar foliage, allowing for side-by-side comparison.

Five-Needle Pines

The five-needle pines that look the most alike, and are grouped in one chart, are the western white pine (*P. monticola*), eastern white pine (*P.*

strobus), and Himalayan white pine. All three hybridize with one another when given the chance (Graham 1990). Western and eastern white pines are notoriously difficult to tell apart. The former is native to most of the major and many of the minor mountain ranges of the PNW and is also found as low as sea level in Washington and British Columbia. Though the eastern white pine has an even more expansive native range in the Midwest and eastern United States and Canada, little of the vast forests that awed the first settlers remains, as the area has been heavily logged since colonial times, when eastern white pine trunks were the timber of choice for ship masts for the British Navy.

With more than two hundred registered cultivars of all shapes and sizes, the eastern white pine is perhaps the most prevalent of all ornamental pines. The western white pine is far less common; the species is rarely planted or seen outside its native range, except in arboreta, and there are far fewer cultivars. Refer to the ID charts for images of the bark and the cone scales to differentiate between these two species. The Himalayan white pine is native to the valleys and foothills of the Himalayas. Though the cones and foliage are very similar to those of the eastern and western white pines, those of the Himalyan pine are considerably longer; this includes the cone stalk, which is by far the longest of any pine in this book. The thin soft needles, up to twelve inches long, arch gracefully away from the branch ends like ballerina skirts.

The foliage of the five-needle limber, Korean, and Swiss stone pines, also grouped in one chart, is similar among the three, but the cones quickly differentiate them. The limber pine is a species of the interior mountains of the western United States and Canada, with a token presence in the Wallowa Mountains in northeast Oregon; the Korean pine is native to eastern Asia, and the Swiss stone pine to mountainous areas of Europe. The species of all three are uncommon ornamentally, but cultivars are becoming more available.

Ponderosa pine: emerging needles and seed cones

	Foliage: Fascicles of 2 needles				
	***Pinus* subgenus Seeds wind-dispersed**				
	P. contorta var. *contorta* Shore pine PNW NATIVE		*P. densiflora* Japanese red pine Native to Japan and East Asia		
Needles and Form	 1"–3" (l); twisted	 To 50'; more irregular in wind	 2½"–4½" (l); thin	 To 100'; irregular open shape	
Cones and Twigs	 1½"–2" (l); no stalk; **prickles, points back**	 Cone closeup	 1¼"–2" (l); heavy cone set	 Needles held 1–2 years, give open look	
Bark and Buds	 Brown-gray bark	 Pointy and pitchy	 **Younger bark red**	 Purple, reflexed scales	
Other	Z7, but some cultivars to Z5		'Umbraculifera' popular multistemmed cultivar; some striking yellow cultivars; Z4		

P. heldreichii Bosnian pine Native to the Balkan Peninsula		*P. mugo* Mugo pine Native to mts of Europe	
3"–4" (l); very stiff, curved, sharp	Slow-growing to 80'; dense pyramid	To 3" (l); long white sheath; rigid	One of few pine family species in nature as a multistemmed **shrub**; wide dense mound with age to 8' (h) x 16' (w)
2"–3½" (l), **blue** then brown; perpendicular to twig	Needles persist 5–6 years; curve forward	To 2½" (l), points back	2"–3" (l), stiff; point forward; **bright sheaths**
		Bark obscured by dense foliage and not useful for ID	
Scaly with age	**Gourd-shaped**		**Pitchy pillars**
aka snakebark pine; a few smaller cultivars; Z5		aka *P. mughus*; many dwarf cultivars; Z2	

	Foliage: Fascicles of 2 needles (continued)			
	***Pinus* subgenus**			
	Seeds wind-dispersed			
	P. nigra Austrian black pine Native to Europe, Turkey, and N. Africa		*P. thunbergii* Japanese black pine Native to Japan and S. Korea	
Needles and Form				
	3½"–6" (l), thick and stiff	50'–80', fast-growing	2½"–4½" (l)	50'–80'; irregular form
Cones and Twigs				
	2½"–4" (l); **scales raised**	Stiff needles	1½"–2½" (l); **flat** unarmed scales	Stiff needles
Bark and Buds				
	Gray furrowed bark	**Dome-like buds**	Furrowed bark	**Long buds and white scales** of 'Thunderhead'
Other	Looks like Japanese black pine; species common; Z4		Looks like Austrian black pine; cultivars more common than species; Z5	

		Pinus subgenus	
		Seeds bird-dispersed	
P. sylvestris Scots pine Native to Eurasia		*P. pinea* Italian stone pine Native to Mediterranean coast	
1"–3" (l), **blue-green**, twisted	30'–60'; irregular form	4"–5" (l), stiff; short basal sheath	40'–80'; flat-topped with age
1"–3" (l); points back; short stalk	Holds needles 3 years	4"–6" (l); **dense**; 3 seasons to mature	Stiff, thick needles
Younger bark red	Pointy red buds can have some resin	Fissured orange-brown bark	Recurved frilly bud scales
Most common pine in Europe; Z2		Large edible seeds; **uncommon**; Z8	

	Foliage: Fascicles of 3 needles		
	***Pinus* subgenus Fire-adapted, seeds wind-dispersed**		
	P. attenuata PNW NATIVE* Knobcone pine		*P. ponderosa* Ponderosa pine
Needles and Form	 3"–7" (l), thin and flexible	 30'–50'; multi-trunked	 5"–10" (l), thick, sharp
Cones and Twigs	 3"–6" (l); **hard knobs** on exposed side	 Long needles	 3"–6" (l), purple then brown, **painful prickles**
Bark and Buds	 Reddish furrowed bark	 Tawny, pillar-shaped with angled shoulders	 **Thick fire-resistant bark**, plated, red with age
Other	Uncommon; persistent cones need fire to open; Z7		Most common pine in the American West; Z3

	Strobus subgenus	Seeds bird-dispersed
PNW NATIVE*	*P. bungeana* Lacebark pine	Native to China
 60'–100'; single trunk	 2½"–4" (l), stiff, pointy	 30'–50'; low branching
 Stiff needles	 To 3" (l), raised scales, prickles, stalk	 Glossy needles
 Large; rounded shoulders	 Exfoliating **bark looks like camo**	 Tawny brown; reflexing scales; no resin
Crosses with Jeffrey pine (*P. jeffreyi*)	Drought-tolerant once established; Z4	

Foliage: Fascicles of 5 needles

Strobus subgenus Seeds bird-dispersed

	P. albicaulis PNW NATIVE* Whitebark pine		*P. aristata* Rocky Mt. bristlecone pine
Needles and Form	To 2¾" (l), thick and stiff	To 50', stunted at tree line (young trees shown)	1"–1¾" (l), thick and stiff; grooved
Cones and Twigs	To 3" (l), purple with **thick scales**, sessile	Tufted-looking	2"–4" (l), **long thin prickles**; pitchy
Buds and Bark	**Whitish thin scaly bark**	Small, tawny red, pointy, fibrous	Bark obscured by foliage; needles of the very similar Great Basin bristlecone pine (*P. longaeva*) lack grooves and have no or few resin specks
Other	Subalpine tree; cone scales stay closed; seeds cached by birds; rare; cultivars uncommon; Z3		Holds needles many years

Native to western US	*P. parviflora* 'Glauca' Japanese white pine	Native to Japan and Korea
8'–40'; dense, slow-growing	2"–3" (l); **dense bright stomata**	To 45'; wide spreading branches
	\n\nYoung cone\n\n	
Resin specks on needles	To 3" (l), sessile, holds onto cones	Needles sweep forward
Small, reddish-brown, pitchy	Young bark thin, old bark fissured	Red, fibrous scales; no resin
Sunny well-drained location a must; Z4	Species uncommon; cultivars **set cones at young age**; Z4	

	Foliage: Fascicles of 5 needles (continued)			
	***Strobus* subgenus Seeds bird-dispersed**			
	P. cembra Swiss stone pine Native to mountains of Europe			*P. flexilis* Limber pine
Needles and Form	 3"–4" (l), moderately thick and flexible	 To 75'; branches arch up; branching low to ground		 2"–4" (l), thin and flexible
Cones and Twigs	 **To 1½"–3½" (l);** scales stay closed	 Branch ends arch up	 **Very hairy new twigs**	 3½"–7" (l); **thick scales**; sessile
Buds and Bark	 Tawny-gray, fissured, and flaky	 Small and pointy, with some resin		 Buff-colored, pitchy
Other	Species rare; smaller dense cultivars more common; Z4			Species rarely planted

'Vanderwolf's Pyramid' PNW NATIVE*	*P. koraiensis* Korean pine Native to China, Korea, Japan, and Russia	

To 30'; **branches arch strongly upward**; blue-green hue	2½"–5" (l), flexible and thick; bright bands	To 90'

Rounded scale edges curl back / Dense upturned branch ends	3½"–6" (l); **pointy scales** curve back	**ID by feel of thick triangular needles**

Bark silvery and a bit flaky	Smooth young bark, rough mature bark	Pointy with some resin
Most prevalent in wild in Rocky Mts; Z4	Species rare; smaller dense cultivars more common; Z4	

	Foliage: Fascicles of 5 needles (continued)		
	Strobus subgenus Seeds wind-dispersed		
	P. monticola PNW NATIVE* Western white pine		*P. strobus* Eastern white pine
Needles and Form	2″–5″ (l), thinnish	Thin tree to 100′	2″–5″ (l), thin
Cones and Twigs	4″–10″ (l); **scales recurve at stalk**	Soft needles	4″–8″ (l); stalk; pitchy
Buds and Bark	**Breaks into small chunks**	Pointy; tawny buff color	**Spreading furrows**
Other	Cultivars rare; very similar to and crosses with *P. strobus*; Z3		Many smaller cultivars; species less common

Native to eastern and Midwest US, and Canada	*P. wallichiana* Himalayan white pine	Native to Himalayas
30'–60'; oval crown	6"–10" (l), thin and soft	30'–50'; low branching
Soft and wispy; needles point up	6"–12" (l); **long stalk**, pitchy	**Needles arch down and away from** twig end
Small, pointed, no resin	Older bark plated	Crown-shaped, wide base
Crosses with *P. monticola*; Z3	Species usually planted; few cultivars; Z5	

Pseudotsuga: The Douglas-Fir Genus
Pinaceae: Pine Family
Needles with Short Stems and Small Circular Leaf Scars

The Douglas-fir genus (*Pseudotsuga*) comprises four or so species, depending on the source. Two are native to western North America; the others are rare Southeast Asian species that are not seen horticulturally. Europeans first encounter with the genus was with the species that is native throughout western North America, the species the genus is named for: Douglas-fir (*P. menziesii*). Old World botanists were initially thrown off by how it looks a little bit like a lot of other conifers and tried hard to force it into a genus already known to them, variously labeling it a true fir, a spruce, and a hemlock, but eventually recognizing it as unique and warranting a genus of its own, *Pseudotsuga*, meaning false hemlock.

The range of the coastal Douglas-fir (*P. menziesii* var. *menziesii*) (fig. 2-59), one of two naturally occurring varieties, extends from northern Vancouver Island

Fig. 2-59: Coastal Douglas-fir

south into Northern California, including the Cascade and Sierra Nevada Ranges; a second inland variety, the blue-needled Rocky Mountain Douglas-fir (*P. menziesii* var. *glauca*), is common throughout the Rocky Mountains and can also be found in parts of Eastern Oregon and Washington and scattered in higher elevations of Arizona, Utah, and New Mexico.

The big-cone Douglas-fir (*P. macrocarpa*) has a much more limited range than its smaller-coned brethren. Native to the leeward side of the coastal mountains of Southern California and higher up on mountain ranges just inland, it bears cones up to six inches long. This species is not used ornamentally.

The coastal Douglas-fir has enjoyed great success outside its native range ever since the Scottish botanist David Douglas sent seeds back to Britain in 1827 that he had collected on the Washington side of the Columbia River near Fort Vancouver. One can visit specimens in Scotland and England grown from those original seeds. Planted in the 1880s, Dughall Mor—Big Douglas in Gaelic—was for many years the tallest known tree in Britain until an even taller Douglas-fir was discovered nearby.

Many conifer species native to the Pacific slopes of the American West are the tallest, fastest-growing, and most massive trees on the planet. This includes the Douglas-fir, a tree that uniquely combines two seemingly incompatible traits: rapid growth and dense wood of superior strength. Known as the Oregon-pine in many countries, Douglas-fir is grown in plantations the world over for its prized timber.

Following World War II, Douglas-fir was integral to the reforestation of Western Europe, particularly the United Kingdom, France, and Germany. A friend tells stories of how after the war her father climbed Douglas-firs in Oregon to harvest cones that were sent to Europe. He used a special tool for raking the cones out of the trees, earning five dollars per burlap bag of cones. However, shifting sentiment toward the Douglas-fir has made its presence in Europe controversial. Some now view it as a species that is disrupting native forests and think it ought to be treated like a weed and removed. Others recognize its economic importance as a plantation tree whose high-quality timber fetches higher prices than native species. And in the face of climate change, some conservationists consider its ability to grow large quickly critical for long-term carbon sequestration. It's strange to think of such a familiar and beloved native PNW conifer engendering such disagreement and acrimony abroad. But in Germany in 2012 Greenpeace forcibly removed two thousand newly planted Douglas-firs and then dumped them like trash on the doorstep of the Bavarian minister of agriculture. In France, anonymous destruction of Douglas-fir plantations is common. Abroad, Douglas-fir is a conifer that has become a victim of its own success.

FOLIAGE

Note: All characteristics from here on describe the coastal Douglas-fir.

The two-sided 1-inch to 1½-inch Douglas-fir needles (fig. 2-60a) have short stems like hemlocks—though the stems don't lie parallel to the twig—and small slightly raised circular leaf scars (fig. 2-60b) like true firs. The upper side has a central groove, and a midrib separates faint stomatal bands on the underside. The needles tend to lie flat in the shade and to be at odd angles to the stem in the sun. Though most commonly a pure green, the foliage can also be blue-green. Douglas-fir foliage is softer to the touch than that of true firs and spruce.

Fig. 2-60a: Needles 1–1½ inches long

Fig. 2-60b: Short stems and small circular leaf scars

FEMALE SEED CONES

Douglas-fir cones, up to four inches long and maturing in one growing season, are one of the most easily recognizable cones in the pine family, and often the most obtainable (figs. 2-61a–c). Not only do they have prominent three-pronged exserted bracts—a trait of all species in the genus—that are *always* described as looking like mouse tails and mouse behinds, they also set loads of cones in all parts of the tree starting from a young age. One is never at a loss to find a Douglas-fir cone.

Far less commonly seen, however, because of how rapidly they develop, are the beautiful immature Douglas-fir cones, with magenta bracts that resemble flowers far more than they do the dull brown cones that fall to the ground after seed release. At this early stage of development, the most noticeable parts are the long, brilliant bracts. A branch of these young cones looks perfectly at ease in a vase or in an ikebana arrangement and will last far longer than flowers. Be on the lookout for them in spring at the branch ends of the previous year's growth.

Fig. 2-61a: Spring cones with brilliant magenta bracts

Fig. 2-61b: Ripening cone with three-pronged bracts

Fig. 2-61c: Mature cone after seed release

MALE POLLEN CONES

Small pollen cones of Douglas-fir set in spring on the undersides of the branches (fig. 2-62). Once pollen has been released, start looking for the immature seed cones, which develop quickly thereafter.

Fig. 2-62: Pollen cones at pollen release

BUDS

The buds of Douglas-fir differentiate it from similar-looking conifers: ruby-red to reddish-brown, hard, pointy, and triangular like tiny spear heads (fig. 2-63). Plus, the buds are clearly visible, never concealed by needles like the shy buds of so many true fir species.

Fig. 2-63: Ruby-red to reddish-brown, hard pointy buds not enclosed by needles

BARK

In youth, Douglas-fir bark is thin and bumpy with resin blisters (fig. 2-64a), like that of young true firs and young pines, but in time forms deep rutted fire-resistant bark that insulates the vascular cambium (fig. 2-64b).

Fig. 2-64a: Young bark with resin blisters

Fig. 2-64b: Mature bark with distinctive corky ruts

FORM

Growing up to 300 feet tall, Douglas-firs stand perfectly straight like soldiers. The branchlets, which often hang straight down from the main branches, can fool you into thinking it's a spruce. Douglas-firs can be rather narrow when growing among other trees or in the wind, and rather wide when growing singly in an open sheltered location.

SEEDLINGS

Douglas-firs seed down at will, and volunteer trees can be found wherever the tree grows. Many oddly placed Douglas-firs get their start this way. Because conifers aren't typically weedy, an individual little tree can go unnoticed for many years until it is large enough to attract attention. Douglas-fir and grand fir seedlings look similar, but by the end of the first growing season, both will have set recognizable terminal buds. Also, Douglas-fir cotyledons are pointy (fig. 1-9d, on page 26), whereas those of the grand fir (fig. 2-27, on page 74) are blunt.

CULTIVARS

There are a number of Douglas-fir cultivars, many with blue needles, but the buds and cones will always tell you it's a Douglas-fir.

Tsuga: The Hemlock Genus
Pinaceae: Pine Family
Needles with Short Stems Parallel to Twig

Hemlock (*Tsuga*) is a genus of nine species split between North America and Asia. Three of the Asian hemlocks are rare Chinese species; two are native to Japan, including one that is becoming more common horticulturally, the northern Japanese hemlock (*T. diversifolia*). Of the two hemlocks native to the eastern United States and Canada, one is a rare endemic of the Southern Appalachians, the Carolina hemlock (*T. caroliniana*). The other, the Canadian hemlock (*T. canadensis*), is common ornamentally and has an expansive native range in the United States, from the upper Midwest to the Northeast and south to Virginia, as well as in southeastern Canada.

The two hemlocks native to the PNW—the

Fig. 2-65: Mountain hemlocks in the wild

mountain hemlock (*T. mertensiana*) (fig. 2-65) and western hemlock (*T. heterophylla*)—are both coastal and montane species. As coastal species, their ranges overlap from the Kenai Peninsula in Alaska to the United States–Canada border, with the western hemlock extending its coastal presence from the border into Northern California. As montane species, their ranges overlap—albeit at different elevations—in the Cascades and Rocky Mountains of southern British Columbia, and western Idaho and Montana, with the mountain hemlock extending its montane presence in isolated populations from the Cascades into the Sierra Nevada Range of California.

The shade tolerance of the hemlock genus as a whole sets it apart from all other genera in the pine family, which are largely sun-loving (the mountain hemlock is an exception); hemlocks are also the least resistant to drought (Farjon 1990). Western hemlocks in PNW forests with dry summers work around this by germinating and growing on fallen trees. The surface of a freshly downed tree is prime unoccupied real estate held above the highly competitive forest floor—lucky are the seeds that fall and germinate on such a spot. In PNW coastal forests, where wind is the most common cause of disturbance and of downed trees, both western hemlock and Sitka spruce (*P. sitchensis*) seeds germinate on fallen trees (Van Pelt 2007).

Decay transforms dead trees into a spongy, absorbent substance (the technical term is punky) and into veritable water storage tanks that irrigate young trees through the dry summers. One commonly sees young western hemlocks all lined up in a row along these nurse logs, which decay away as the young trees mature (fig. 2-66). When you see western hemlocks looking strangely like a cultivated row among the disorder of a wild forest, you can be sure they shared the same nurse log early in life. When I read that "forest colonnade" is the lovely term forest ecologists give this phenomenon (Van Pelt 2007), I got

the small thrill I always get when I learn there's a name for something I've observed.

Moreover, western hemlocks have such an affinity for germinating and growing on Douglas-fir (*Pseudotsuga menziesii*) bark, it is not uncommon to see young western hemlocks appearing to grow directly out of the thick lower bark of a living Douglas-fir (fig. 2-67). But the young trees are usually growing in the jumble of sloughed-off bark

Fig. 2-66: Young western hemlocks along a nurse log

Fig. 2-67: Western hemlock growing out of the base of a Douglas-fir

Fig. 2-68: Mountain hemlock (tall) with Pacific silver fir volunteer

that accumulates deeply enough at the base of older Douglas-firs to provide a little platform above the forest floor (Van Pelt 2007). One often sees the base of a Douglas-fir ringed with an atoll of seedlings and young trees—it's an endearing sight. It looks as if the Douglas-fir is playing big brother to the little hemlocks. Western hemlocks occasionally seed down in the residential landscape but typically require supplemental water in the dry season to survive.

The native PNW mountain hemlock—a lovely slow-growing tree with a small footprint—stands apart from all others as being the only subalpine hemlock in the world and the only one tolerant of sun and drought. Perhaps this is the reason specimens sold at nurseries, which are typically dug from the wild, survive domestication so well—the seemingly impossible transition of being yanked off a mountainside and then dropped into a lowland landscape. I had seven such mountain hemlocks in my yard; all but one thrived (with irrigation).

An unexpected bonus of these dug-up trees is the wild seed bank carried in their soil. Keep an eye out for seedlings growing out of the original root ball; my dug-up mountain hemlocks produced several Pacific silver firs (*Abies amabilis*) and additional mountain hemlocks. In figure 2-68, the young Pacific silver fir was still a seed when the mountain hemlock was planted. However, it will soon become too large to stay where it is, as Pacific silver firs grow much faster and become much taller than mature mountain hemlocks.

I could have moved it when it was still small, but at this point it's destined to be harvested and brought indoors as a small Christmas tree.

The Canadian hemlock and the Carolina hemlock are both threatened in the wild by an introduced insect, the hemlock woolly adelgid (*Adelges tsugae*), which feeds on the foliage. The insect is less prevalent in the northern part of the Canadian hemlock's range, where harsher winters knock populations back, but the adelgid appears to be adapting to the cold and pushing farther north and west (Limbu et al. 2018). Hemlocks are the rare conifers that can dominate an understory. Their dense evergreen boughs exclude light and trap the moisture they require in the forest, creating a cool damp microclimate that supports hundreds of plant and animal species, a microclimate disappearing along with the hemlocks where mortality rates from the insect are high. Forests under adelgid attack transition over a few short decades to warmer, drier deciduous hardwood forests, though the transition has been known to occur in as few as ten years (Ellison et al. 2018). Fortunately, native PNW hemlocks are already adapted and resistant to the insect, as it has been present in western North America for twenty thousand years.

FOLIAGE

Flat two-sided hemlock needles attach to the twig by pegs (pulvini) (fig. 2-69), like spruce (*Picea*) needles; however, hemlock pegs are much shorter and less noticeable, such that it is often easier to feel them than to see them with the naked eye. Grooves on the twigs terminate at the pegs, like they do in spruce. Looking at the base of hemlock needles with a hand lens reveals that the needles have short stems that lie parallel to the twig, a feature that differentiates hemlocks from true fir and spruce. With the exception of the mountain hemlock, which has stomata on both sides of the needles, two stomatal bands brighten

Fig. 2-69: Two-sided needles with grooves, very small pegs, and stems parallel to the twig

the bottom sides of hemlock needles. The needles of all hemlock species in this book are grooved on the upper surface, though the grooves of the mountain hemlock are shallow and extend only partway up the needle.

FEMALE SEED CONES

Female hemlock seed cones are small and woody, some of the smallest cones in the pine family, maturing in one growing season on the previous year's shoots (fig. 2-70a). They are purple, reddish, or yellow when young and tan to brown when mature. Again, the mountain hemlock stands apart—it has the largest cones (up to three inches long) of all hemlock species. In a heavy-cone-set year, the intense purple of a branch loaded with cones can make your eyes water (figs. 2-70b,c). As with most cones in the pine family, early in their development the bracts are visible but are quickly overtaken by the rapidly growing cone scales. The mountain hemlock cones in the images grew from three-quarters of an inch to nearly three inches in about five weeks.

Fig. 2-70a: Mature cones from the previous season on Canadian hemlock 'Pendula'

Fig. 2-70b: Mountain hemlock cone in late June

Fig. 2-70c: Mountain hemlock cones in early August

MALE POLLEN CONES

The small male pollen cones of hemlock, less than a quarter-inch long, form on the previous season's shoots, maturing from reddish-purple to yellow with a tinge of pink at pollen release (fig. 2-71). They are not typically useful in species ID.

Fig. 2-71: Male pollen cones on last season's shoots

BUDS

The unusually small terminal buds of most hemlocks are barely visible with the naked eye and typically not useful in species ID. The larger (for a hemlock) round deep-red buds of the northern Japanese hemlock are an exception (fig. 2-72).

Fig. 2-72: Typically very small indistinct buds; northern Japanese hemlock an exception

BARK

The smooth bark of young hemlocks develops narrow fissures with age. Most often a brownish-gray color, it is not distinct enough from species to species to

Fig. 2-73: Unusual bark on wild mountain hemlock

be useful in ID. But in the wild, the bark of an old mountain hemlock sometimes forms beautiful checks, with horizontal and vertical fissures so distinct they looked as if cut with a cleaver (fig. 2-73). Hemlock bark is not fire-resistant.

FORM

The form of hemlock species varies considerably by species, though all are known for having drooping leaders (fig. 2-65). This is helpful when identifying a tree in the wild, as hemlocks are the only pine family species in native PNW forests with this trait (Alaska-cedar also has a drooping leader); however, this feature is less helpful in a cultivated landscape, as there are many other ornamental species with leaders that droop.

Variable Form of Mountain Hemlock

Since mountain hemlocks are dug from the wild and grow from seed, one sees a great deal more variability in form and needle color than in genetically identical cultivated clones (figs. 2-74a,b). The branches can droop noticeably (an adaptation for shedding snow) or not at all. Needles can be blue-green, deep green, or any shade in between. Also, one often sees mountain hemlocks sold in groups of two or three, as they commonly grow this way in the wild. The entire grouping is dug up and sold as a unit. All these variables can throw one off on the way to species ID.

DWARF MISTLETOE

A dwarf mistletoe (*Arceuthobium tsugense*), with a number of subspecies, grows parasitically on younger limbs of mountain hemlock and western hemlock, as well as on noble fir (*A. procera*) and Pacific silver fir, which dug-up plants often bring with them from the wild (fig. 2-75). With severely reduced branches and leaves, the dwarf mistletoe looks twiggy and defoliated, more like a mini staghorn coral one might see on a reef than a flowering plant. Even though its avocado-green color is due to chlorophyll, this species is a poor

Variable Form of Mountain Hemlock

Fig. 2-74a: Green foliage and horizontal branches

Fig. 2-74b: Blue-green foliage and drooping branches

photosynthesizer, an obligate parasite depending almost entirely on the host for sugar, minerals, and water.

The small pale female flowers are thought to be pollinated by both wind and insects. The sticky seeds, forcefully ejected from the small oval fruit, adhere to surfaces. Newly germinated seeds of nonparasitic flowering plants typically develop true leaves quickly to start making sugars through photosynthesis before energy stored in the cotyledons runs out. In contrast, after a parasitic mistletoe seed germinates on the branch and grows down through the bark, the plant spends two to five years underground inside

Fig. 2-75: Dwarf mistletoe on mountain hemlock

the host developing root-like structures before the first shoots appear, with the branch typically swelling at the infection site about a year in advance. Dwarf mistletoe can also cause witches'-brooms to form. The best strategy is to remove infected branches to limit the spread within the tree and from tree to tree. Other species of dwarf mistletoe in the *Arceuthobium* genus affect other native conifers.

CULTIVARS

The vast majority of hemlock cultivars have foliage similar to the species; the most common cultivars by far are from the Canadian hemlock, of which there are hundreds, with 'Pendula' being the most prevalent (fig. 2-76). The short dark-green needles of cultivars of the northern Japanese hemlock make them a standout in the garden and worth seeking out. Cultivars of the two hemlocks native to the PNW are less common but not rare.

Fig. 2-76: Canadian hemlock 'Pendula'

Bark beetle galleries on conifer

Tsuga   Hemlock Genus

	Foliage: Needles with short stems parallel to twig Cones: Small and woody			
	T. canadensis Canadian hemlock Native to eastern US and Canada		*T. diversifolia* Northern Japanese hemlock Native to Japan	
Needles and Twigs				
		Needles to ¾" (l), wider at base, rounded tips; some **needles press along upper stem and show 2 stomatal bands on underside**, differentiating it from other hemlocks		**Dark green needles** to ½" (l); **blunt**, notched tips; snow-white stomatal bands; unequal lengths but same width along entire needle; shorter needles pop up
Buds		Very small red buds not distinctive		**Deep ruby-red round buds** most distinct of the hemlocks
Cones and Form				
	To 1" (l) with a short stalk	To 100'; younger specimen shown	To 1" (l); nearly sessile	To 80' in wild; shorter in cultivation
Bark		'Pendula' bark shown, nondescript brown bark		Nondescript brown bark
Other	Species rare in the landscape; 'Pendula' most common of the many cultivars; Z3		Cultivars more common than species; 'Loowit' common cultivar; Z4–5	

T. heterophylla Western hemlock PNW NATIVE*		*T. mertensiana* Mountain hemlock PNW NATIVE*	
	Blunt needles to ¾" (l); unequal lengths but same width along entire needle; shorter needles pop above longer ones; a few needles press along upper stem		Only hemlock in world with **stomata on both sides of needles**; blue-green to green needles to ¾" (l) point forward, encircle twig and look star-like
	Very small indistinct buds		Tiny buds not distinct
	To 1" (l); green then brown	To 150'; draping branches	To 3" (l); purple to yellow then brown	Smaller tree; layered branches
	Grayish-brown bark		Gray reddish-brown bark forms fissures at young age
Thrives in heavy shade; tallest of all hemlocks; Z6		Tolerant of sun and low water; native habitat is tree line; Z4–5	

CHAPTER 3

Cupressaceae: The Cypress Family

Introduction to the Cypress Family

What's true of all conifer families is especially true of the cypress family. The 140 or so species are spread thinly over approximately thirty genera, with just over half home to one species (monotypic) and only three claiming species in the double digits. This doesn't include subspecies or naturally occurring varieties. Cypress-family species are native to every continent except Antarctica. Twenty-five species across thirteen genera are included in the ID charts in this book. Table 3-1 shows the number of species in each genus worldwide, compared with how many are included in the ID charts and how many of those are native to the PNW. Keep in mind that the number of species recognized in each genus varies depending on the source.

The approximately eighteen remaining genera, too numerous to list here, are native to Argentina, Australia, Africa, Chile, China, Japan, New Caledonia, New Guinea, New Zealand, and Spain.

Table 3-1. Cypress Family Genera and Species Numbers

Native Genera	Worldwide	Book	PNW
Juniperus Juniper	52	9*	1
Chamaecyparis False-cypress	6	3	2
Thuja True arborvitae	5	2	1
Calocedrus Incense-cedar	3	1	1
Sequoia Coast redwood	1	1	1
Hybrid Genus			
× *Cupressocyparis*	1	1	½
Nonnative Genera			
Cupressus Cypress	15	2	0
Taxodium Baldcypress	2	1	0
Cryptomeria Japanese-cedar	1	1	0
Metasequoia Dawn redwood	1	1	0
Platycladus Oriental arborvitae	1	1	0
Sequoiadendron Giant sequoia	1	1	0
Thujopsis Staghorn-cedar	1	1	0

*includes one hybrid species

FOLIAGE TYPES

The small leathery leaves of species in the cypress family take one of four forms: scale-like and flattened, scale-like and rounded, awl-like, or linear, with linear foliage being an exception. Determining which type of foliage your specimen has is the first step toward species ID. But the foliage in the cypress family is trickier than foliage in the pine family, which sorts neatly by genus, in that the foliage of each has features unique to that genus only. This is not the case in the cypress family.

Flattened Scales

This book includes six genera in the cypress family with flattened scales, which look and feel as if they've been run through a pasta maker, like linguine (fig. 3-1).

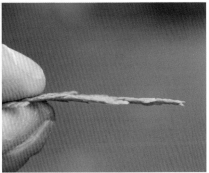

Fig. 3-1: Flattened scales: top and side views

Rounded Scales

Cypresses and many junipers have rounded scales, which roll easily in your fingers like spaghetti (fig. 3-2).

Fig. 3-2: Rounded scales

Awl-Like Foliage

Awl-like foliage is wide at the base, pointy at the tip, and forms a small triangle (fig. 3-3). This book includes six species in the cypress family across three genera with foliage that is exclusively awl-like. But although most species display either rounded scales or awls, some junipers have both types.

Fig. 3-3: Awl-like foliage

Linear Foliage

Linear foliage is the exception in the cypress family (fig. 3-4). This book includes three species across three genera with this type of foliage, which at first glance might lead one to think these species are in the pine family; characteristics to look for that differentiate them are discussed later in this section.

Fig. 3-4: Linear foliage

FOLIAGE: A CLOSE LOOK

To identify a genus or species in the cypress family, one must take a close look at the foliage. Note that the foliage on the fast-growing branches can be up to twenty times larger (fig. 3-5) than the foliage on the frond-like twiglets (Farjon 2005a). Also, the larger foliage is not pressed against the twig as tightly as the smaller foliage. It is important to remember that the smaller foliage of the twiglet is used in genus and species ID. It is small enough that you will probably need a loupe to see the details.

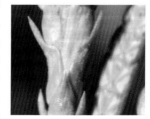

Fig. 3-5: Larger foliage of branch

Scale-Like Foliage: What Is a Scale?

In the cypress family, each small foliage segment is a single leaf. These small leathery leaves overlap one another like scales on a fish, leaving only a portion of each leaf exposed. The scales press down tightly against one other, adhering to the twig for all or nearly all their length; in some species, the apex of the scale is not attached to the twig. These scale-like leaves form opposite pairs: a lateral pair and a facial pair (fig. 3-6). Together the two pairs form what looks like a unit of foliage composed of four scales.

In species with flattened scales, the lateral pair folds in the long direction. The lovely botanical word for this is conduplicate. It not only sounds nice; it also has a wonderful mouthfeel when you say it out loud. The facial pair is flattened and embraced on the sides by the conduplicate lateral pair.

A number of observable characteristics about this unit of foliage will help you ID a specimen to genus and species. First, note how completely the lateral pair embraces the facial pair. Is there separation between the two lateral scales, or do they join at the base? It can help to think of this feature in terms of necklines. Does the lateral pair form a shallow V-neck (fig. 3-7), an open V-neck (fig. 3-8), or a plunging neckline (fig. 3-6)? Second, do the two pairs of scales line up (figs. 3-6, 3-8), or does the facial pair poke above the lateral pair (fig. 3-7)? Third, note the shape of the scale apices. Are they rounded (fig. 3-7) or pointed (figs. 3-6, 3-8)?

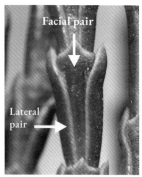

Fig. 3-6: Plunging neckline and pointy apices

Fig. 3-7: Shallow V-neck and rounded apices

Fig. 3-8: Open V-neck and pointy apices

Stomatal Bloom on Scales

In some species with scale-like foliage, stomata leave a distinctive light-colored pattern. (Refer to the pine family introduction for more on stomata.) This pattern or lack of pattern is often helpful in genus and species ID. Sometimes the stomata run along the edges of the scales (fig. 3-7), in effect highlighting their shape. Other times the stomata form patterns on the scale surfaces (fig. 3-8). For example, the stomatal bloom on the surface of flattened western redcedar (*Thuja plicata*) scales is typically described as butterfly-shaped, but it looks more like cat eyes to me (fig. 3-8). Stomatal bloom typically appears on the underside of foliage but sometimes is found on both sides.

Awl-Like Foliage: What Is an Awl?

An awl looks like a scale that is partially pulled away from the twig or partially free of the twig. If you could glue awls onto the twig, they would look like overlapping scales. However, they don't form pairs like scales. They are typically arranged alternately around the twig. Awls can be prickly or soft to the touch. In some species, awls flare out (fig. 3-9); in others, they curl in (fig. 3-10).

Most species in the cypress family display either scales or awls, but some in the juniper genus have both. Also, the initial juvenile foliage of every species in the cypress family is entirely awl-like before transitioning to adult foliage by the end of the first growing season. In some cultivars this juvenile foliage is fixed, never transitioning to adult foliage. Refer to the "Cultivars with Juvenile Foliage: Cypress Family" section in the introduction for more on this subject.

Fig. 3-9: Awl-like foliage flared out

Fig. 3-10: Awl-like foliage curled in

Linear Foliage: In the Cypress Family?

The cypress family has five species across four genera with linear foliage. Three of these species are found in residential and commercial landscapes: the coast redwood (*Sequoia sempervirens*), dawn redwood (*Metasequoia glyptostroboides*), and baldcypress (*Taxodium distichum*). One way to think of linear foliage is as awls that are pulled away from the twig. Look at the leaf bases to differentiate linear foliage from the foliage of species in the pine family; the leaf bases of the cypress family species extend and press down along the twig (decurrent). The twigs are literally wrapped in foliage, giving them a bright green color (fig. 3-11). This never occurs in the pine family. If twigs in the pine family are green, it is not due to the foliage—the twig itself is green.

Scale-like foliage is considered an adaptation to drying conditions that began about 23 MYA (Eckenwalder 1976). Linear-foliaged conifers in the cypress family have traditionally been seen as relics, species that didn't adapt to the changing climate, left behind by evolution to become the lone survivors of conifer lineages that had otherwise died off (Eckenwalder 1976). It follows

Fig. 3-11: Decurrent foliage wraps twig

that in the wild these species are found in wet areas. Baldcypresses grow in swamps. Coast redwoods are found along the coast with ample fog drip. And the dawn redwood, thought to be extinct until a population was discovered in China in 1944, is riparian.

Until recently these species, along with a number of others, were in their own family, Taxodiaceae, the baldcypress family. The separation of the baldcypress and cypress families was based largely on the foliage, but foliage is considered a much less reliable differentiator than reproductive structures, such as seed cones and pollen cones (Eckenwalder 1976). Even to the naked eye the globular seed cones of these linear-foliaged species look very similar to those with scales, especially to those in the cypress genus. Because of these features, as well as other cone characteristics visible under high magnification, and DNA testing, all species in the baldcypress family but one have been moved into the cypress family. DNA testing showed the Japanese umbrella-pine to be unique enough to warrant its own family. The baldcypress family is now devoid of species, but botanists still refer to these moved-over species as taxodiaceous.

Botanists have long looked for the missing link—a species that represents an intermediate step—between these linear-leaved species that never adapted to a drying planet and those with scale leaves that did. When the dawn redwood was first discovered, some considered it to be that species. The foliage is linear and deciduous, like that of the baldcypress, and the orientation of the foliage to the twig in opposite pairs is like many species in the cypress family. This view has not taken hold.

But sometimes the thing you've been searching for has been right in front of you all along. The scale-leaved species in the cypress family are now considered by many botanists to be that missing link, the descendants of taxodiaceous species that changed and progressed (Eckenwalder 1976). Fossils provide glimpses into geologic time. From these glimpses botanists map the evolutionary history and relationships of extinct and living conifers, a map that is redrawn and comes more into focus as new extinct and living species are discovered.

Linear Foliage Look-Alikes

One complicating factor is that many of the characteristics of species with linear foliage in the cypress family can also be found in plants in the yew family (Taxaceae). However, the cones and form of yew family species are very different.

TWIGLETS SHED AS A UNIT

All conifers shed a portion of their foliage seasonally, but this process is fundamentally different in the pine family than in the cypress family. All twigs in the cypress family drop from the branch as one piece. The leaves do not fall singly, as they do in most genera in the pine family. If you look on the ground around a tree in the cypress family, you'll see piles of twiglets. Each piece of foliage is anatomically part of the twiglet or branch, attaching at the cortex (Farjon 2005a), which lies just beneath the epidermis. In the pine family, the abscission layer forms

Fig. 3-12: Brown inner branches: seasonal shedding

between the needle and the twig; in the cypress family it forms between the twig and the branch.

This shedding of entire branches is called cladoptosis, a Greek word meaning falling branch. Each spring as new foliage emerges older foliage retreats farther back on the branch, becoming a little more shaded, a little less productive, until the point is reached where it draws more resources from the tree than it supplies through photosynthesis. In the cypress family, when all the oldest nonproductive branches turn brown at once, most typically in the fall, it can look alarming, like the tree is in distress (fig. 3-12). But this is a natural phenomenon, seasonal maintenance the tree performs to remain vigorous. It is more commonly known as cedar flagging (referring to species with cedar in their common names, not true cedars), but occurs on all species in the cypress family. The tree is fine as long as it's the old foliage browning and dropping and not foliage at the branch ends or at the top of the tree, in the crown.

FEMALE SEED CONES

Be sure to review the content on cones in the pine family introduction before reading this section, as the two are compared.

Anatomy and Evolution

Seed cones in the pine family are typically used instructionally to represent a typical conifer cone, but there are fundamental differences in anatomy and evolutionary history between cones of the cypress family and those of the pine family. The seed scales and bracts, what botanists call the bract-scale complex, have evolved in opposite directions in the two families and swapped roles—to a point. In the pine family (in brief), the seeds and seed wings rest on a woody seed scale, the seed scale attaches to a reduced bract, and the bract attaches to the axis. In the cypress family, the situation is reversed: the seed scales are highly reduced, vestigial, or missing altogether (Farjon 2005a), typically not large enough to see with the naked eye or a loupe, and the bracts are enlarged and thickened with what's called intercalary growth, making up the visible exterior woody part of the cone. And, in the same way that seed scales in the pine family remain tiny until the ovules are fertilized, bracts in the cypress family enlarge only after fertilization is assured. In instances where the seed scales are highly reduced but still visible, they often appear as protuberances on the cone scales, as can be seen in those of the Japanese-cedar and baldcypress genera (Farjon 2005a).

171

One would not be foolish in assuming the bracts have taken over the role of hosting the seeds, because, where else is there for the seeds to go? Not foolish, but incorrect. In the cypress family, over time, the ovules made their way from the seed scales to the base of the bracts and from there relocated onto the cone axis itself (Farjon 2005a). Evolution is far more ingenious than we can imagine—who would have predicted that? Once the seed scales no longer had a job to do, they disappeared or became highly reduced; and once the bracts didn't need to be there for the seed scales to attach to, they were free to do other things, like become the woody part of the cone (Farjon 2005a).

CONE TYPES

This evolution of the bract-scale complex in the cypress family has resulted in seed cones that look very different than those of the pine family. For each genus, the extent to which tissue around the bract has enlarged and how it has enlarged drives the shape and size of the cone, which is typically no more than an inch long. Also, a significantly shorter axis supports many fewer bracts.

Please read this note on terminology before continuing further: Even though the visible woody parts of seed cones in the cypress family develop from bracts, the overgrowth transforms them into what are commonly referred to as scales. For simplicity, from this point forward, bracts are referred to as scales.

Soccer Balls, Flower Buds, Fleshy Cones

Diamond-, pentagon-, and hexagon-shaped woody scales are responsible for the pleasing geometry of the round or roundish cones of many genera in the cypress family (fig. 3-13). Typically, each scale of these little soccer balls is armed to some degree with a protuberance (umbo), which is the original bract poking through the overgrowth (Farjon 2005a). In some species in the cypress genus, the cones are so dense they feel like actual wood, hard like mahogany or some other exotic species high on the Janka hardness scale. Substantial dark gaps open up between the scales of mature cones, allowing you to see the entire scale surface and all of its edges.

The scales of other genera are less woody, more linear, and bud-shaped when closed, with slight curled back protuberances at the tips (fig. 3-14). In these cones, growth around the original bract has mostly elongated and thickened very little.

In a few genera, the cones are fleshy and rubbery when immature, the texture of large moles or warts, but only juniper cones remain fleshy at maturity (fig. 3-15). Except for the two species in the baldcypress genus, the cones of the cypress family never self-destruct as in the true fir and true cedar genera in the pine family.

Fig. 3-13: Soccer-ball cones   Fig. 3-14: Flower bud cones   Fig. 3-15: Fleshy cones

SEEDS AND SEED WINGS

Cone and cone scale size drive seed and seed wing size. Compared to those of the pine family, in general the smaller cones and cone scales of the cypress family produce significantly smaller seeds and seed wings, to the point that you must be careful while shaking them from the cone into your collection envelope, as once they drop to the ground, they become lost among the rest of the organic litter.

Each scale on a cone in the cypress family hosts two or more seeds and each seed has two wings, unlike in the pine family, where each scale always has two seeds with one wing each. In many genera in the cypress family, the two wings nearly encompass the seed, which bulges up in the middle like a dome. The seeds and seed wings of the incense-cedar (*Calocedrus decurrens*) are among the largest in the cypress family and are notable for their uneven wings (fig. 3-16).

Fig. 3-16: Japanese-cedar cone and seeds (left) Incense-cedar cone and single seed (right)

NO TERMINAL BUDS (WITH EXCEPTIONS)

One thing that seems very odd at first is that most plants in the cypress family do not have terminal or axillary buds. This is in contrast to the pine family, where buds are often used to identify conifers to species. The scales or awls at the twig tips curl in a bit to shield the growth tips, but even with a loupe this feature is inconspicuous. (Many species form small male pollen cones in fall and winter at the branch tips, which could be mistaken for buds.) Notable exceptions to this are the handful of deciduous conifers in this family (the baldcypresses and dawn redwood), which do have terminal and axillary buds.

BARK

Bark in the cypress family is similar across many genera and species, and typically has a fibrous, stringy texture and a tawny cinnamon-red color. Descriptions of bark are included only for those genera and species that deviate from what is typical.

Calocedrus: The Incense-Cedar Genus
Cupressaceae: Cypress Family
Flattened Scales

Only one of the three species in *Calocedrus* is found outside of the Far East, the incense-cedar (*C. decurrens*) (fig. 3-17), native to Oregon, California, northern Baja, and a wee bit of western Nevada in the Lake Tahoe area. (In older publications you will find this species in *Libocedrus*, a genus of five species native to New Zealand and New Caledonia.)

The incense-cedar is used extensively in urban forestry, as it can endure considerable abuse, including heat, drought, wind, car exhaust, and poor or even hazardous soil. This, in addition to its somewhat narrow form, makes incense-cedars popular highway trees, where they not only survive but somehow also manage to seed down rather readily. When stuck in traffic along roadways where incense-cedars are planted, look

Fig. 3-17: Incense-cedar

for these plucky seedlings and young trees getting their start in life under the most inhospitable urban conditions. Typically, you see them well out of the irrigation zone, with tire-splash their sole source of supplemental water, pressed up against a guardrail directly in the blast zone of passing semis, or in some other way situationally compromised. Seedlings of all species are delicate creatures, but the rapidly developing and extensive roots of incense-cedars give them an advantage over most other conifers right from the seedling stage, which helps make them drought- and wind-resistant from day one

(Powers and Oliver 1990). Even so, these volunteer highway trees don't tend to live long lives
and seem to cry out to be rescued from their dire
circumstances.

In the residential landscape, their narrow
form makes incense-cedars popular hedge trees,
although they require quite a bit more space than
the typical two-foot-wide arborvitae hedge (refer
to the *Thuja* genus). If incense-cedars are growing in or near your yard, be on the lookout for
the seedlings (fig. 3-18). In the spring and early
summer, their two impressive cotyledons, up
to 1¼ inches long and looking a bit like rabbit

Fig. 3-18: Incense-cedar seedling

ears, make them easy to spot among weeds and other volunteer seedlings.
The cotyledons are three times as long and nearly twice as wide as those of
the western redcedar (*Thuja plicata*) and Port-Orford-cedar (*Chamaecyparis*

Foliage

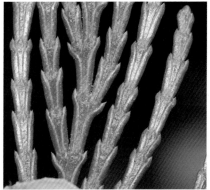

Fig. 3-19a: Long narrow scales

Fig. 3-19b: Close-up of scales

Fig. 3-19c: Branch ends with fan-like sprays

lawsoniana). The seedlings quickly develop prickly juvenile foliage that is much shorter than the cotyledons, and by the end of the first growing season adult foliage appears.

FOLIAGE

Incense-cedar leaves are longer than any other species in the PNW with scale-like foliage, making the twiglets appear feathery and, in combination with the narrow growth habit, giving the tree its distinctive look. Individual scales are shaped like champagne flutes or vases, with lateral and facial scales of approximately the same length (figs. 3-19a,b). With a hand lens, note that the lateral scales do not join at the base and that the apices are pointy, with the facial scales creating the profile of an idealized wave. They are a pure green without any visible stomatal bloom. The branches arch up at the ends, but this characteristic is obscured by sprays of foliage that fan out in all directions (fig. 3-19c).

FEMALE SEED CONES

The one-inch seed cones of incense-cedars are always described as looking like duckbills, but this describes how they look when they are mature after seed release—the state they're in when you find them on the ground. Before this they take the shape of unopened tulips. Maturing over one growing season, the cones begin kelly green, brighten to yellow, and then deepen to cheddar-gold and caramel before aging to a final brown (fig. 3-20), a color sequence the cones of many species with flattened scales pass through, including those in *Thuja* and *Chamaecyparis*. In heavy-cone-set years, the branch tips look as if they've been dipped in yellow mustard and, come winter, you will wonder where all the cones went. The incense-cedar drops all its mature cones

Fig. 3-20: Tulip-shaped cones when ripening, then duck-bill-shaped

directly after seed release. If you are looking for cones after the end of the growing season, you will have to search on the ground.

MALE POLLEN CONES

Large numbers of small incense-cedar pollen cones appear in late fall before the Christmas holiday. The bright cones form individually at the twig ends like yellow Q-tips, displaying nicely against the dark-green fan-like foliage, making incense-cedar sprays a common element in seasonal wreaths and bouquets (fig. 3-21). The winter holiday season is a celebration of conifers; the green of the traditional red and green colors of Christmas is supplied by conifers. But why is it that only when flowering trees and shrubs have died back

Fig. 3-21: Seasonal bouquet of conifer foliage: noble fir, white pine, and incense-cedar with pollen cones

do we invite conifers indoors, and then only during the holidays? Many conifer species set pollen cones that are much larger and more colorful than those of the incense-cedar but go unnoticed when they appear in spring, during a time when most gardeners and florists are enamored with flowering plants.

Conifers are the best plants to befriend—their evergreen foliage is a constant one can rely on. If fragrance is what you're after, the foliage of most species in the cypress family, especially those with cedar in their common names, is fragrant year-round. The wood is also aromatic. Many incense sticks are made from compressed incense-cedar sawdust; incense is derived from the Latin word *incendere*, as in incendiary materials.

Everyone over a certain age has the specific smell memory of a freshly sharpened number two pencil—that's incense-cedar with a whiff of graphite—an aroma that transports me directly back to grade school. Incense-cedar wood is ideal for pencils because it doesn't splinter when whittled. Each time you shave off the outer layer, the aroma is released anew. At one time eastern redcedar, which is actually a juniper (*Juniperus virginiana*), was the wood of choice for pencils in the United States, but when supply diminished the incense-cedar became the go-to wood. Today, incense-cedar is mostly used in more expensive high-quality pencils.

BARK

Incense-cedars form vivid bark at a fairly young age. The cinnamon-red young bark is fibrous and peeling. With some age, narrow and deep irregular fissures develop that look like they've been gouged out in haste with a woodworking tool (fig. 3-22). The fissures part like turbulent water around socket-like branch scars. The effect is that in certain lighting the trunk appears to writhe and to watch you—tree bark that wouldn't be out of place in a Vincent van Gogh painting or a Grimm's fairytale. With even more age, the bark becomes thick and hard, almost wood-like.

Fig. 3-22: Writhing bark

INCENSE-CEDAR RUST

The foliage of incense-cedars is susceptible to a fungal pathogen evident in the spring. Its orange Day-Glo color and jelly-fish consistency are hard to miss, looking as it does like a life form that splatted down from outer space (fig. 3-23). The fungus has a complex life cycle requiring an alternate host, which means it must infect more than one species in a specific sequence to complete its life cycle and survive. In the case of incense-cedar rust (*Gymnosporangium libocedri*), the alternate host can be one of a number of deciduous species in the rose family, including pear and apple. Incense-cedars tolerate infections well, but on fruit trees both foliage and fruit are infected, and I can personally attest to the fact that in wet springs the fungus can ruin one's entire crop of pears. On fruit the fungus looks more powdery than gelatinous.

Incense-Cedar Rust

Fig. 3-23: Rust on a two- to three-year-old incense-cedar and on a developing pear

CULTIVARS

Most of the dozen or so registered incense-cedar cultivars are compact versions of the species, though a few are variegated. The species is planted far more commonly than cultivars, however.

Chamaecyparis: The False-Cypress Genus
Cupressaceae: Cypress Family
Flattened Scales

True cypresses have rounded scales and are in the cypress genus (*Cupressus*). False-cypresses have flattened scales and are in the false-cypress genus (*Chamaecyparis*). To muddy the waters further, conifer taxonomists disagree about where species in *Chamaecyparis* belong, with a minority saying the lot of them ought to be moved into *Cupressus*, in which case they would no longer be false-cypresses. One argument for this change is that, while it is uncommon for a plant to hybridize with another outside its own genus, when given the chance many false-cypresses hybridize with true cypresses, creating what you might call a true/false hybrid.

Fig. 3-24: Port-Orford-cedar

One well-known example is the Leyland-cypress (× *Cupressocyparis leylandii*), a hybrid of the Alaska-cedar (*Chamaecyparis nootkatensis*) and the Monterey cypress (*Cupressus macrocarpa*), which brings up another point of contention: where to place the Alaska-cedar. In addition to *Chamaecyparis* and *Cupressus*, some botanists place it in *Xanthocyparis* or *Callitropsis*. This can make finding the species in a book organized by botanical names a bit time-consuming. Although unlikely to remain in *Chamaecyparis*, the Alaska-cedar is most commonly sold as a *Chamaecyparis* in the horticultural trade, which is where it is placed in this book.

Chamaecyparis is one of a number of conifer genera, including *Calocedrus* and *Thuja*, whose species are split geographically between North America and East Asia. Three of the six species are native to North America, including the Port-Orford-cedar (*C. lawsoniana*) (fig. 3-24), and three are native to Japan and Taiwan. These six are the remains of what was once a highly successful genus with a continuous distribution of species throughout East Asia and across North America. When sea levels were lower, plant and animal species traveled between the two continents over the Bering land bridge. But the genus did not adapt well to the cooling and drying out that began worldwide about 23 MYA. The ice ages of the Pleistocene led to the extinction of many species, reducing *Chamaecyparis* to its current six scattered species.

These six species are found predominantly along the coast no more than 120 miles from the sea where there's abundant rainfall and humidity. The Alaska-cedar is also found in higher elevations of the Cascades, where it intermingles with western redcedar (*Thuja plicata*). *Chamaecyparis* species are known for being adapted to difficult circumstances other species cannot withstand, a recurring theme with conifers. Coastal species must be able to tolerate high concentrations of salt, which is so toxic to most plants it essentially clears out the competition for those species tolerant of it (Laderman 1998). Plants very close to shore are hit directly with ocean spray, but coastal fog is also salty. Minute salt particles tossed into the air by breaking waves attract water vapor, which condenses around them, forming fog. Water droplets held in suspension are what make fog visible—water vapor is invisible. Salt-tolerant species benefit from other elements in sea-spray that coastal fog is rich in, including phosphorous, calcium, magnesium, and nitrogen. Fog is essentially a delivery system that transports moisture and nutrients from the sea into coastal forests (fig. 3-25). Along much of the Pacific, coastal fog is most common in summer and early fall, providing valuable moisture to the forest during what are typically droughty seasons and contributing significantly to annual water intake.

In addition to salt, most *Chamaecyparis* species, including the two native to the PNW, must contend with difficult soil. The soil of coastal Alaska-cedars stratifies into depleted and toxic layers, with elements migrating out of the upper layer and accumulating in high concentrations in the

Fig. 3-25: Coastal salt-tolerant species

lower layer. Port-Orford-cedars grow in soil high in heavy metals and low in nutrients, a combination few species can tolerate. The third species native to North America, the Atlantic white-cedar (*C. thyoides*), is found on the East Coast growing in peat, an anaerobic soil with few nutrients available to plants.

The three *Chamaecyparis* species from East Asia face similar difficulties. Cultivars of the East Asian species are very popular, but you'd probably have to visit an arboretum to observe the species, as they are rarely if ever planted in the residential or commercial landscape.

Foliage

Fig. 3-26a: No stomata and pointy apices on Alaska-cedar

Fig. 3-26b: Stomata at edges and rounded apices on Port-Orford-cedar

Fig. 3-26c: Drip tips of Port-Orford-cedar

FOLIAGE

You'll need a loupe to differentiate *Chamaecyparis* foliage from that of other genera and species with flattened scales. The edges of the lateral and facial scales of all *Chamaecyparis* species form an X pattern where they overlap (figs. 3-26a,b). To differentiate among *Chamaecyparis* species, note whether there is stomatal bloom, as well as the shape of the scale apices. The bloom of some species highlights the edges (fig. 3-26b), while others have no bloom (fig. 3-26a). In some species the apices are rounded (fig. 3-26b), and in others they are pointed (fig. 3-26a).

The foliage of many coastal conifers, including the two native PNW *Chamaecyparis* species, is designed to harvest rain and condensation from fog. This adaptation essentially converts overhead irrigation into drip irrigation: water droplets that collect on the foliage are directed to the branch ends, where they drip off the tips onto the root zone (fig. 3-26c). Moisture and nutrients are also taken in directly by the foliage.

FEMALE SEED CONES

With the exception of the Alaska-cedar, the cones of *Chamaecyparis* species mature in one growing season. Alaska-cedar cones require two growing seasons, a trait the species shares with the true cypresses. The small, woody, soccer-ball-shaped cones of all *Chamaecyparis* species, no more than ½ inch in diameter, grow in profusion at the branch ends (fig. 3-27a). The middle of each scale is armed with a horn, which can be prominent or slight, depending on the species (figs. 3-27b–d). Also pay close attention to the scale edges. In some species the edges are wavy (fig. 3-27c), and in others they are so straight they look as if cut with a sharp knife (fig. 3-27d).

MALE POLLEN CONES

The very small *Chamaecyparis* pollen cones form at the branch tips in spring and are typically an indistinct yellow. But those of Port-Orford-cedar are a showstopping crimson (fig. 3-28), differentiating it from other species in the genus found in the PNW. On certain dwarf cultivars with congested foliage, such as the 'Chirimen' Hinoki-cypress (*C. obtusa*), the pollen cones can be so densely packed that it seems as if something's amiss, like the plant is afflicted with a pathogen, particularly when the cones are brown after pollen release.

Female Seed Cones

Fig. 3-27a: Masses of cones at branch ends

Fig. 3-27b: Alaska-cedar: large horns and slightly wavy scale edges

Fig. 3-27c: Port-Orford-cedar: slight horns and wavy scale edges

Fig. 3-27d: Hinoki-cypress: moderate horns and straight scale edges

SPECIES UNDER DURESS

Port-Orford-Cedar Plant Destroyer

The Port-Orford-cedar is in decline in its native range, a small area straddling southwest Oregon and northwest California, from an introduced water mold (*Phytophthora lateralis*), which attacks the roots. The pathogen is also rampant in horticultural plantings. The genus of the water mold is aptly named—*Phytophthora* means plant destroyer. Few things are sadder than watching this destroyer of plants kill off a grouping of Port-Orford-cedars one at a time, like a slow-moving execution, with all stages of the disease visible in a glance. The bad news is difficult to deliver to those who inquire about

Male Pollen Cones

Fig. 3-28: Crimson pollen cones of Port-Orford-cedar

their beloved failing trees: nothing can be done to stop this fatal disease. After initial infection, established trees perish in one to four years. After dead or diseased trees are removed, the water mold stays alive in the soil for up to ten years, depending on how wet the soil is (BLM/USFS 2003). Fungal spores follow the water gradient downhill and spread uphill (and downhill) on the wheels of lawnmowers, tractors, and wheelbarrows, as well as on the soles of shoes and the paws of pets and wild animals.

This disease was first detected in the Seattle area in the 1920s and moved south in horticultural plantings and from there into wild populations in southwest Oregon by the 1950s. The water mold is now found throughout Port-Orford-cedar's native range and also in Europe, where the Port-Orford-cedar is extremely popular. The good news is that horticultural varieties are now available that are grafted onto resistant root stock developed by Oregon State University, and plant pathologists have identified specimens in the wild that appear to be naturally immune. A program for planting resistant seed in Port-Orford-cedar's native range has begun, but it will be many years before these trees are old enough for researchers to know whether the trees will remain resistant over the long term (Sniezko et al. 2012). A concern is that rare species like the Port-Orford-cedar with long life spans and patchy island-like ranges can experience delayed extinction (Laderman 1998).

Alaska-cedar: Dying of the Cold on a Warming Planet

The Alaska-cedar is one of the most northerly species in the cypress family. Although native to the Cascades of Oregon, Washington, and British Columbia, as well as the Olympic Mountains, it is most common as a coastal species, growing in an uninterrupted range from Vancouver Island north to past Valdez Bay in Alaska, from just above high-tide line to timberline. (It is also found in a few isolated pockets in northwest California and Eastern Oregon and British Columbia.) Starting about 12,000 years ago, the Alaska-cedar flourished, expanding into territory freshly exposed by retreating glaciers. Then, during a 550-year period called the Little Ice Age (1300–1850), it retreated to its current range, to ice-free areas where, until recently, snow cover has been ample late into spring.

Snow, like goose down, is a natural insulator, and for some of the same reasons. The space in and among snow crystals traps air in a three-dimensional maze. The lighter, drier, and fluffier the snow, the more gently it lands, the deeper it piles up, and the more insulating it is. Anyone who has experienced real winters knows this type of snow by the sounds it makes—it squeaks and crunches underfoot as millions of crystals rub against each other and break. Each flake is actually an aggregate of snow crystals that join as they bump into one another on their haphazard fall to the ground. Up to a billion crystals compose one cubic foot of snow. The crystals of warmer, denser, less insulating snow are lubricated by a thin film of water, allowing them to slide more quietly when tramped on.

In coastal Alaska and Canada, snow is changing to rain earlier in the season, and the roots of the Alaska-cedar are acclimatizing earlier for spring. Without the insulating snow, the ground is exposed, and the roots are vulnerable to freezing when the inevitable frigid spring weather system blows through, resulting in a paradoxical problem: warmer temperatures are causing Alaska-cedars to freeze to death. To learn more about this phenomenon, refer to *In Search of the Canary Tree*, Lauren Oakes's personal account of the unglamorous, soggy, calorie-deprived field research she and her team conducted in the panhandle of Alaska. Her words on how scientists like her who study climate change manage to live hopeful lives are particularly affecting.

Another problem is that the Alaska-cedar, a valuable timber tree, regenerates poorly after clear-cutting. The cones require two growing seasons to mature. The seeds require two winters to break dormancy and have poor germination rates. In many areas, the Alaska-cedar grows in close association with western hemlock (*Tsuga heterophylla*), which seeds down vigorously after a disturbance. In certain areas where mixed forests are left to regenerate naturally after clear-cutting, Alaska-cedar is often outcompeted by western hemlock, and the forest transitions to pure western hemlock (Dunsworth 1998).

PORT-ORFORD-CEDAR SEEDLINGS IN THE LANDSCAPE

It's a contradiction that the Port-Orford-cedar, a species with a tiny distribution in the wild, seeds down so readily outside its native range. Look for the seedlings wherever this tree is planted (figs. 3-29a–c). But look carefully—they remain invisible until your eyes adjust to their small scale. The two cotyledons and first juvenile leaves rise no more than an inch above the soil. Typically, where there's one there's many, and you discover a virtual seedling forest at your feet. It's fun to scoop up bunches of seedlings, plant them in trays, and follow the changes they go through on their way to becoming adult trees. Without irrigation, almost none of the seedlings in figure 3-29c made it through their first droughty PNW summer.

Fig. 3-29a: Seedling with two cotyledons and first juvenile leaves   Fig. 3-29b: Young two- to three-year-old tree

Fig. 3-29c: Seedling forest

CULTIVARS

Port-Orford-Cedar

The willingness of Port-Orford-cedar seeds to germinate and the species' propensity for throwing variants are the reasons this conifer has so many cultivars. A conifer grower can observe countless seedlings in the seedbed, easily keeping watch for those that might exhibit unusual characteristics. Many have been selected for their especially blue foliage, such as 'Van Pelt's Blue' (fig. 3-30a), but the shape and X pattern of the scales, as well as the cones, will tell you it's a Port-Orford-cedar. Other cultivars have been selected for their fixed juvenile foliage, which looks nothing like the foliage of the species.

Fig. 3-30a: Port-Orford-cedar 'Van Pelt's Blue'

Fig. 3-30b: Alaska-cedar 'Green Arrow'

Fig. 3-30c: Twisted cupped foliage of Hinoki-cypress cultivar

Fig. 3-30d: Variegated foliage of Hinoki-cypress cultivar

189

Fig. 3-30e: Threadleaf Sawara-cypress cultivar limbed up

Fig. 3-30f: Pea-sized ¼-inch cones of Sawara-cypress cultivar

Fig. 3-30g: Limbed-up Sawara-cypress cultivar with juvenile foliage

Alaska-cedar

Cultivars are sometimes selected for displaying a more intense version of a characteristic the species is known for. Chionophiles are species that, like the Alaska-cedar, have adaptations for thriving in winter conditions. The branches of the Alaska-cedar droop dramatically, giving it a weeping form, an adaptation for shedding snow and limiting broken limbs. Many popular Alaska-cedar cultivars carry its natural weeping habit to an extreme, with the effect that many look lugubrious, even ghoul-like. Some, like 'Green Arrow', are so skinny and droopy they look positively anorexic, like they haven't the strength to lift their limbs (fig. 3-30b). If conifers had an undertaker, it would be the Alaska-cedar, a species that appears eternally burdened. These cultivars make a statement wherever they are planted, and the anorexic forms are especially useful in small backyards or tight spots, as tall trees with a small footprint are uncommon. Look to the foliage, cones, and form to identify it as an Alaska-cedar.

Hinoki-Cypress

Though in Japan the Hinoki-cypress is the most highly prized and revered of all conifers, you rarely if ever see the species in the residential or commercial landscape. However, cultivars of the Hinoki-cypress are extremely popular and come in all shapes and sizes, from large trees to miniature bun-shaped shrubs. You can identify the majority of them by their foliage, which is very similar to the species: dark-green, cupped, and twisted (fig. 3-30c); yellow-tinged cultivars are also common (fig. 3-30d). Many also set cones. In the ID chart, 'Gracilis' is used as a representative cultivar, as it is one of the most popular.

Sawara-Cypress

Cultivars of the Sawara-cypress (*C. pisifera*) are everywhere you look; how-ever, almost none bear any resemblance to the species. The majority fall into two groups. The first group is characterized by stringy threadleaf branches with a rag-mop-like appearance (fig. 3-30e). They come in all sizes, from smaller mounds to those that eventually grow into small trees, which are often limbed up. Some of the threadleaf cultivars set cones, which helps in ID. *Pisifera* means pea-like, which refers to the small size (¼ inch) and shape of the cones (fig. 3-30f). Be aware that there is a newer cultivar of the western redcedar called 'Whipcord' with threadleaf foliage that looks very similar—it also takes a rag-mop form, but the foliage is darker green and the foliage segments are longer. The second group of popular cultivars has blue feathery juvenile foliage (fig. 3-30g). Again, some are mound-shaped, and others grow into small trees with time and are often limbed up.

Atlantic White-Cedar

Cultivars of the Atlantic white-cedar, a denizen of swamps in the eastern United States, are less common and typically have fixed juvenile foliage. They require wet soil, and the foliage tends to bronze in winter, characteristics they share with the species.

× *Cupressocyparis*: The Leyland-Cypress Genus
Cupressaceae: Cypress Family
Flattened Scales

The Leyland-cypress (× *Cupressocyparis leylandii*) (fig. 3-31) is a hybrid of two North American Pacific Coast conifers, the Alaska-cedar (*Chamaecyparis nootkatensis*) and Monterey cypress (*Cupressus macrocarpa*), creating a hybrid genus with one species. The two trees grow nowhere near each other in the wild. They met in cultivation on the other side of the Atlantic, where Monterey cypress pollen fertilized Alaska-cedar cones on a Welsh estate in the late 1800s. In the early 1940s, the Leyland-cypress came full circle when rooted cuttings came back across the Atlantic. It would be another twenty years before it entered the horticultural market in the United States.

Fig. 3-31: Improperly placed Leyland-cypresses growing next to 'Emerald Green' arborvitae

CHARACTERISTICS

This repatriated tree has a combination of parental traits. The flattened scales that form an X pattern with no stomatal bloom are like those of its Alaska-cedar mother, except the foliage is a much deeper green (fig. 3-32). The few cones it sets are larger, like those of its Monterey cypress father. The stems age from green the first year into a bright cinnamon that contrasts nicely with the dark foliage. Leyland-cypress' branching breaks strongly for its Monterey cypress mother with no trace of the drooping habit of its father. The branches rise from the trunk in tight Vs (fig. 3-33) and remain straight for their entire length, like arms thrown up in the air after victory, giving the tree its distinctive diamond shape.

Fig. 3-32: Dark green flattened scales in X pattern and cinnamon-colored twigs

Fig. 3-33: Branches in tight Vs

LEYLAND-CYPRESS HEDGES

Three factors make Leyland-cypress a popular hedge tree for securing privacy. The dense foliage responds well to shearing. The tree holds onto its branches all the way to the ground. And since it grows up to three feet a year—it is more vigorous than either parent—one can have that privacy in no time. That's the lure, anyway, but its fast growth has a dark side. In Britain, Leyland-cypress' rapid growth is the source of so much acrimony between neighbors (sometimes even leading to violence) over blocked light and compromised views that, in 2003, Parliament passed legislation regulating its maintenance. The Leylandii Law, as it is called, is a section of the Anti-social Behavior Act. A twenty-nine-page booklet, "Hedge Height and Light Loss," establishes guidelines for local authorities mediating disputes. Her Majesty's government is even so kind as to provide an Excel spreadsheet with ten criteria for calculating whether there are grounds for action against a neighbor. You input slope of the property, compass direction, setbacks, hedge length, hedge height, and so on, after which you arrive at a final authoritative number, called the Effective Hedge Height, that, if greater than two meters, allows an official complaint to go forward. Let's hope it doesn't come to this in the colonies.

The problem isn't with the tree of course, it's with how it's planted, or mis-planted, in locations where the tree is expected to be narrow and slow growing. The results, especially if not corrected early on, are unfortunate. In figure 3-31, you can see a row of Leyland-cypresses that has taken control of the small backyards of a few homes, with no outdoor space left for the home-owners. You can also see by their flats tops that these trees were even sheared at some point, but their fast growth makes this an onerous task few can keep up with. To their right is a row of well-behaved 'Emerald Green' arborvitae (*Thuja occidentalis*), an appropriate if uninspired choice for a tight narrow space. Housing developers are fond of planting Leyland-cypresses because, even when young, the trees take up enough space to make a newly planted landscape look somewhat filled in and more appealing to prospective buyers. Once the house is sold it becomes someone else's problem—given enough time, a big problem. The trees in the image (fig. 3-31), taller than the houses and nearly as wide, would be quite expensive to remove and to replace, leaving the homeowners with the grim prospect of starting the backyard landscape from scratch. These trees work well as a stately row for dividing space on a large piece of property where there are no houses close by (fig. 3-34). The impulse to plant trees like these for the short-term gain of a quick landscape must be resisted.

Fig. 3-34: Properly placed row of Leyland-cypresses

Platycladus: The Oriental Arborvitae Genus
Cupressaceae: Cypress Family
Flattened Scales

The Oriental arborvitae genus (*Platycladus*) has one species, the Oriental arborvitae (*P. orientalis*). This species was formerly in the *Thuja* genus and is often still sold as *T. orientalis*. *Platycladus* means broad branch, in reference to this species' defining characteristic of flat somewhat vertically oriented fronds. It is native to East Asia but is rarely if ever planted outside arboreta. However, many cultivars, such as the popular 'Aurea Nana' (fig. 3-35), have similar foliage characteristics as the species.

Fig. 3-35: Fifteen-foot Oriental arborvitae cultivars, presumed to be 'Aurea Nana'. The graves these shrubs watch over date back as far as the 1870s. 'Aurea Nana' was registered as a cultivar in 1867 in France.

FOLIAGE

Many of the popular cultivars of Oriental arborvitae carry the foliage characteristic of the species to its logical conclusion. The flat fan-like sprays align vertically and tightly, like the pages of a book, with little or no space in between (figs. 3-36a,b). It's as if the twisted foliage of the Hinoki-cypress kept on twisting until reaching an ideal space-efficient order. The foliage is dense to the point that no light reaches the interior, where fronds are brown and dead from lack of sunshine.

195

Fig. 3-36a: Parallel fronds

Fig. 3-36b: Vertical flat branchlet with cones

FEMALE SEED CONES

Though the disposition of the foliage alone is enough to identify Oriental arborvitae, the unique cones verify the ID. When young they are rubbery like erasers and a pale powdery green. Each of the six or eight scales has a prominent tip that hooks back, giving the cone the look of a jester's hat (fig. 3-37a). The tips are especially evident when cones are younger, as the scales overgrow them somewhat during maturation. Their powdery coating reflects light and contrasts against the foliage, making them easy to spot on a drive-by, as they often form in large numbers. Fronds full of these quirky cones, easily mistaken for leaf galls, are a curious addition to an indoor arrangement. The cones develop over one year and become woody when mature, with the outside maintaining a slight powdery color. Wingless or largely wingless seeds the shape of small almonds can often be found inside opened cones (fig. 3-37b).

Fig. 3-37a: Spring cone

Fig. 3-37b: Almond-shaped seed

196

MALE POLLEN CONES

The pollen cones of the Oriental arborvitae are tiny, but if you happen to be looking when they set in masses in late winter and early spring, you see that they are a lovely salmon color and worthy of attention for the brief time they are on the plant (fig. 3-38).

Fig. 3-38: Tiny salmon-colored pollen cones

CULTIVAR FORM

The most popular Oriental arborvitae cultivars, such as the 'Aurea Nana', are wide shrubs with foliage all the way to the ground. Often, dwarf conifer cultivars that are composed and tidy when young become looser and more gangly with age. This is not true of most Oriental arborvitae cultivars. Known for looking perpetually pruned without ever being sheared, many grow incrementally, like nested dolls, increasing in size over time while managing to stay the same. This quality gives them many uses. You often see them in cemeteries and other formal settings that require an eternally maintained look, as if landscaping elves come in and prune overnight, as seen in the spectacular old specimens in figure 3-35. They are also good for a low-maintenance hedge and add whimsy to the landscape as a small grouping, but be warned that most of the cultivars grow slowly and require patience. Although you can shear them, it is not necessary and is also ill-advised, as you'd be shearing away their character.

The species and its cultivars are tolerant of a wide range of soils and conditions, including heat, drought, and cold (USDA zones 5–6), making them a good selection east of the Cascades. Deer find them slightly less tasty than the

'Emerald Green' arborvitae (*Thuja occidentalis*), but they are also a target, especially in winter (fig. 3-39).

Berckmann's Blight on Cultivars

Unfortunately, Oriental arborvitae cultivars are highly susceptible to a fungal infection called Berckmann's blight (*Seimatosporium berckmansii*). In wet areas of the PNW, the fungus can cause areas of brown foliage. The cultivars' most redeeming quality, the dense foliage, inhibits air circulation, creating higher humidity and a cozy environment for this fungal disease. Luckily, some recently introduced cultivars are less susceptible to the blight.

Fig. 3-39: Two graveside deer-pruned 'Aurea Nanas'

Thuja: The True Arborvitae Genus
Cupressaceae: Cypress Family
Flattened Scales

The five species in *Thuja*, the true arborvitae genus, are split between North America and East Asia in a distribution similar to that of *Chamaecyparis* and *Calocedrus*. The three East Asian species (not mentioned beyond this sentence) have very restricted native ranges; cultivars are rare. This is in contrast with the extensive native ranges of the two North American *Thujas*. The western redcedar (*T. plicata*) and the eastern white-cedar (*T. occidentalis*) are found along coasts of the Pacific and Atlantic Oceans, respectively, as well as in the interior of the continent. It follows that both species can tolerate a wide range of conditions, from wet temperate coastal environments to cold dry inland continental climates. Both are also tolerant of a wide range of soils.

Fig. 3-40: Western redcedar

The western redcedar (fig. 3-40) is found as far north along the Pacific Coast as Port Protection, Alaska, about midway up the Alaskan Panhandle. Its range in Washington, Oregon, and California narrows from north to south: in Washington you find it from the coast to east of the Cascade crest; in Oregon to just west of the crest until Gold Beach, where its range constricts abruptly to no more than thirty miles from the sea and remains that way until the southern end of its range, a hundred miles into California.

Western redcedar also has a presence in the Rocky Mountains of British Columbia, Alberta, Idaho, and Montana. Many disjunct island populations occur between the Cascades and Rockies, suggesting there was at one time a continuous distribution connecting the two mountain ranges.

Western redcedar intermingles with Alaska-cedar (*Chamaecyparis nootkatensis*) in the northern part of its range, as well as in higher elevations of the Cascades and in the Olympic Mountains in Washington. Both species figured prominently in the marine travel of native peoples, who carved canoes out of light, buoyant, easy-to-work western redcedar and canoe paddles out of light, stiff Alaska-cedar. Secondary aromatic compounds make the wood of all species with cedar in their common names aromatic and rot-resistant, an essential quality in wood for seafaring vessels.

LONG-LIVED AND DECAY-RESISTANT

Old-growth stumps of slow-to-decay western redcedar often remain for hundreds of years. Stumps of trees felled with axes and two-man cross-cut saws from the early days of logging bear deep mouth-shaped wounds for receiving the ends of saw boards. Lumberjacks wielded their tools from atop the boards, which were placed just above the wide buttressed bases to allow for narrower and quicker cuts. Groves of these ancient stumps haunt second- or third-growth forests or forests now set aside for recreation. Like natural standing graves, they persist eerily in defiance of the swiftness with which they were removed.

In its native range, the eastern white-cedar is not nearly as grand or long-lived as the western redcedar. Until recently, 250 to 350 years was considered its maximum potential life span. But ancient grizzled thousand-year-old-plus specimens, whose slow growth rates rival those of the bristlecone pines, have been discovered on the limestone cliffs of a remarkable land formation called the Niagara Escarpment. The Escarpment, most famous for the same-named falls that plummet off its eastern edge, runs east to west in a 650-mile sinuous arc from the southern shore of Lake Ontario to the western shore of Lake Michigan, cutting across Canada and through Lake Huron along the way.

In some places the arc takes the form of lakeside cliffs; in others the limestone has been eroded down to no more than a low rise; and in yet others it is subterranean, the ground has yet to erode away around it. In the waters of Lake Huron and Lake Michigan, where it is largely submerged, the Escarpment's undulating spine surfaces intermittently as small islands. Researchers had to become rock climbers to study eastern white-cedar specimens whose inaccessible cliffside location has protected them from human consciousness and encroachment.

This vertical forest is thought to be the most extensive and least disturbed old-growth ecosystem in eastern North America, one that's existed undetected right under everyone's noses. Each ancient tree takes a unique form. One specimen has the distinction of being one of the oldest as well as one of the smallest, growing on average a scant .007 of an inch in each of its 1,213 years to reach 8.6 inches in girth (as of 2007). Measuring the height of a tree named The Snake was trickier. Certain laws of nature don't seem to apply in how it issues from a tiny slit in the rock, growing upside down for its entire length toward the cliff base, as if trying to reach proper ground, with a trunk that folds in five tight U-turns before branching out and producing foliage. I love reading about discoveries like this; it gives me faith in the resilience and craftiness of nature. At the same time, I hate reading about discoveries like this; the media attention strips the species of the obscurity that has served to protect it.

Beyond the Niagara Escarpment, the eastern white-cedar enjoys a wide continuous range from the Maine and New Brunswick coasts west all the way to Winnipeg. To the south its continuous range encompasses all the Great Lakes except Lake Erie, with dozens of isolated populations sprinkled as far south as Tennessee and North Carolina, places of refuge where, in addition to the limestone cliffs of the Escarpment, the species hid out during the ice ages of the Pleistocene, when ice sheets covered most of its present-day range (Kelly and Larson 2007). Though the species is rarely planted in the landscape in the PNW, it is the source of countless cultivars, including the omnipresent narrow hedge tree, the 'Emerald Green' arborvitae, also known as 'Smaragd'.

ARBORVITAE: TREE OF LIFE

A number of stories describe why *Thuja* are called arborvitae, the tree of life. All involve Europeans' first experiences with one of the two North American species. The story that is widely accepted as being true describes how, in the winter of 1535, the eastern white-cedar saved the lives of Captain Jacques Cartier and his crew while they were exploring the Saint Lawrence River. Twenty-five sailors had already died, and the rest weren't far behind; all were suffering horribly with scurvy, a vitamin C deficiency that causes gums to bleed and swell, teeth to loosen and fall out, and joints to swell to grotesque sizes, as well as other external and internal hemorrhagic symptoms. Scurvy was also a common winter affliction of the local Iroquois, one of whom, Domagaia, shared their remedy.

Domagaia instructed Cartier to make and drink a decoction of the foliage and bark of a tree the Iroquois called *annedda* and to use the leftover pulp as a poultice for their swollen gums and joints. In his journal Cartier

Foliage

Fig. 3-41a: Western redcedar: draping, braided-looking fronds

Fig. 3-41b: Eastern white-cedar 'Emerald Green': twisted and cupped fans of very thin foliage

Fig. 3-41c: Western redcedar: distinct stomata and indistinct resin glands

Fig. 3-41d: Eastern white-cedar 'Emerald Green': no stomata and visible resin glands

wrote at length of their miraculous and rapid recovery. "After drinking it two or three times" they "were cured of all diseases." Furthermore, "some of the sailors who had been suffering for five or six years from the French pox [syphilis] were by this medicine cured completely" (Durzan 2009). (This last point is considered an embellishment by Cartier to curry favor with the king of France.)

The story is true, but debate and scientific research continue about whether the conifer in question, which came to be known as "Arbre de Vie," was *T. occidentalis*, as the foliage and bark of other conifers in Eastern Canada, including the red spruce (*Picea rubens*), have been tested and also been shown to be rich in vitamin C, as well as most amino acids (Durzan 2009).

One hundred and seventy-five years after Cartier, Meriwether Lewis and William Clark navigated northwest by river from St. Louis as far as they could until encountering a rather large obstacle, the Rocky Mountains. After ditching their boats, they crossed the mountains on horseback, not knowing what trees they might find on the other side for constructing new boats. To say the least, it was their good fortune that the range of western redcedar, the best wood in the West for boats, incudes the west slopes of the Rocky Mountains of Idaho, right where they emerged from their overland journey. *Thuja occidentalis* was familiar enough to Lewis and Clark that they immediately recognized *Thuja plicata* as an arborvitae but, giving the tree its due, upgraded its name to giant arborvitae. They built a small fleet of five vessels from western redcedar trunks in which they followed the Snake and Columbia Rivers to the Pacific Ocean. *Thuja* to the rescue again.

Many books have been written on the countless uses native peoples had for western redcedar. It was like a cultural keystone species: from birth until death there was hardly a moment of life that didn't involve some component of the tree, with no part of it going to waste. At birth babies were diapered in shredded cedar bark, in death carved cedar trunks were erected as memorials and mortuaries, what the Haida call *gyáa' aang*, or man stands up straight, more commonly known as totem poles. From clothing, medicine, and storage to structures, transportation, and cooking, there was no plant species in all of North America that native people had more uses for (Moerman 1998).

FOLIAGE

Taken as a whole, the fronds of the western redcedar and the eastern whitecedar look very different (figs. 3-41a,b). Those of the western redcedar drape from the branches in long graceful sprays that look braided. The twisted and cupped fan-like fronds of the eastern white-cedar are held close to the branch. However, a close inspection reveals the scales to be similarly shaped but with different markings (figs. 3-41c,d). The lateral scales of both spread apart and do not join at the base. The apices of the scales come to distinct points, with those of the lateral pair pulling away slightly from the twig. Under the magnification of a loupe, the outline of the facial scales looks like the profiles of perfectly symmetrical volcanic peaks.

Western redcedar foliage typically has stomatal bloom on the lower surface in a distinct cat's-eye pattern you come to recognize. But be aware that the intensity of the bloom can vary from bright to almost nonexistent, depending on the season and the tree. Eastern white-cedar foliage has faint stomata but visible flame-shaped resin glands on both sides just below the apices of the facial scales. Eastern white-cedar foliage is also very thin, the thinnest of all species with flattened scales seen in the PNW. With the large number of cultivars in every shape and size, running the foliage between your fingers, particularly of those without cones, can be an effective ID technique. Once you've handled enough fronds with flattened scales, you come to know this species and many of its cultivars by touch.

FEMALE SEED CONES

The diminutive ½-inch-long *Thuja* seed cones form in masses at the branch ends in spring and mature in one growing season (figs. 3-42a–c). Before reaching maturity and releasing seeds, the linear scales overlap like the petals of a small rosebud just beginning to open. The tip of each scale has a slight protrusion that usually browns in advance of the rest of the cone. The cones are similar in size and shape across the genus and can be relied on to identify a species as a *Thuja*.

MALE POLLEN CONES

The small *Thuja* pollen cones form at the branch tips in spring and are typically indistinct, but those of the western redcedar are an eye-catching dark red and black (fig. 3-43).

EASTERN WHITE-CEDAR CULTIVAR: 'EMERALD GREEN' ARBORVITAE

We all tire of 'Emerald Green' arborvitae hedges. They are so common, the workhorse of housing developers, the bread and butter of many conifer

Female Seed Cones

Fig. 3-42a: Masses of young rosebud cones at branch ends

Fig. 3-42b: Masses of mature rosebud cones at branch ends

Fig. 3-42c: Spring cone, up close: tips of scales slightly pointy, brown early

Male Pollen Cones

Fig. 3-43: Dark red and black pollen cones of western redcedar

Fig. 3-44a: Long rows of field grown 'Emerald Green' arborvitae

Fig. 3-44b: Dying 'Emerald Green' arborvitae hedge

growers (fig. 3-44a). The lack of variety can make one scream. But there's a good reason they're so popular—they get the job done. If planted properly, they grow into a lush, green, aromatic fence taller than any HOA or building code would ever allow, one typically requiring little maintenance or fuss. The most practical of all conifers, they are not meant to draw attention or to be admired like other landscape plants, but to delineate and occupy a perimeter like a row of tree soldiers, blocking visual blight, buffering noise, creating an enclosure and sense of space. What they have is a niche; the one thing the 'Emerald Green' is good at, it is the best at. They are, in a word, dependable. Many other eastern white-cedar cultivars are available, in a plethora of shapes and sizes, typically with the same foliage as the 'Emerald Green'.

The caveat to an arborvitae hedge's dependability is proper siting, planting, and irrigation. The 'Emerald Green' needs both good drainage, for when it rains, and water every two to three weeks, when it doesn't. If deprived of either, the hedge often perishes, like a row of dominoes, often failing one tree at a time in an orderly fashion (fig. 3-44b). If the problem is lack of water, individual trees can be replaced and the watering problem rectified. If the issue is root rot due to poor drainage, the pathogen remains in the soil and you have a bigger headache when it comes to replacement trees. Keep in mind that 'Emerald Green' is the most susceptible to root rot of all the eastern white-cedar cultivars, so proper drainage is critical to its long-term success. If the planting site is soggy clay soil in a low-lying area, you can create a raised berm to improve drainage around the roots.

An 'Emerald Green' arborvitae hedge with dense foliage from regular shearing supplies deer with a nice buffet, as deer intuitively know what the Iroquois knew, that *Thuja* foliage is vital for surviving winter when fresh produce is scarce or nonexistent. The deer likely benefit more from ingesting the foliage directly than drinking *Thuja* tea as the Iroquois and Cartier and his crew did, as by weight it contains nearly as much vitamin C as oranges. It makes one wonder if the Iroquois didn't learn about the benefits of adding *Thuja* foliage to their diets from observing the winter foraging habits of deer. Once deer have discovered a hedge, not much can be done to prevent them from dining out on it.

WESTERN REDCEDAR FORM AND CULTIVARS

Each old-growth western redcedar develops a unique form, but younger trees take predictable shapes. The teardrop shape of very young trees (fig. 3-45a) bears little resemblance to the pyramidal form they take as they age (fig. 3-45b).

Fig. 3-45a: Young western redcedar   Fig. 3-45b: Western redcedar pyramidal with age

A number of cultivars share the same foliage as the species; one called 'Whipcord' has stringy foliage nothing like the species.

DRIVE-BY ID SKILLS: THREE FALSE CEDARS

We often focus on identifying conifers through a close inspection of the foliage and cones, but you can differentiate among similar-looking trees at a distance by familiarizing yourself with characteristics that give a species its definitive look. To differentiate among western redcedar, Alaska-cedar, and Port-Orford-cedar (*Chamaecyparis lawsoniana*) as you whiz by in your car, observe the arc of the branches and the disposition and size of the fronds, particularly midway up the tree.

Branches of western redcedar sweep down from the trunk before arching up at the ends, like crooked smiles (fig. 3-46a). As mentioned in the *Chamaecyparis* section, Alaska-cedar branches are known for their theatrics, often rising straight up from the trunk for quite a distance before suddenly flopping at the ends like hooks (fig. 3-46b). Large western redcedar fronds, which drape heavily from the branches, can give the tree an overall saggy appearance and fool one into thinking it's an Alaska-cedar, whose fronds hang without any lift, as if flattened in an iron press. To differentiate between the two by form alone, focus your eyes on the branch ends, remembering that an upward swoop means western redcedar and a downward droop means Alaska-cedar. The gesture of Port-Orford-cedar branches is subtle by comparison. The branches extend out from the trunk fairly horizontally before nodding bashfully at the tips (fig. 3-46c). This trait in combination with its smaller and lighter fronds gives Port-Orford-cedars a well-kept, groomed appearance, while both western redcedars and Alaska-cedars past a certain age look sloppy.

Drive-By ID Skills: Three False Cedars

Fig. 3-46a: Western redcedar: branch ends arch up

Fig. 3-46b: Alaska-cedar: branch ends droop

Fig. 3-46c: Port-Orford-cedar: branch ends nod

Thujopsis: The Staghorn-Cedar Genus
Cupressaceae: Cypress Family
Flattened Scales

The single species in the staghorn-cedar genus (*Thujopsis*) is endemic to Japan, *T. dolabrata*. (There are also two naturally occurring varieties.) This conifer goes by a number of common names: staghorn-cedar, elkhorn-cedar, hatchet-leaved arborvitae, Hiba arborvitae, and so on. No one name seems to be more commonly used than any other. When I look at the foliage, I see staghorns, not hatchets, so that's the common name I'll use.

Thujopsis means *Thuja*-like, which is fitting, as the staghorn-cedar and the western redcedar (*Thuja plicata*) have much in common. In the wild both enjoy a temperate maritime climate, growing as understory trees alongside shade-loving hemlocks (*Tsuga*). In the case of the staghorn-cedar, that *Tsuga* is the northern Japanese hemlock (*T. diversifolia*), while the western redcedar keeps company with the western hemlock (*T. heterophylla*). Paradoxically, given enough time and age and lack of disturbance, the western redcedar and staghorn-cedar both become the tallest trees in the forest, rising above the canopy with their crowns in the sun. This may explain their adaptability in the landscape, where they do well in full shade or full sun, though they look better in locations with some afternoon shade and supplemental water. Their natural ranges also both extend into mid-elevations of the mountains.

Even though the staghorn-cedar has many outstanding qualities to recommend it as a landscape plant, including being easy to propagate and care for, it is uncommon to rare. You're unlikely to find this species at a typical retail nursery; you'll have to visit ones that specialize in conifers, which happily there are many of in the PNW.

FOLIAGE

It is difficult to overstate the surprising beauty of the staghorn-cedar's foliage. I never tire of introducing it to those unfamiliar with the species, as they tend to express audible delight upon seeing it for the first time, just as I did. The lateral scales spread far apart from the facial scales, making the scales the widest of all species with flattened foliage. The stomata take full advantage of this large canvas, painting the undersides a brilliant chalk-white (fig. 3-47a). Only the perimeters are left green, like frames. This feature makes the staghorn-cedar one of the easiest conifers to ID. It is also a

Fig. 3-47a: Brilliant stomatal bands on underside of foliage

Fig. 3-47b: Upper side of foliage

conifer you could ID blindfolded. The thick pliable foliage feels more like braided vinyl than plant material, and the apices of the facial scales are so raised up and pronounced you can actually count them with your fingertips (fig. 3-47b).

FEMALE SEED CONES

The staghorn-cedar also has unique flower-shaped seed cones that are fleshy and powdery green when immature (fig. 3-48a) and woody when mature (fig. 3-48b). The edges of the cone scales tend to darken in advance of the rest of the cone, creating contrast.

Fig. 3-48a: Rubbery maturing seed cones

Fig. 3-48b: Woody mature cone

MALE POLLEN CONES

Tiny (1/16 inch) staghorn cedar pollen cones form at the branch ends, releasing pollen in late winter or early spring.

FORM

The staghorn-cedar is difficult to ID from form alone; its pyramidal profile resembles so many others (fig. 3-49), including a young western redcedar. But as soon as you walk up to it, and touch and flip over a frond, the mystery is over. It doesn't become as large as many of the other false cedars, making it a more practical choice for most landscapes.

CULTIVARS

The majority of the two dozen or so registered staghorn-cedar cultivars have the same foliage as the species. The forms range from mounding shrubs to full-size variegated trees.

Fig. 3-49: Full-size variegated cultivar

Incense-cedar bark

Cupressaceae   Cypress Family

	Calocedrus Incense-cedar genus	*Chamaecyparis* False-cypress genus	
	C. decurrens Incense-cedar PNW NATIVE*	*C. lawsoniana* Port-Orford-cedar PNW NATIVE—endemic	

Foliage and Branches	 **Long fluted scales**	 With male cones	 **X-shaped bloom**	 Blue-green tint
	 Feathery branchlets		 **Branch ends nod**, more so with cones	

Cones	 Spring	 Summer	 Mature	 Spring	 Summer	 Mature
	1″ (l); tulip, then duckbill-shaped			⅓″; **wavy edged-scales, slight horns**		

Form and Bark	 Branches arch up	 Reddish-gray-brown bark vertically fissured	 Pyramidal; layered; tips blue-green esp. with cones	 Reddish-brown vertically fissured bark
Other	Popular privacy tree; Z5		Used as large barrier hedge; many cultivars, many with juvenile foliage; Z5	

C. nootkatensis Alaska-cedar PNW NATIVE*		*C. obtusa* Hinoki-cypress 'Gracilis' Native to Japan and Taiwan	
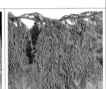		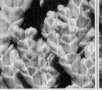	
No bloom	**Drooping fronds**	Some bloom	**Twisted, cupped**
		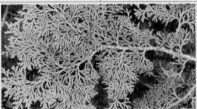	
Branchlets and fronds hang straight down		Open layers, dieback at center common	
Spring yr 1	Summer yr 2 · Mature	Spring · Summer	Mature
½"; **large horns**; 2 seasons to mature		⅓"; small horns, **smooth-edged scales**	

Drooping branches give the tree a shaggy look	Shaggy red-brown bark	Smaller tree, open layered growth	Reddish stringy bark
A number of even more droopy, narrow cultivars; Z4		Many cultivars of all shapes and sizes with same foliage; 'Gracilis' most common; Z4	

Cupressaceae   Cypress Family

	× *Cupressocyparis*		*Platycladus*		
	× *Cupressocyparis leylandii* Leyland-cypress Hybrid		*P. orientalis* Oriental arborvitae 'Aurea Nana' Native to China, Korea, Russia		
Foliage and Branches	 Little or no bloom	 **Very dark green**	 Little or no bloom	 **Parallel fronds**	
	 Branches attach at tight V angles		 Tiny pink male cones on branch		
Cones	Hybrid of Alaska-cedar and Monterey cypress; ranges don't overlap	 Mature	 Spring	 Summer	 Mature
	To 1"; sets few cones		To 1"; **rubbery then woody**		
Form and Bark	 Large tree, low branching, diamond-shaped	 Tawny bark	 ID by shrubby, wide form; old specimens shown	Bark obscured by dense form	
Other	Often planted wrongly as hedge tree for small spaces; becomes large fast; Z6		Old healthy specimens stunning; many other similar cultivars; formerly in *Thuja*; monotypic; Z5–6		

Thuja True arborvitae genus Cones: Rosebud shaped				*Thujopsis*
T. occidentalis Eastern white-cedar 'Emerald Green' Native to US and Canada		*T. plicata* Western redcedar PNW NATIVE*		*T. dolabrata* Staghorn-cedar Native to Japan
Little or no bloom	**Twisted fans**	**Cat's-eye bloom**	Looks braided	**Chalk-white below**
Fan-like branches; **thin foliage**		Fronds drape, branch ends arch up		Feels like vinyl
Spring	Summer / Mature	Spring	Summer / Mature	Summer / Mature
½" when mature; **rosebud-shaped**		½" when mature; **rosebud-shaped**		½", **fleshy** when young
Dense and narrow; most common hedge tree; often sheared	Stringy tawny bark	Large pyramidal tree; wide scalloped flare at base	Reddish-brown bark peels away in stringy vertical strips	To 30'; pyramidal
Many cultivars in smaller sizes; the species not planted in PNW; Z2–3		Long-lived tree; some cultivars but the species more commonly planted; Z5		ID by feel and stomata; a few mounding cultivars; monotypic; Z5

Cryptomeria: The Japanese-Cedar Genus
Cupressaceae: Cypress Family
Awl-Like Foliage over Entire Plant

Geology isn't usually thought of as a driver of human history, but geologic processes have defined the boundaries of many nations, and there is no more definitive boundary than the sea. If Japan were not an island nation and were still attached to the Eurasian continent, as it was up until about 15 MYA, there very well might not be a Japan, and the Japanese-cedar (*Cryptomeria japonica*) (fig. 3-50) might very well be extinct. At one time *Cryptomeria* species were found across Eurasia, but by 5 MYA, all were extinct except for *C. japonica*, now endemic to four of the thousands of islands that make up Japan. Japan was a lifeboat for this species, as well as others, when it gained its geologic independence from the continent.

Fig. 3-50: Mature Japanese-cedar at Iseli Nursery

During more recent geologic history, during the twenty or so warm and cold pulses of the ice ages of the Pleistocene, the Japanese-cedar alternately advanced inland from coastal refugia toward the interior mountains and fell back to the coasts, like a slow-moving botanical tide. Many of the coastal areas where it took refuge during the cold pulses are now beneath the Sea of Japan and North Pacific (Tsukada 1982).

The windward and leeward coasts of Japan experience different climates, particularly during the winter monsoon, when cold Siberian air fortified with moisture from the Sea of Japan brings heavy snow to the western side, while the eastern Pacific side remains sunnier and drier. Japanese-cedars, known as sugi in Japan, have adapted to these differing coastal climates. It has long been observed that the branchlets of those on the Sea of Japan side, ura-sugi, are more slender and the awls softer, whereas the branchlets of those along the Pacific, omote-sugi, are rougher and the awls harder (Tsumura et al. 2014). Some populations have characteristics intermediate between the two. Studies confirm that the genotypes of ura- and omote-sugi have diverged somewhat from the intermittent isolation imposed by glaciers and the interior mountains (Moriguchi et al. 2019).

At the end of the Pleistocene, the Japanese-cedar again moved inland and north from the coasts but encountered a force as nonnegotiable as glaciers—human activity in the form of logging and managed forests. Today's wild Japanese-cedar forests are highly fragmented and reduced, accounting for well under 1 percent of all *Cryptomeria* forests; the other 99 percent have been planted. The Japanese-cedar is Japan's largest and longest-lived native tree and its most important managed tree, accounting for 45 percent of all plantation forests, with the Hinoki-cypress (*Chamaecyparis obtusa*) accounting for another 25 percent. Though the native Japanese-cedar forests have been highly exploited, Japan's ancient Shinto religion is suffused with a reverence of nature. The advanced age of planted Japanese-cedar specimens near temples and lining avenues rivals the maximum life span of those in the wild, which can live more than a thousand years. In certain areas of Japan where humans have lived for thousands of years, wild and planted trees intermix indistinguishably.

By the 1600s, Japan's natural tree reserves were severely depleted, and isolationism prohibited importing timber from other lands. In a move that seems ahead of its time, timber felling was reduced to allow forests to regenerate, and trees were planted and harvested at a sustainable rate. Faced with the same problem around the same time, Europe looked outside its borders for a solution, exploring and exploiting distant lands to maintain supplies of natural resources such as timber.

It is counterintuitive to think of thousand-year-old forests as being the work of humans, but this is the case with the Japanese-cedars in China, where this species was once thought to be native. In the early 1700s, when Europeans first encountered the ancient and now well-known Japanese-cedar

Foliage

Fig. 3-51a: Awls curve in toward the twig

Fig. 3-51b: Awls (with frost) free of twig for most of their length

Fig. 3-51c: Branches with pollen cones in winter

forests in eastern China, they understandably assumed the forests were naturally occurring. But these forests are composed of trees or descendants of trees that were most likely introduced during the intermittent periods of cultural exchange between China and Japan (Farjon 1999), an exchange that goes back nearly two thousand years and pre-dates the maximum life expectancy of the species. Many sources cite two natural variants or two species of the Japanese-cedar, one native to Japan and one to China, but the slight differences in characteristics of the trees in China are considered artifacts of the limited genetic stock of the introduced trees (Farjon 1999).

FOLIAGE

The Japanese-cedar and the giant sequoia (*Sequoiadendron giganteum*) share a number of characteristics. Both are large trees with awl-like foliage and stringy tawny-red bark. If one must make an ID by foliage alone, note the size and texture of the awls. Japanese-cedar awls are thicker and fleshier and are free of the twig for more of their length (figs. 3-51a–c) compared with those of giant sequoia. Also, Japanese-cedar awls curve inward toward the twig, whereas those of the giant sequoia curve back. And although not as prickly as the giant sequoia, Japanese-cedar foliage ranges from slightly prickly to the touch to quite prickly.

FEMALE SEED CONES

Japanese-cedar seed cones mature in one growing season. If you look carefully, in late winter you will see nascent goblet-shaped cones at the branch tips not long after the pollen has flown (fig. 3-52a). As the cones mature and their features become more distinct, claw-like extensions on each scale, often tipped in purple, are visible—one at the center and several toward the edge (figs. 3-52b–d). A delightful short vegetative shoot often extends beyond the peak of the cone, like an antenna (fig. 3-52c). Up to about ¾ inch in diameter,

Fig. 3-52a: Cones in late winter just becoming visible (¼ inch)

Fig. 3-52b: Cone in early summer

Fig. 3-52c: Cone scale extensions tipped in purple

Fig. 3-52d: Mature cone after seed release

the roundish cones release seeds late in the season. You will not typically be at a loss to find cones on Japanese-cedars, as they set cones at a fairly young age in large numbers and hold on to them for a few years. If you look back along the branches, you see successive generations of cones.

MALE POLLEN CONES

Pollen and seed cones of Japanese-cedars appear on the same tree but on different branches. Pollen cones cluster densely at the branch ends in winter, tinging the entire tree in yellow (fig. 3-51c) and appear on young trees after a couple of years. In Japan, pollen from plantations of pure Japanese-cedar that were aggressively planted after World War II blows into the cities, causing severe allergies.

FORM

Japanese-cedars hold on to their branches all the way to the ground, are dense with foliage, broadly conical (fig. 3-50), and supported by a buttressed base. These lovely trees would do well either as a single specimen or planted in a row to separate large formal spaces.

CULTIVARS

The foliage of many Japanese-cedar cultivars looks just like that of the species. A few, such as 'Black Dragon', set cones readily, but many others do not. In many instances you will have to rely on your familiarity with the foliage of the species to make an ID. However, when confronted with an upright cultivar like 'Spiralis' with dreadlock-like awls (fig. 3-53a) or a dense mounding cultivar like 'Tenzan' (fig. 3-53b), you'll have to put more thought into it and learn to recognize awls even when they're acting bizarre.

First, you must convince yourself that the foliage you're staring at is indeed composed of awls. It helps to ask yourself what it is not. Is it rounded or flattened scales? No. Is it linear foliage like the coast redwood (*Sequoia sempervirens*)? No. The only option left is awls. Then you must eliminate the possibility that it is a juniper. Look for juniper berries and note the growth habit. Junipers with awl-like foliage are typically either ground covers or dense, spreading, low shrubs, forms not seen in Japanese-cedar cultivars. Plus, in many juniper species, dense stomata brighten the undersides of the awls, whereas Japanese-cedar foliage is faintly sprinkled with stomata.

'Elegans' is one of a number of cultivars with juvenile foliage (fig. 3-53c). A well-defined central stem keeps it upright and composed as it ages. The foliage is known for bronzing in winter.

Fig. 3-53a: Twisted weird awls of 'Spiralis': conifer dreadlocks

Fig. 3-53b: Densely packed awls of 'Tenzan'

Fig. 3-53c: Juvenile foliage of 'Elegans'

Sequoiadendron: The Giant Sequoia Genus
Cupressaceae: Cypress Family
Awl-Like Foliage over Entire Plant

Fig. 3-54: Hedgerow of the Gods

The giant sequoia (*Sequoiadendron giganteum*) (fig. 3-54) is the sole species in its genus. At one time it kept company with the coast redwood in the *Sequoia* genus, but was moved into its own genus based on differences between the cones. It is difficult not to speak of sequoias and redwoods in the same breath. One is the yin to the other's yang. While the coast redwood is the tallest tree in the world, the giant sequoia is the most massive; and while *Sequoia* is a maritime, shade-tolerant species, *Sequoiadendron* is a sun-loving species of the interior Sierra Nevada Range, with ten to twelve feet of winter snow and dry summers.

When Europeans first encountered giant sequoias in 1852, descriptions of their immense size strained credulity for those who hadn't experienced them firsthand. The commodious platform of the first felled tree famously hosted cotillions of more than thirty dancing couples, including a small orchestra. Slices of the massive trunk went on tour across the United States and through Europe. For the equivalent of about $15 today, one could be in the presence of a cross-section of giant sequoia. Within a few years of its discovery, seeds of giant sequoia made it to Britain, where it is often called the Wellington, and where the oldest and largest ornamental specimens in the world are found.

The giant sequoia's brittle wood, unsuitable for most purposes, has saved it from the extreme logging pressure that has reduced old-growth coast redwood to 5 percent of its original numbers. Seventy-five groves of giant sequoias survive in the wild, portions of which have been logged, but all of which are now protected. These seventy-five groves are fragments of what was once a much larger natural distribution. At one time its range extended east into Nevada. As summers became warmer and drier and winters cooler and wetter, the giant sequoia migrated west to the Sierra Nevada Range, first to the leeward side, then pulling back farther to the western windward slopes where it is found today. Though no new groves have been established since the end of the Pleistocene about 12,000 years ago, a few groves have expanded in size.

FOLIAGE

The green to blue-green awl-like foliage of the giant sequoia is very prickly and irritating to the skin. The awls curve out and are lightly sprinkled with stomata on all surfaces (figs. 3-55a,b). Smaller fronds resemble whisk brooms.

Fig. 3-55a: Close-up of turned-out awls with scattered stomata

Fig. 3-55b: Branch with pollen cones

FEMALE SEED CONES

Mature giant sequoia seed cones—up to three inches long and with diamond-shaped scales of four equal sides—look like small hand grenades (figs. 3-56a,b). The cones mature over two growing seasons, but giant sequoia is the only conifer in the world whose cones remain on the tree in a green ready state with viable seeds for up to twenty years or more. While on the tree, the green cones continue to photosynthesize; the cones grow at the end of twiglets that lengthen each year, allowing you to count the growth rings and determine their age (Weatherspoon 1990).

The green cones lie in wait for when they are most needed, when the next fire sweeps through and they discharge huge quantities of seeds into the forest. It is no coincidence that the average interval between fires (sixteen to twenty-two years) in a giant sequoia forest (Swetnam et al. 2009) is nearly the same as the maximum life expectancy of a giant sequoia cone, with a mature tree holding as many as twenty thousand green viable cones at one time (Weatherspoon 1990).

Giant sequoia seeds are too small and low in nutrition to be of interest to foraging animals (Weatherspoon 1990), but the scales of the succulent green cones are an important food source for the Douglas squirrel and the tiny larvae of a long-horned beetle, both of whom trigger yearly seed release on a smaller scale. The squirrels inadvertently dislodge seeds as they feed on the carbohydrate-rich scales and also cache the green cones in large numbers. The female adult long-horned beetle lays her eggs directly on the green cone. The larvae hatch and chew their way through the cone, including the vascular tissue, cutting off the scales' water supply and initiating the drying out process. From the outside it appears as if the cone scales turn brown in a random order, but the pattern reflects the meandering feeding path of the larvae (Weatherspoon 1990).

Female Seed Cones

Fig. 3-56a: Cones green and photosynthetic for more than twenty years

Fig. 3-56b: Mature cones look like small hand grenades

MALE POLLEN CONES

The pollen cones of giant sequoia appear in winter singly at the branch tips (fig. 3-55b), differentiating it from the Japanese-cedar (*Cryptomeria japonica*), the tree one is most likely to mistake for a giant sequoia, which also has awl-like foliage. But Japanese-cedar pollen cones form in masses at the branch ends.

FORM AND BARK

Young giant sequoias (less than a hundred years old) that one typically sees in the landscape tend to have perfect symmetry and are impressive when flanking a long formal entryway, like a hedgerow of the gods, giving one the sense of arriving somewhere important (fig. 3-54). They get large quickly and are often unwisely planted in spaces nowhere near big enough. The roots are notorious for busting up driveways and sidewalks. The wide buttressed base, evident even on a young tree, foretells of the enormous mass it is preparing to support (fig. 3-57). As they age their form becomes irregular and var-

Fig. 3-57: Wide buttressed base and spongy bark

ies from tree to tree. Like so many species in the cypress family, giant sequoia bark is cinnamon-red. With age the bark thickens into a spongy layer of fire protection up to two feet deep that gives a little when you press on it, like stiff dough.

CULTIVARS

Most giant sequoia cultivars have the same foliage as the species, though it may be variegated or especially blue. 'Pendulum' is a very popular cultivar (fig. 3-58) whose highly irregular growth habit allows each specimen to take a unique shape. Most branches droop straight down, but some also grow straight up or at 90 degrees. For some reason, housing developers are fond of planting them on street corners. I've seen a few grow horizontally nearly all the way across intersections before someone noticed and pruned them back to the side-

Fig. 3-58: Old large 'Pendulum'

walks. This is another one of those cultivars that looks manageable in a nursery pot but in time can become a menace if not allotted enough space.

Cupressaceae   Cypress Family

Foliage: Awl-like over entire plant	
Habit: Large tree	

Cryptomeria japonica   Japanese-cedar   Native to Japan

<table>
<tr>
<td rowspan="2">Foliage and Branches</td>
<td>

Somewhat prickly **awls curl in**

</td>
<td>Foliage segments less pressed to the twig than those of the giant sequoia</td>
</tr>
<tr>
<td colspan="2">

Clusters of pollen cones at branch ends in midwinter (shown with frost)

</td>
</tr>
<tr>
<td>Cones</td>
<td>

Spring   Summer   Mature

</td>
<td>Cones to 1″, tinged with purple in spring; **each scale with several projections**; matures from green to brown</td>
</tr>
<tr>
<td>Form and Cultivars</td>
<td>

Species   'Elegans'

</td>
<td>Species: To 100′, pyramidal with branches that arch up at mid-tree and top, less so near ground
Cultivar: 'Elegans' popular upright cultivar with prickly juvenile foliage</td>
</tr>
<tr>
<td>Bark</td>
<td>

</td>
<td>Stringy tawny bark</td>
</tr>
<tr>
<td>Other</td>
<td colspan="2">Many smaller cultivars with same foliage as species and many with juvenile foliage that bronzes in winter; monotypic; Z5–6</td>
</tr>
</table>

Sequoiadendron giganteum   Giant sequoia   Endemic to California

Branchlets look like whisk brooms

Very prickly awls turn out

Pollen cones appear in late winter **singly** at branch ends

Before seed release   After seed release

To 3", **shaped like hand grenades**; take 2 seasons to mature; remain green and viable on tree up to 20 years

Species: young tree   'Pendulum'

Species: To 100' in the landscape, very symmetrical and stately looking; massive trunk flares out at base
Cultivar: 'Pendulum' looks cute in pot but gets big and grows in unpredictable directions—note lamppost for scale

Stringy reddish-brown bark feels spongy when pressed

Long-lived tree; most massive tree in the world; monotypic; Z6

Cupressus: The Cypress Genus
Cupressaceae: Cypress Family
Rounded Scales

In the PNW, areas west of the Cascades are typically too wet for cypresses and east of the Cascades too cold. Baker's cypress (*Cupressus bakeri*) is one honorary species native to the PNW, a small population of which seems to have lost its way and wandered over the border from California into Oregon. It is exceedingly rare, found on a total of nine small sites.

Cypresses' natural home in the United States is California, where six to eleven of the genus' fifteen or so species are native, making it home to more cypress species than anywhere else on the planet, most of which are endemic. Some, like the

Fig. 3-59: Smooth Arizona cypress 'Blue Ice'

Monterey cypress (*C. macrocarpa*), are coastal species. Others, like the Baker's cypress, are located in inland mountains. Nearly all have been reduced to a small number of isolated stands. Some botanists consider a number of the scattered California species to be remnants of what was once a continuous distribution of a single species, and that their divergent characteristics are due to different environments. Five cypresses make up the "Arizona cypress complex." A complex is a group of closely related plants with overlapping

230

characteristics, plants that may be actively differentiating into species. Some botanists give all five cypresses in the Arizona cypress complex the rank of species; some downgrade them to subspecies or varieties. One of these, the smooth Arizona cypress (*C. arizonica* var. *glabra*), is popular horticulturally (fig. 3-59). Outside California and Arizona, cypresses are native to Central America, the Mediterranean, and Asia.

FOLIAGE

All species in the cypress genus have rounded scales that roll easily in your fingers (figs. 3-60a,b). Rounded scales are the most highly adapted to hot dry climates of all the cypress family foliage types. The scales overlap tightly, leaving a diamond-shaped portion exposed.

Fig. 3-60a: Rounded scales   Fig. 3-60b: Branch tips with pollen cones

FEMALE SEED CONES

Cypresses set globular cones that mature over two growing seasons (figs. 3-61a–c). As large as more than one inch in diameter, they are much larger than similarly structured cones in the false cypress genus (*Chamaecyparis*). The shape and size of bonbons (a French word that appropriately means "hard"), cypress cones remain very hard and woody after seed release. Pine cones are typically the cone of choice for wiring onto holiday trees and wreaths, but if you can locate some, cypress cones can be a more interesting choice.

Female Seed Cones

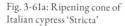

Fig. 3-61a: Ripening cone of Italian cypress 'Stricta'

Fig. 3-61b: Mature cones of Italian cypress 'Stricta'

Fig. 3-61c: Ripening cones of smooth Arizona cypress 'Blue Ice'

MALE POLLEN CONES

Cypress male pollen cones form at the branch ends in winter (fig. 3-60b).

CYPRESSES IN THE PACIFIC NORTHWEST

Surprisingly, the droughty warm summers west of the Cascades seem to give the cultivars of a couple of cypress species enough of a break from the rain that they do well in sunny locations, as long as they have good drainage.

Italian Cypress

Most of the popular Italian cypress (*C. sempervirens*) cultivars can be identified by their narrow tubular form and light-brown lumpy cones, which they readily set to the point you can spot them on a drive-by. Although the species is native to the Mediterranean region and parts of Asia, its natural range is not thought to include Italy, as the common name would have you think; however, recent research suggests a small population in the Campania area may have survived the ice ages of the Pleistocene (D'Auria et al. 2020).

Wood of the Italian cypress has been used by humans for thousands of years. Valued for its rot-resistance since pre-Roman times, it was used to line wells. Much of the Roman Empire was built with Italian cypress wood, depleting natural reserves to the point the Romans grew it in plantations, a profitable enterprise referred to as a "daughter's dowry" (D'Auria et al. 2020). The Romans admired narrow Italian cypress cultivars with a narrow upright form occurring in nature, preferentially selecting and planting them ornamentally, obscuring the line between wild and cultivated for future generations.

Today, Italian cypresses are often placed in widely spaced rows, a configuration that lends formality to an informal setting or another layer of ostentation to a pretentious setting. In a garden aiming for a more natural look, particularly one with limited space, an Italian cypress placed singly among low-lying plants and conifers adds a nice counterpoint, rising like a finger your eye can't help but follow (figs. 3-62a,b). Its very small footprint allows you to put it just about anywhere with sun and good drainage.

Fig. 3-62a: Yellow cultivar of Italian cypress   Fig. 3-62b: Italian cypress 'Stricta'

Smooth Arizona Cypress

Cultivars of the smooth Arizona cypress are increasingly popular and, as members of the Arizona cypress complex, are sold under a number of aliases:

C. arizonica, *C. arizonica* var. *glabra*, or *C. glabra*. Blue is a foliage color people seem particularly drawn to. Foliage of smooth Arizona cypress cultivars like 'Blue Ice' or 'Blue Pyramid' is the mesmerizing hue of a tropical lagoon. Smooth refers to the bark, which peels away to reveal a deep red underlayer (fig. 3-59), a striking scaffolding for the foliage. Over time, fibrous shaggy bark accumulates over the gleaming red underlayer. But these trees are perhaps loveliest in winter, when pollen cones contribute a third tone and tip the powdery blue branches for a brief time in a deep sulphur yellow (fig. 3-60b). The female seed cones are powdery, ½-inch, blue-green boxes with curlicue-like extensions at the middle of the scales (fig 3-61c). Most smooth Arizona cypress cultivars are a USDA zone or two more hardy (zones 5–6) than the species and might make a go of it east of the Cascades.

Monterey Cypress

The majority of Monterey cypresses planted ornamentally are cultivars with yellow juvenile foliage. Refer to the Cultivars section for more on this topic.

Juniperus: The Juniper Genus
Cupressaceae: Cypress Family
Rounded Scales, Awls, or Both Rounded Scales and Awls

With approximately fifty-two species, the juniper genus (*Juniperus*) is by far the most successful in the cypress family. Junipers are found throughout the Northern Hemisphere. Subarctic tundra, semi-arid desert, and temperate and tropical islands are a few of the environments they find accommodating. One species is native to the Southern Hemisphere. Most are adapted to arid or semiarid conditions—some to cold and dry, some to hot and dry. Junipers are typically indifferent to soil type, but in the landscape many perish from root rot in wet poorly draining soil. Place them in a sunny spot with sharp drainage. An inhospitable roadside berm

Fig. 3-63: Chinese juniper 'Torulosa': green fire

suits them just fine. Few plants are as unfazed by asphalt's radiant heat as junipers. Many you can water the first season and never again.

For a number of reasons, junipers are a challenge to ID in the field. Junipers are shape-shifters. In one of many examples, the common juniper (*J. communis*) is an upright tree of open woodlands in Europe and Asia, and a low-growing shrub in the PNW. Junipers hybridize easily to the point that the parentage of a number of cultivars can only be guessed at. Many junipers have two types of adult foliage. The cones are similar across the genus.

Junipers lack buds. Lastly, a microscope is required to answer the question botanists pose in breaking the junipers with rounded scales into two main groups: Are the scale edges smooth or minutely wavy? Horticulturally, junipers largely defy systematic treatment, but there are characteristics to look for to make the best possible ID, and a number of cultivars are so common you come to recognize them, such as the 'Torulosa' Chinese juniper (*J. chinensis*) (fig. 3-63).

FOLIAGE

Some adult juniper species have awls, some have rounded scales, some have both. Rounded scales are a characteristic that junipers share with cypresses, to which they are closely related. Like those of cypresses, each scale has a resin dot that can be either active or inactive.

Awl-Like Foliage

Some junipers don't follow the rules written for them. All foliage in the cypress family wraps the twig (decurrent). That is, except for a few of the junipers with awl-like foliage. But one can take advantage of this exception by splitting this group of junipers into two camps: those without decurrent awls and those with decurrent awls.

Non-decurrent Awls

Juniper awls that are not decurrent end where they connect to the twig (fig. 3-64a), allowing you to wiggle them back and forth 180 degrees where they attach, as if they're hinged (figs. 3-64b,c), a characteristic botanists call articulated or jointed. The twigs themselves are brown, except for the new growth at the tips.

- The common juniper, the most widespread conifer on the planet, has four naturally occurring varieties. The variety native to the PNW (*J. communis* var. *saxatilis*) is a sprawling low shrub. At its most robust near tree line in the Cascades, you'll also sometimes spot it in surprisingly shady locations as low as 3,500 feet elevation, close to the Cascade crest. However, popular pillar-shaped cultivars, such as 'Compressa', are probably derived from *J. communis* var. *communis*, an upright shrub or small tree native to Europe and Asia. But plant tags don't typically indicate the variety, and in some cases

Awl-like Foliage

Fig. 3-64a: Twig with non-decurrent awls: lighter at tip, darker farther back

Fig. 3-64b: Non-decurrent awls

Fig. 3-64c: Non-decurrent awls on yellow cultivar

Fig. 3-64d: Dense decurrent awls on 'Blue Star' juniper

cultivars have been in circulation for so long information on their origins has been lost.

- The shore juniper (*J. rigida* ssp. *conferta*) is a prostrate shrub found in the wild in coastal Japan, where it grows in pure sand. The species, as well as a number of cultivars, many variegated, are popular

237

Fig. 3-64e: Decurrent awls of Japanese garden juniper 'Nana'

Fig. 3-64f: Cascading habit of Japanese garden juniper 'Nana'

landscape plants sold as ground covers. Many sources give the shore juniper the rank of species, and it is often sold as such (*J. conferta*).

Foliage of the common and shore junipers can be difficult to tell apart. A subtle distinction can be seen in the stomata, which in both are densely white on the undersides of the awls. But those of the common juniper cover more of the awl surface, leaving narrower green margins than those on the stomata of the shore juniper. The awls of both are very prickly. Both species are dioecious.

238

Decurrent Awls

Junipers with awls that are decurrent behave as you would expect: the base of the awl extends down along the twig, making the twig green along the entire length. You will not be able to wiggle the awls back and forth, as you can in junipers with awls that are not decurrent.

- Cultivars of the single-seed juniper (*J. squamata*) are very popular. However, to lay eyes on the species you'd probably have to travel to Asia where it is native, as it is rarely planted, even in arboreta. Cultivars are typically low and dense mounding shrubs with crowded prickly vibrant blue foliage. The 'Blue Star' juniper, a witches'-broom cultivar, is the most popular (fig. 3-64d). The species is monoecious.

- The trailing habit of the Japanese garden juniper (*J. procumbens*) (figs. 3-64e,f) makes it a natural fit for rock gardens and as a bonsai subject. On the underside of the awls, a central faint green line separates two wide bands of stomata. White specks that are sometimes evident on the upper side of the awls are not dots of resin, as one might assume, but small stomatal circles, distinguishing it from all other low-growing junipers with awls. 'Nana' and 'Green Mound' are two popular cultivars. The species is monoecious.

- Most cultivars of the Chinese juniper (*J. chinensis*) have rounded scales with some awls, like the species. However, the foliage of a few cultivars is entirely awl-like, which is why the species is mentioned here. (The species is rarely seen in the landscape.) These cultivars are typically more a low shrub than a ground cover.

Rounded Scales or Rounded Scales and Awls

Many more juniper species have rounded scales than have awls; however, many of those with scales also have some awl-like foliage (fig. 3-65a). In junipers with both types, awls are especially evident after pruning or shearing, as new growth tends to be predominantly awl-like and lighter in color. Horticulturally, this group of junipers is a sticky wicket.

Shrubby Forms: The Chinese-Savin-Pfitzer Juniper Conundrum

The Chinese juniper and the savin juniper (*J. sabina*) are closely related. The Pfitzer juniper (*J. × pfitzeriana*) is a hybrid of the two. All three have many

Rounded Scales or Rounded Scales and Awls

Fig. 3-65a: Rounded scales and awls on Tam juniper

Fig. 3-65b: Tam juniper

Fig. 3-65c: Sheared Tam juniper

Fig. 3-65d: Pfitzer juniper limbed up

Fig. 3-65e: Pfitzer juniper 'Daub's Frosted'

shrubby cultivars, in a plethora of growth rates and colors, all of which are maddeningly difficult to differentiate. (The species are rarely sold horticulturally.) What they have in common is dense growth that covers the ground entirely and outcompetes other plants.

Fig. 3-65f: Pfitzer juniper gold cultivar

Fig. 3-65g: Creeping juniper 'Pancake'

- Shrubby Chinese juniper cultivars tend to have an irregular form, with branches reaching up at sharp angles and in different directions. Sometimes they're vase-like, at other times more open and wind-blown-looking. Sargent's juniper (*J. chinensis* var. *sargentii*) is a naturally occurring variety of the Chinese juniper that in nature is a shrub with a vase-like shape. It is treated as its own species by some (*J. sargentii*) and is popular horticulturally, with many of its own cultivars. The Chinese juniper is dioecious.

- In the wild all varieties of the savin juniper are shrubs. This is also true of its cultivars. The Tam juniper ('Tamariscifolia'), the most prevalent cultivar (figs. 3-65b,c), is perhaps best identified by its strong smell of cat urine. Its deep green, boat-shaped foliage layers beautifully: the small side twigs attach to the branch at upright angles, a feature distinguishing it from other shrubby junipers, giving the plant an orderly appearance. The species can be either monoecious or dioecious.

- The Pfitzer juniper, a vigorous hybrid of the Chinese and savin junipers, was once thought to be a cultivar of the Chinese juniper. This hybrid and its cultivars are collectively known as the Pfitzer Group but are still often sold as cultivars of the Chinese juniper. The Pfitzer juniper's prickly blue-green foliage forms ascending layers that are more open than those of the Chinese and savin junipers. The branch ends nod gently at the tips. The Pfitzer juniper is commonly used in rows as a mass planting, becoming with time quite large and messy looking. Some try to tame and tidy it by limbing it up into what looks like a small tree (fig. 3-65d). Many of the Pfitzer cultivars are recognizable by their vigorous growth and layered look (figs.

3-65e,f). Many are variegated. A number are second-generation cultivars, that is, a cultivar derived from a cultivar.

This group of Chinese-savin-Pfitzer junipers represents the bulk of shrubby junipers with rounded scales or rounded scales and awls. But there are hundreds and hundreds of cultivars with this combination of form and foliage; many will look other than described. Also, shrubby junipers are often sheared into smooth mounds, removing much of their characteristic shape (fig. 3-65c). With this category of junipers, a practical approach is best. If faced with an anonymous juniper that defies ID, observe its habit and growth rate and deal with it accordingly. When purchasing these junipers, be sure to select and place them carefully; many become large quickly and have prickly awls irritating to the skin, creating a potentially unpleasant maintenance situation. Rassling with an overgrown prickly juniper can leave you feeling as if you've had a run-in with a porcupine. Additionally, most don't grow back when pruned into the wood. If properly placed, these are plants you can largely forget about once they're in the ground.

Many of these shrubby cultivars have been around a long time and are inexpensive and easy to propagate. The Pfitzer and Tam junipers fall into this category and are typically sold by big box stores. Specialty nurseries carry more unique and recently introduced (and more expensive) cultivars.

Creeping Juniper: Ground Cover

The creeping juniper (*J. horizontalis*) has all scales and no awls. Native to most of Canada, scattered populations also can be found in the United States from Montana and Wyoming east to New England, with a wayward population in Alaska. Its natural habitats are both bogs and stream banks. Cultivars tend to be low growing, from flat against the ground to about six inches high, such as 'Pancake' (fig. 3-65g), with trailing branches that eventually root down. But even this species has a few cultivars that are somewhat upright and can fool you into thinking they're something else, but the low ones are the most common. The creeping juniper is useful thanks to its greater tolerance of wet soils than other junipers. The species is almost always dioecious.

Juniper Trees

Though most ornamental junipers in the PNW are shrubs, some are noteworthy small trees.

- 'Torulosa' Chinese juniper, aka 'Kaizuka', aka the Hollywood juniper, is a deservedly popular small tree with deep green foliage (fig. 3-63). Its awkward reaching form gives it the look of green fire. A female cultivar, it sets lighter-colored cones, irregularly round like the gibbous moon. It is often planted against buildings, where it somehow grows in the long direction naturally without looking cramped, as most trees planted close to structures eventually do.

- The Rocky Mountain juniper (*J. scopulorum*) and the eastern redcedar (*J. virginiana*) are closely related. The two species split the country between them. The Rocky Mountain juniper is native to every western state but California. The eastern redcedar is native to every eastern state. Their ranges overlap in the middle of the United States, in the states that stack on top of one another like blocks, from North Dakota south to Texas, and where they interbreed in what is called a hybrid swarm. Cultivars of these two species are easily confused, to the point that a number formerly attributed to eastern redcedar have been reassigned to Rocky Mountain juniper, including the popular 'Blue Arrow'. Many other cultivars credited to one or the other may actually be from hybrids of the two (Auders and Spicer 2012). In the wild as younger trees, both junipers take the shape of a teardrop, a characteristic captured in many cultivars, including 'Blue Arrow'. To confuse things further, though uncommon, there are a few low shrubby cultivars of these two junipers. Both have all scales and are dioecious. Many botanists also recognize the seaside juniper (*J. maritima*) as a species, which is very similar to the Rocky Mountain juniper. It is found in Puget Sound and the southern tip of Vancouver Island.

FEMALE SEED CONES

Unlike every other conifer genus in the pine and cypress families, the entire juniper genus is neither all monoecious nor all dioecious. It differs from species to species. Some are monoecious, some are dioecious, some can be either. A berry-like juniper cone is not what comes to mind when you think of conifer cones (figs. 3-66a,b). The powdery coating of the small succulent cones reflects light and contrasts against the darker foliage. Those of some species are powdery green, others are powdery blue; some mature from green to blue, and those of a few species not seen in the PNW are orangey red. The cones' fused scales do not open at maturity, but the edges are delineated, allowing you to count the number of scales, which range from one to four depending on the species. The scales of some species have slight curlicue extensions. Except for serotinous cones that open in response to fire, one can typically assume cones that remain shut harbor wingless seeds. Junipers are the only species in the cypress family with seeds dispersed by animals, mainly birds, making juniper the only genus in the cypress family to have increased in the number of species since the ice ages of the Pleistocene. A juniper seed's hard coating ensures its viability after it has been discharged from a bird's digestive tract.

Female Seed Cones and Male Pollen Cones

Fig. 3-66a: Powdery blue cones with visible scale edges and minute extensions on common juniper

Fig. 3-66b: Close-up of emerging seed cone and spent pollen cones on monoecious juniper

MALE POLLEN CONES

Small unremarkable pollen cones develop on the branch tips of junipers in late winter and early spring (fig. 3-66b). They age from yellow to dull brown and are not useful in plant ID.

HOW TO USE THE JUNIPER AND CYPRESS ID CHARTS

In nature, most conifers are trees. The pine family has a few species that are shrubs; almost all of the dozens of shrubby cypress family species are junipers. At a certain point, plant habit is a judgment call. When does a ground cover become a low shrub? When is a large shrub more of a small tree? Many junipers straddle these categories. Cultivars muddle the issue even further. Junipers' variable form and two adult foliage types drive the organization of the ID charts, resulting in three charts for the juniper genus, one of which it shares with the cypress genus:

- Foliage: awl-like over entire plant

  Habit: ground cover or low shrub
- Foliage: rounded scales or rounded scales and awls

  Habit: small tree
- Foliage: rounded scales or rounded scales and awls

  Habit: ground cover or low shrub

Although a number of junipers in the wild are trees with all awls, species and cultivars with this combination of foliage and form are rare horticulturally and not included in this book.

Cupressaceae   Cypress Family

Foliage: Awl-like over entire plant	
Habit: Ground cover or low shrub	
Juniperus Juniper genus Cones: Fleshy	
Awls do not wrap twig	
J. communis Common juniper PNW NATIVE*	*J. rigida* subsp. *conferta* Shore juniper Native to coastal Japan

Foliage	 Short wide awls; single wide central dense stomatal band	 Awls to ⅔″ (l); single wide central dense stomatal band
	 Glossy, points forward	 Prickly awls open out
Form	 Ground cover or low shrub	 Can cover a large area  Yellow cultivar 'All Gold'
Other	Most common conifer in world; many upright cultivars; species not planted; dioecious; Z2	'Blue Pacific' cultivar has longer awls; dioecious; Z5–6

J. squamata	*J. procumbens* 'Nana'
Single-seed juniper	Dwarf Japanese garden juniper
'Blue Star' juniper Native to Asia	Native to mountains of Japan

Very dense blue foliage; somewhat prickly; 2 stomatal bands separated by midrib; waxy coating	Short awls to ⅓" (l); low to the ground; foliage light blue-green

Foliage sweeps forward	Prickly awls

Spreading mound	Tends to cascade with age

Can die out in the middle with poor drainage; species has similar foliage; monoecious; Z4	Popular in rock gardens and as bonsai subject; monoecious; Z4

Cupressaceae   Cypress Family

Foliage: Rounded scales or rounded scales and awls

Habit: Small tree

Cupressus   Cypress genus   Cones: Woody

C. arizonica var. *glabra* Smooth Arizona cypress (Blue upright cultivars) Native to AZ, NM, and Mexico	*C. sempervirens* Italian cypress 'Stricta' Native to Europe, Asia, and N. Africa

Foliage

Very blue; distinct stomata

Deep green

Resin dots often prominent

Tight scales

Cones

To 1″, squarish

Mature

Knobby to 1½″

Form

'Blue Ice' 15′ (h) x 4′ (w); red flaky new bark

'Blue Pyramid', 15′ (h) x 7′ (w)

Narrow pillar

Other

Species Z7; some cultivars Z5–6

ID by form and cones; formal looking; Z7–8

Juniperus Juniper genus Cones: Fleshy		
J. chinensis Chinese juniper 'Torulosa' Native to Asia	*J. scopulorum* Rocky Mountain juniper (Blue upright cultivars) PNW NATIVE*	
 Upswept branches, deep green foliage	 Upright twig	
 Tight scales look braided	 'Moonglow'; male clone	
 To ½"	Fleshy gray-green cones; female clone	Cultivar will be either all male or all female
 Awkward and wide; to 8' (h) in 10 years	 'Moonglow' to 15' (h)	 'Wichita Blue' to 15' (h)
Species dioecious; Z5	Blue pillar-shaped cultivars most common; species dioecious; Z3	

Cupressaceae   Cypress Family

Foliage: Rounded scales or rounded scales and awls			
Habit: Ground cover or low shrub			
Juniperus Juniper genus Cones: Fleshy			
J. chinensis cultivars Chinese juniper Native to Asia	*J. horizontalis* cultivars Creeping juniper Native to US and Canada		

Foliage	 Mostly scales	 Mostly scales	Short side branches; blue-green foliage; 'Wiltonii' foliage shown
	The foliage of many *J. chinensis* cultivars tends to look more dense and the branches tend to stick up at distinct angles, giving plant a **vase-like shape**	 Roots down eventually	Trailing habit; species and many cultivars bronze in winter
Form	 'Sea Green'; 5' (h) x 7' (w)	 'Wiltonii' to 4" (h)	 'Pancake' to 2" (h)
Other	A few *J. chinensis* cultivars are all awl-like; dioecious; Z3	Roots down at the nodes eventually; many cultivars grow flat or very low; a number of yellow cultivars; tolerant of wetter conditions and heavier soils than other junipers; dioecious; Z3	

J. sabina	*J. × pfitzeriana*
Savin juniper 'Tamariscifolia'	aka *J. chinensis* 'Pfitzeriana'
Native to Europe, Asia, N. Africa, and	Hybrid of *J. chinensis* × *J. sabina*
Russia	Pfitzer juniper

Mostly scales; awls toward inside and where recently pruned	Scales and awls; prickly

Twiglets at tight angles to twig	**Nodding tips**

Dense, covers wide area with age; to 3' (h); ascending tips	To 7' (h); older specimens often limbed up; nodding tips
Perhaps best diagnostic characteristic is odor of cat urine; tolerates urban conditions if drainage good; fast-growing; grows out from a central point; does not root down; tidy layered look as it ages; either monoecious or dioecious; Z3	Branches tend to look messier than other juniper cultivars; more space between layers; develops a thick trunk with time; tolerates urban conditions if drainage good; many yellow, blue, green, and smaller cultivars; Z4

Metasequoia: The Dawn Redwood Genus
Cupressaceae: Cypress Family
Needles Wrap Twig and Woody Cones

Metasequoia is a genus of one species, *M. glyptostroboides*, the dawn redwood. It's one of only four species in the cypress family with foliage that is both linear and deciduous (fig. 3-67). The dawn redwood was known from the fossil record and was thought to have gone extinct about 5 MYA. Then, in 1944, a population was identified in China. And though today's extant dawn redwood has been given a different species name than that of the extinct dawn redwood (*M. occidentalis*), botanists have observed that their characteristics are virtually indistinguishable and that the two are most likely the same species (LePage et al. 2005).

For two years between China's war with Japan and the founding of the People's Republic of China in 1950,

Fig. 3-67: Dawn redwood in winter tinged in pink from pollen cones

China opened its doors to international scientists. During this interregnum, Chinese botanists sent plant material and seeds to sites around the world, and teams of American botanists visited China and brought the same back to the United States. Then China returned to isolationism, and another thirty years would pass before botanists from the international community set foot inside China and again laid eyes on the dawn redwood in its native habitat.

Discovering a living tree previously known only from two-dimensional fragments of ancient rock is the thing botanists' dreams are made of. Many new species of angiosperms are discovered each year, typically small herbaceous plants or shrubs, and on occasion a tree from a remote area of the tropics. A new conifer tree species is rare, let alone a redwood. Redwoods capture people's imaginations. The word carries with it the weight of so many superlatives. The announcement of a new redwood species was, to say the least, rousing to the botanical community and to the world.

One reason the dawn redwood was so easily identified from fossils is that it hasn't changed much since the early Cretaceous when it first appeared. This is unusual. Genetic mutations occur regularly in all species such that most don't persist more than ten million years before going extinct. The longevity of a species is driven by its life cycle, specifically, how long it takes to reach sexual maturity. The longer the maturation process, the longer the species persists. On average, flowering plant species don't last beyond 3.5 million years. Being slow to produce seed, the species longevity of conifers is at the high end of the range, up to ten million years (LePage et al. 2005). At 140 million years and still going, the dawn redwood is a genetic time capsule, an order of magnitude older than any other conifer species, a phenomenon that continues to perplex scientists (LePage et al. 2005). Another reason the dawn redwood was easy to ID from fossils is that its range was enormous, making *Metasequoia* fossils rather common, as well as affordable. Since the late Cretaceous, three land bridges have been exposed, submerged, or rearranged as sea levels fluctuated and land masses were reconfigured, allowing for intermittent movement of plant and animal species between continents. Asia is considered the dawn redwood's point of origin. From there it traveled to North America over the Bering land bridge. From North America it proceeded across two more land bridges into Northern and Southern Europe. That's the entire Northern Hemisphere, including all the way to the Arctic (LePage et al. 2005).

The Arnold Arboretum of Harvard received dawn redwood seeds from China in 1948 and redistributed them to arboreta across the United States and the rest of the world, including the Hoyt Arboretum in Portland and the Washington Park Arboretum in Seattle. Both have specimens grown from those seeds, which represent direct genetic links to the last five thousand survivors of this species in China and the dawn of the Cenozoic. Horticulture has brought this botanical discovery to the backyards and parks of the world, including a number of small cultivated varieties.

FOLIAGE

Dawn redwood's soft deciduous foliage forms in opposite twiglets on the branch, and the needles form in opposite pairs on the twiglet (fig. 3-68a). Faint stomatal bands lighten the undersides to a creamy green (fig. 3-68b). The needles have raised midribs on the upper sides and tips that are rounded but not sharp. Anatomically part of the stem, the needles extend along and wrap the stem in foliage, making the two the same color. This means that during the

Fig. 3-68a: Opposite twiglets and opposite needles

Fig. 3-68b: Underside of spring foliage

Fig. 3-68c: Deteriorating fall foliage

Fig. 3-68d: Foliage of yellow cultivar

growing season the twig is green. As the foliage deteriorates in the fall, both the needles and the stem age to brown (fig. 3-68c). With yellow foliage and yellow twigs, cultivars such as 'Ogon' perhaps illustrate this point best (fig. 3-68d). It is not surprising then that the needles and twigs don't part company in the fall when the foliage dies back. The two remain joined and are shed as a unit.

FEMALE SEED CONES

Each one-inch seed cone of dawn redwood develops on its own shoot, complete with foliage. Early in development, the female seed cone appears a distance back from the tip of the shoot, with a few leaves poking out of the top, and seems to consume the stem as it matures (fig. 3-69a). At full size it's the shape of a tiny hornet's nest (fig. 3-69b). At seed release, the cone scales open wide, often with enough space in between that you can see through them (fig. 3-69c). The *Metasequoia* cone fossil in figure 3-69d dates back to the extinction event that ushered in the Cenozoic, about 66 MYA, and is from the Hell Creek fossil beds near the Black Hills in Wyoming.

Fig. 3-69a: Spring   Fig. 3-69b: Summer   Fig. 3-69c: Mature   Fig. 3-69d: Fossilized

MALE POLLEN CONES AND FORM

Dawn redwood pollen cones (fig. 3-70) set in autumm and are visible on the leafless tree all winter. The dark pink stems and pairs of lighter tawny pink cones dangle from the branch ends like tassels, tingeing the perimeter of the tree in color. This characteristic, in combination with the upswept branches, make this species fairly easy to ID in winter, even at a distance or on a drive-by (fig. 3-67). In summer the form is somewhat concealed by the foliage (fig. 3-71).

Male Pollen Cones and Form

Fig. 3-70: Pollen cones dangle from branch ends   Fig. 3-71: Upswept branches

BUDS

The only species in the cypress family to set buds are the few that are deciduous, including the dawn redwood. The opposite, creamy white to light pink buds are not well secured to the twig and break off when nudged (fig. 3-72).

Fig. 3-72: Delicate opposite buds

CULTIVARS

Many dawn redwood cultivars bear all yellow, partly yellow, or creamy foliage for at least part of the season. Some are small and better suited to yards with limited space. One popular full-sized cultivar, 'Ogon', also known as 'Gold Rush', has delicate feathery yellow foliage (fig. 3-68d). All require the same conditions as the species: sun and moist well-drained soil. The Chinese name for the dawn redwood, water-fir, refers to its riparian habitat in the wild. The species is hardy to USDA zone 4.

Taxodium: The Baldcypress Genus
Cupressaceae: Cypress Family
Needles Wrap Twig and Woody Cones

The baldcypress genus (*Taxodium*) has two species. The Montezuma baldcypress (*T. mucronatum*), native to Mexico, Guatemala, and the southernmost tip of Texas, is not hardy in the PNW. Hardy to USDA zone 4, the baldcypress (*T. distichum*) is native to the southeastern United States and is found in cultivation across the country, as well as in Europe, where it was introduced in 1640. A fast-growing tree that can live more than 1,500 years, it is still uncommon ornamentally in the PNW.

It is often the case that a species flourishes in cultivation under conditions in which it cannot compete in the wild. This is especially true of the baldcypress. It is actually quite obliging, capable of growing in anaerobic swamps or on dryer soil, and is both cold- and heat-tolerant. But as drainage improves just upslope from the swamps where it thrives in the wild, flowering trees muscle it out. In the wild it has a niche, occupying real estate only a few trees on the planet can survive.

The two *Taxodium* species have a number of adaptations that make them the only conifers in the world able to grow in water. Odd ghostly structures that appear as misshapen creatures rising from the dead extend up from their submerged roots through the water. It is generally reported that these pneumatophores, more commonly called knees, deliver oxygen to the root system; however, research has never been able to support this view. The pneumatophores of other species, like mangroves, have openings in the bark (lenticels) for gas exchange and specialized cells that move oxygen from the knees to the roots, neither of which baldcypresses possess (Briand 2000). Additionally, it has been observed that baldcypresses in deep water lack knees and that those on dry land sometimes form knees if close to water. When knees do form, they must spend at least part of the year above water for the tree to survive.

In addition to wobbly saturated soil, baldcypresses in the southeast must contend with hurricane-force winds, a deadly combination that topples most trees. Their three-dimensional grid-like root system provides superior anchorage. Where the knees intersect the horizontal lateral roots, vertical roots extend deep into the soil. Aboveground, wide buttressed tree bases that look like part trunk and part root lend additional stability, encircling the tree like a ring of crutches that help keep baldcypresses upright under the most shaky conditions imaginable.

BALDCYPRESSES OF BLUE RIVER RESERVOIR

In 1971, seventy-five baldcypresses were planted at the newly filled Blue River Reservoir, formed from damming the Blue River just off the McKenzie Highway in Central Oregon east of Eugene. The reservoir depth fluctuates up to a hundred vertical feet yearly, with the lowest levels just before October 1, the start of the water year. The baldcypresses were part of a larger effort to vegetate and beautify the barren mucky areas exposed by the draw-down of the water, stabilize the soil, and increase habitat for aquatic wildlife (Skeesick 1991).

In late spring, when the water is at its highest, just the crowns of the bald-cypresses are above water (fig. 3-73a). In late summer, after the drawdown has begun, the trees are about half submerged (fig. 3-73b), though a few closer to shore are entirely above water. And in late fall, all are entirely above water (fig. 3-73c), revealing that these baldcypresses, which spend a portion of the year in very deep water, survive without forming knees.

Because Blue River Reservoir is in a natural area in the Willamette National Forest, where one expects to see only native trees, the presence of an unusual horticultural species like the baldcypress creates a kind of botanical cognitive dissonance, as if two ecosystems separated by thousands of miles or millions of years had somehow defied space or time to come together, as the baldcypress and the dawn redwood were native to the PNW until about 5 MYA.

The cataclysmic Holiday Farm Fire swept through this part of Oregon in the fall of 2020; fortunately, the fire skipped over the baldcypresses and the area directly surrounding them.

FOLIAGE

Baldcypress' soft deciduous foliage forms in alternate twiglets on the branch, and the needles form in alternate pairs on the twiglet (figs. 3-74a,b), differentiating it from the dawn redwood. The upper surface of the foliage is smooth, without grooves, and the tips are pointy but not sharp. In fall the foliage is beautifully multitoned (fig 3-74c). As with all species in the cypress family, the twiglets drop as a unit (fig. 3-74d).

Baldcypresses of Blue River Reservoir

Fig. 3-73a: Just the crowns above water in late spring

Fig. 3-73b: Emerging from the water in late summer

Fig. 3-73c: On dry land in late fall

FEMALE SEED CONES

The soccer-ball-shaped seed cones (up to 1½ inches) of the baldcypress are hard and woody like cypress cones. Look for the puckered edges of the scales to differentiate them (fig. 3-75a). The seed cones of both species in the baldcypress genus have a number of adaptations for a watery environment. Almost all conifer seeds are wind-dispersed (anemochory). The two baldcypress species are the only conifers in the world whose seeds are spread by water (hydrochory). To make the journey from seed to young tree, baldcypresses must navigate between the aquatic and terrestrial domains.

Baldcypress cones are the only cones in the cypress family to break apart at maturity (fig. 3-75b). The seeds remain bonded to the scales, which function like lifeboats. Buoyant seeds and scales travel together by water to points unknown, in some areas more than a mile from the parent tree, farther than wind-dispersed seeds (Renner 1992). Coated with a pungent, sticky, water-repellent resin that serves as a wetsuit, seeds can remain dry and viable in water for two and a half years (Wilhite and Toliver 1990), allowing them to survive more than one flood season. Eventually the seeds must find ground on which to germinate. Each seed is equipped with a hook for snagging and holding on to solid earth. Mind you, for germination to occur, this bit of earth cannot be the least bit dry—it must be saturated with water but not flooded. Ideally, this place is peaty or mucky, the kind of stuff you sink into up to your ankles, and is often a spot retreating flood waters have exposed. Then it's a race with time. The seedling must grow like mad to ensure its top

Foliage

Fig. 3-74a: Alternate twiglets

Fig. 3-74b: Alternate needles pointed but not sharp

Fig. 3-74c: Multitoned fall foliage

Fig. 3-74d: Twiglets drop as a unit

will be above water for the majority of the year when the water level rises again. And it does, growing up to thirty inches the first year (Wilhite and Toliver 1990).

Female Seed Cones

Fig. 3-75a: Cone scales with puckered edges   Fig. 3-75b: Reassembled cone

MALE POLLEN CONES

Baldcypress male pollen cones are similar in appearance to those of the dawn redwood (*Metasequoia glyptostroboides*). The cones of both dangle in long tassels, except baldcypress cones are arranged randomly and not in opposite pairs like those of the dawn redwood.

BARK AND FORM

The bark of the baldcypress is brownish-gray with narrow furrows. The straight narrow trunk tends to shed the lower branches as it ages (fig. 3-76).

Fig. 3-76: Baldcypress in summer

263

CULTIVARS

It's unclear why the baldcypress is not more popular horticulturally in the PNW. So few plants can tolerate saturated soil, making baldcypress a natural fit for tricky low-lying spots where water collects. If you don't have room for a full-sized tree, there are a number of small cultivars with the same foliage as the species, though you might have to seek them out at a specialty nursery.

Sequoia: The Coast Redwood Genus
Cupressaceae: Cypress Family
Needles Wrap Twig and Woody Cones

The coast redwood (*Sequoia sempervirens*) is the only species in the *Sequoia* genus (fig. 3-77), and the only species in the cypress family with linear foliage that is also evergreen. The other species with linear foliage, the dawn redwood (*Metasequoia glyptostroboides*) and the two baldcypresses (*Taxodium* spp.), are deciduous. In fact, the first botanist to describe the coast redwood placed it in the baldcypress genus, giving it the species name *sempervirens,* which means always green, to differentiate it from the deciduous species in that genus.

The coast redwood is the tallest tree on Earth, found in the wild along a thin strip of the Pacific Coast from the

Fig. 3-77: Coast redwood

southernmost part of Oregon to south of Monterey, California. Coast redwoods grow to such great size in part because they don't have an off season. Mild temperatures and evergreen foliage allow them to photosynthesize year-round and, being shade-tolerant, they photosynthesize well in low light. Though during the rainy season coast redwoods receive up to 125 inches of rain in the wettest part of their range and as little as 25 inches in the driest part, throughout the entire range little or no rain falls in summer. But the dense fog that forms when warm summer air passes over the cold water of the Pacific supplies coast redwoods with moisture in the dry season. It is hardy to USDA zone 7.

THE CANOPY OF ANCIENT COAST REDWOODS

Canopy science of ancient coast redwoods is a fascinating field pioneered by Stephen Sillett and others. Beginning in the 1990s, Sillett followed his curiosity and climbed with ropes hundreds of feet into the tops of the oldest specimens. The complex architecture he and others discovered in the crowns and the life it supported astonished him and the world.

When the main trunk of an old coast redwood snaps off, it isn't the beginning of the tree's decline, as one might assume. The injury stimulates the tree to do something unthinkable—unthinkable to organisms with flesh and blood, that is. At an already advanced age for most trees, the coast redwood experiences a rebirth, sprouting not just one new trunk but multiple trunks, out of which issue more trunks, all parallel to one another, a phenomenon called reiteration. The tree's structure keeps replicating in a self-similar manner such that some trees have upward of two hundred trunks. Many of these new trunks, up to four feet in diameter, are trees unto themselves. Their branches interconnect. Sometimes the bark grates off as trunks rub against each other in the wind, exposing the vascular cambium, the actively growing part of the tree. The two vascular cambiums, now in physical contact, stitch themselves together, and the two trunks fuse into one (Sillett and Van Pelt 2000). And in and among all the tight spaces and crotches of the crowded crown, forest debris collects. Centuries of it.

The canopy of an ancient coast redwood is nothing less than a second terrestrial plane, firm enough to walk on, an aerial ecosystem of water, soil, and plants, and also animals, like the wandering salamander (*Aneides vagrans*), who may spend its entire life cycle in the canopy, never coming down out of the sky (Spickler et al. 2006). When I say plants, I don't just mean delicate low-growing perennials—though those are there too—there are copses of huckleberry full of berries in season, flowering rhododendrons, and even proper trees like western hemlock (*Tsuga heterophylla*) and Douglas-fir (*Pseudotsuga menziesii*) growing in the crowns of coast redwoods as natural dwarfs. Ancient coast redwoods confound the old expression, "can't see the forest for the trees," because, as Stephen Sillett and Robert Van Pelt have observed, an ancient coast redwood with dozens and dozens of trunks and a rich community of plants growing on it is both a forest and a tree (Sillett and Van Pelt 2000).

VEGETATIVE REPRODUCTION

A coast redwood has a gift for staying alive. When one falls over in wind or is logged, it often regenerates. Large misshapen burls all around the tree base or just below ground are in fact masses of latent buds. In a response not unlike what happens in the canopy, new genetically identical trees sprout from the burls all around where the original tree stood, like an atoll. This new growth occurs surprisingly fast, within two to three weeks of the disturbance (including logging), no matter what time of year the disturbance occurs (Roy 1966). Each new tree in the atoll develops its own root system, a characteristic that delights lumber companies that harvest coast redwoods commercially, as much of a logged forest regenerates on its own without the need for replanting.

The one- to two-foot-thick bark of an old coast redwood insulates the vascular cambium from all but the hottest blazes. After the foliage and many of the branches of an old tree have been burned away, latent buds along the length of the trunk break dormancy. The trunk becomes obscured from the ground all the way to the canopy, looking like a massive pillar of green, what ecologists call a fire column.

FOLIAGE

The linear foliage of the coast redwood is deep green with pointy tips that are sharp to the touch (fig. 3-78a). As with all linear foliage in the cypress family, the base of the needle extends down along the twig, coloring it green, and the twigs are shed as a unit. The foliage has bright stomatal bands on the underside (fig. 3-78b) and individual scattered stomata on the upper side that you'll need a loupe to see. The needles and twigs are alternate.

Fig. 3-78a: Sharp tips and scattered stomata on the upper side

Fig. 3-78b: Two bright stomatal bands on the underside

FEMALE SEED CONES

It's a good thing that the coast redwood has many strategies for reproducing vegetatively, because only a small percentage of the seed it produces is viable. The thin seed coat easily absorbs tannins from the cone, which are lethal to the seed. And with puny wings, the seeds fall quickly and don't get far from the parent tree.

The cones, up to 1¼ inches long, grow on their own twigs. The center of each cone scale is sunken, the edges are wrinkled, and the four sides are somewhat flattened, making each scale look a bit like puckered lips (fig. 3-79). You're most likely to confuse it with a giant redwood cone whose scales are also sunken and wrinkled but are much less flattened and more uniformly diamond-shaped.

Female Seed Cone   **Male Pollen Cones**

Fig. 3-79: Mature seed cone with scales like puckered lips

Fig. 3-80: Spent pollen cones

MALE POLLEN CONES

Small pollen cones form at the branch tips of coast redwoods in winter (fig. 3-80). They age from yellow to a tawny brown and often form in vast numbers, tingeing the tree in color.

BARK

Fibrous coast redwood bark is cinnamon-red with shallow interweaving ruts. Sprays of foliage can often be seen growing directly out of the trunk from buds below the bark (fig. 3-81).

Fig. 3-81: Cinnamon-red bark

FORM

A landscape-sized coast redwood takes the generic shape of a wide column with branches that stick out fairly straight from the tree, though they may curve down or up in certain spots (fig. 3-77). Its form takes a while to learn to ID from a distance. You learn to recognize it by the process of elimination.

CULTIVARS

Cultivars of the coast redwood can be difficult to find. Many have foliage that is the same as the species, although it may be blue-green or variegated. However, some have foliage that looks quite a bit different, such as 'Prostrata', a low-growing form that often sends up vertical shoots (fig. 3-82a); the needles are much lighter in color, not as sharp, and noticeably wider than that of the species (fig. 3-82b). Like the species, it grows vigorously but can be controlled with pruning, making it a good selection for areas without the space for a large upright tree. With summer irrigation and a mild winter, it grows year-round, almost right before your eyes. There is also an upright cultivar with this same unusual foliage.

Fig. 3-82a: 'Prostrata'

Fig. 3-82b: Close-up of newly emerged 'Prostrata' foliage

Cupressaceae   Cypress Family

Foliage: Needles wrap twig **Cones: Woody**					
Habit: Large tree					
DECIDUOUS **Soft foliage**					
Metasequoia glyptostroboides Native to China Dawn redwood			*Taxodium distichum* Baldcypress		

Foliage and Branches	Twiglet	**Opposite needles**	**Rounded tips and grooves**	No grooves	**Alternate needles**	
	Opposite twiglets drop as a unit		Pollen cones	Alternate twiglets		
Cones	Spring	Summer	Mature		Ripening	Mature
	1"; look like hornets' nests				To 1½", break apart at maturity	
Form and Bark	Summer	Winter with pollen cones	Bark stringy gray-brown		Summer	Fall
Other	Dwarf and yellow cultivars with similar foliage; monotypic; Z4				Not common in landscapes; can grow in water	

	EVERGREEN Stiff foliage		
Native to SE US	*Sequoia sempervirens* PNW NATIVE* Coast redwood		

Pointy tips not sharp	**Alternate; sharp tips**	2 wide stomatal bands below

Twiglets drop as a unit	Glossy green foliage; alternate twiglets drop as unit

Water-dispersed soccer-ball-shaped cones at branch ends, ripen in one growing season			Mature cone scales open wide enough to see through	
	Spring	Mature		
	Stemmed cones to 1¼"			Pollen cones

Eventually drops lower branches; indistinct reddish-brown fissured bark		
	Large columnar tree	Tawny-brown bark forms fissures with age

'Peve Minaret' popular cultivar; Z4	A few cultivars including prostrate forms; tallest tree on the planet; monotypic; Z7

CHAPTER 4

Taxaceae: The Yew Family

Introduction to the Yew Family

The yew family (Taxaceae) has approximately thirty-two species spread across six genera. Five species (plus one hybrid species) across three genera are covered in this book. Table 4-1 shows the number of species in these genera worldwide, compared with how many are included in the ID charts in this book and how many of those are native to the PNW. Keep in mind that the number of species recognized in each genus varies depending on the source.

The three other genera, not discussed beyond this paragraph, are native to Asia and the South Pacific: *Amentotaxus*, catkin-yew, six species (Asia); *Austrotaxus*, New Caledonia yew, one species (New Caledonia); *Pseudotaxus*, white-berry yew, one rare species (China).

FOLIAGE

The foliage of all species in the yew family is linear and at first glance similar to needles in the pine family. To tell them apart, look carefully with a loupe at how the needles intersect the twig. A close inspection reveals that yew family needles don't actually stop at the twig, they merge with and become part of it (fig. 4-1). Each unit of foliage can be thought of as having three integrated

Table 4-1. Yew Family Genera and Species Numbers

Native Genus	Worldwide	Book	PNW
Taxus Yew	10	4*	1
Nonnative Genera			
Cephalotaxus Plum yew	8	1	0
Torreya Stinking-cedar	6	1	0

*Includes one hybrid species

Fig. 4-1: Yew family foliage   Fig. 4-2: Pine family foliage

components: the part that hangs free of the twig that we call the needle, the part that extends along and adheres to the twig, and a narrower stem-like isthmus that joins these two together. This marriage of foliage and twig is what makes twigs in the yew family green—they are literally swaddled in foliage. Needles in the pine family never do this. The needle and the twig are clearly delineated from each other (fig. 4-2). Aside from vascular tissue, needle anatomy ends cleanly upon encountering the twig.

Though needles in the yew family attach to the twig in a spiral pattern around the entire circumference,

Fig. 4-3: Two-ranked foliage

274

they more or less lie opposite one another, a characteristic called two-ranked. The isthmus' job is to orient the needle no matter where it attaches on the twig, to achieve this arrangement, twisting to whatever degree necessary. Needles laid flat-out like this are common in shade-loving understory conifers, giving the foliage maximum exposure for collecting as much light as possible for photosynthesis (fig. 4-3). However, be prepared to see needles in the sun to be arched at varying angles to the twig.

YEW FAMILY LOOK-ALIKES

As a source of confusion, four species in the cypress family have linear foliage with the same characteristics as that of the yew family: the coast redwood (*Sequoia sempervirens*), the dawn redwood (*Metasequoia glyptostroboides*), and the two baldcypresses (*Taxodium* spp.). You can rule out the dawn redwood and the baldcypresses as contenders for the yew family; they're deciduous, and all species in the yew family are evergreen. If you're trying to make an ID during the growing season, growth habit further differentiates them, as does the soft foliage of the deciduous species. Plus, all three look-alikes are large single-trunked trees, while yew family species and their cultivars are at best small trees or upright or prostrate shrubs.

However, trying to differentiate a prostrate cultivar of the coast redwood from a yew can be a tricky business. But species in the yew family that are commonly seen in the PNW and their cultivars grow slowly, whereas the few coast redwood cultivars are typically fast-growing. Also, all three look-alikes have smaller roundish woody cones. Plants in the yew family have soft, fleshy cones, and all set small buds, whereas coast redwoods don't set any buds. In summer, when buds aren't present, brown bud scales will be visible on yews (fig. 4-4).

Fig. 4-4: Twig with brown bud scales

FEMALE SEED CONES: ARILS

The female seed cones of species in the yew family challenge one's assumptions about what conifer cones ought to look like. In no part of their development are they woody. Looking more like the succulent fruit or berries of flowering plants, they attract birds, who help disperse the seeds, an uncommon trait for conifers. Species in the yew family are largely dioecious, with separate male and female plants, though there are some exceptions.

Taxus: The Yew Genus
Taxaceae: Yew Family
Needles Wrap Twig and Fleshy Cones

Historically, botanists have had difficulty differentiating among species in the yew genus (*Taxus*) because they all look so darn much alike. A prominent botanist in the early nineteenth century treated all yews as the English yew (*T. baccata*) or as subspecies of the English yew. Geographic separation has often been the sole basis on which many yew species were recognized; if one encountered a yew species in, say, Japan, one could assume it was a different species than one in Europe or other parts of Asia. Botanists differ more on *Taxus* than on perhaps any other conifer genus. Some recognize ten species with a few subspecies, while others cite twenty-four species with fifty-five varieties (Farjon 2010).

Fig. 4-5: Upright English yew cultivar

More recently, DNA testing has lent clarity—to a point. Because yews are such popular landscape plants, cultivated in much of the world since the early 1900s, finding natural populations isolated enough to ensure there is no genetic contamination is increasingly difficult, as they hybridize easily (Farjon 2010). This presents a conundrum for taxonomists. If wild yews have been pollinated by cultivated yews, what seeds down from the wild yews are hybrids. Under these conditions, how can one be sure that wild specimens are genetically pure species?

In addition to the English yew (fig. 4-5), three other yews are commonly seen in the PNW landscape: the PNW native Pacific yew (*T. brevifolia*), the Japanese yew (*T. cuspidata*), and a hybrid of the English yew and Japanese yew (*T. × media*). Two other yew species are native to eastern North America. The Florida yew (*T. floridana*) is a rare threatened species endemic to an isolated stretch of the Apalachicola River in Florida and Georgia. The Canadian yew (*T. canadensis*) is a low shrub native to the eastern United States and Canada that reproduces primarily by layering.

A stroll through an arboretum where one can examine labeled yew species side by side underscores the thorny task faced by botanists. They all do look alike.

FOLIAGE

All species in the yew genus have linear needle-like foliage with pointy tips (figs. 4-6a–c). All foliage is medium to dark green and of similar lengths (¾–1½ inches long). The leaves of all species have dim stomatal bands on the underside. All species have two-ranked needles, as do the prostrate shrubs that grow wider than tall. However, foliage of the narrow multistemmed upright cultivars encircles the twig like a bottle brush (figs. 4-6d,e). Though the foliage of all species in the yew genus is toxic, certain wild grazing species whose ranges overlap that of the Pacific yew seem to be tolerant of the foliage; so, it is important not to plant nonnative yews in areas that foraging animals (or livestock) can access, as they might not differentiate Pacific yew foliage from that of nonnative yews, which is toxic to them.

FEMALE SEED CONES

All species in the yew genus are dioecious (except for the Canadian yew), with separate male and female plants, though the odd monoecious yew is not unheard of. Additionally, sometimes one branch on a plant will switch genders.

Arils

All species in the yew genus bear unusual berry-like cones, called arils, that are an extreme reduction of a typical woody cone down to one cone scale and a single seed (fig. 4-7). The cones emerge from the leaf axils, maturing from green to red in six to nine months (sometimes they can be orange or yellow). The squishy red part is the aril. Each aril incompletely encloses a

Foliage

Fig. 4-6a: Pacific yew branch

Fig. 4-6b: Upper side of Pacific yew foliage

Fig. 4-6c: Underside of Japanese yew foliage

Fig. 4-6d: Encircling foliage of upright cultivar

Fig. 4-6e: Variegated foliage of upright cultivar

Female Seed Cones

Fig. 4-7: Maturing and mature arils of Japanese yew

single hard, green, pointy seed visible through a peekaboo opening at the top of the aril. When unripe, the seed is larger and longer than the still-green aril and pokes above the opening. The aril thickens and elongates as it matures, with the red color telegraphing ripeness. At this point they resemble small pimento-stuffed cocktail olives, only with the colors reversed.

The sweet-tasting aril is the only part of the yew plant that is not toxic. The seed itself is quite toxic, however, and the arils should not be eaten. These diminutive cones are an adaptation that allows animals to consume them in palatable bite-sized pieces. Not having teeth, birds swallow the aril and seed whole. The soft cone scale is digested, while the seed travels with the bird for the length of time it takes to pass through the bird's digestive system and is then dropped intact as waste. Transit time can be surprisingly brief.

Food passes through the system of a small fruit-eating bird in as few as thirty minutes. Also, the yew aril is reported to act like a laxative, perhaps shortening transit time even further. Avian laxative effects in fruit are not uncommon. Research suggests that the less time seeds spend in birds' guts, the less likely the seeds are to be damaged by digestive enzymes and the more likely they are to germinate successfully after being discharged (McKechnie 2010). (Note: In nectar-consuming birds like hummingbirds, transit time is even shorter; in birds that consume proteins such as insects, or fats such as seeds, transit time is longer.)

MALE POLLEN CONES

All species in the yew genus form small round bisque-colored pollen cones that emerge in dense double rows from the underside of the leaf axils, releasing pollen in late winter (fig. 4-8). Before releasing pollen, they look like tight miniature heads of cauliflower raised up on small stalks.

Fig. 4-8: Pollen cones of English yew

CONES AND CULTIVARS

Many yew cultivars set cones. However, because the genus is dioecious, any one cultivar will be either all male or all female, as cultivars are typically clones propagated from cuttings. Males will form mature pollen cones without females nearby, but females will not develop mature cones without males in the vicinity. Female cones grow large enough to see with the naked eye only after they have been successfully pollinated. However, yews are popular enough landscape plants that there are plenty of males around to ensure pollination even if you don't have a male in your yard or neighborhood. And the pollen of any yew species will probably suffice, because, as mentioned earlier, they hybridize easily. If you'd like a yew that sets female cones, be sure to choose a cultivar that's reliably female, like the 'Standishii' English yew. Be aware that not all plant tags declare the gender of the cultivar, as many seem to be of an undetermined sex.

BUDS

The tiny buds of species in the yew genus are indistinct and not useful for ID.

BARK

All species in the yew genus have purplish-red young bark (fig. 4-9a) that becomes tawny brown and stringy with age (fig. 4-9b). However, you will probably only ever notice bark on the Pacific yew, which has no cultivars. All other yews common in the landscape are smaller cultivars with dense foliage that obscures the bark.

Fig. 4-9a: Young red bark

Fig. 4-9b: Thin ⅛-inch bark of a mature Pacific yew

IDENTIFYING YEWS IN THE LANDSCAPE: A PRACTICAL APPROACH

In their native habitats, yews are most commonly understory plants that take the form of a shrub or tree and that are more tolerant of moisture than most other conifers. In the commercial and residential landscapes, unless you have the native Pacific yew tree, you can assume that the plant specimen is a cultivar and not a species. This means that the plant habit is a multistemmed upright shrub (fastigiate), a shrub wider than tall, or a prostrate ground cover. It may also have some interesting leaf characteristics that set it apart from the species even more, such as shorter, fatter needles or variegated foliage.

Faced with a yew cultivar of uncertain origin, one would be hard-pressed to ID it as either the English, Japanese, or hybrid yew, let alone ascertain the cultivar, as the yew genus has more than four hundred registered cultivars, though some are far more commonly planted than others. Here's the practical approach: call it a yew, observe its growth habit, growth rate, and leaf characteristics, and deal with it accordingly. Though the species are shade-dwelling in their native habitats, yew cultivars often do well or better in part to full sun, and those that are variegated may require sun to maintain their color or scorch if they receive too much sun. One important difference is that the English yew is hardy to USDA zone 6 and the Japanese yew and hybrid are hardy to zone 4.

SHEARING AND MOVING

Latent buds beneath the bark allow yews to grow back even when sheared to bare wood. This quality makes them popular hedge plants, as well as victims of topiary. The elaborate maze gardens once popular in Europe were created with English yews. Yews are also highly tolerant of being dug up and moved.

Yews hundreds of years old have been successfully moved, including one as long ago as 1880 in Britain and another in Germany in 1907. In the churchyard near Dover (most ancient English yews in Britain needed the sanctuary of a churchyard to be spared the axe), it took nine days to move the tree sixty feet; in Frankfurt, seventeen days were needed to move the tree just over two miles (Hageneder 2013). It was like a very slow-moving parade; crowds of people turned out to witness the tree roll, on average, seventy-five yards a day on logs through the streets of Frankfurt to its new home. The move was part of an even larger effort to relocate the entire botanical garden—the yew was one of 4,340 transplanted specimens. The English yew is one of only three native conifers in all of the British Isles, along with the Scots pine (*Pinus sylvestris*) and the common juniper (*Juniperus communis*), the most common conifer in the world. (Flowering plants add just two more evergreens to this list: holly and boxwood.)

Though yews grow slowly, some species like the English yew can live well over a thousand years and achieve great size. In the wild, the oldest known

Pacific yews approach three hundred years in age, but they are not tolerant of fire and, as such, in the PNW, reach the greatest age where fires occur least frequently.

YEWS UNDER THREAT: WAR AND THE WAR ON CANCER

Many yew species around the globe are vulnerable, threatened, or endangered. In the Old World there was so much demand for English yew wood for the construction of the British longbow, the primary weapon of the British Army, that much of continental Europe and Britain were depleted of yews by the late sixteenth century, forcing them to switch to firearms, which were at the time an inferior weapon to the longbow and would remain inferior for two hundred more years. Longbows were composed of compressible yew heartwood on the inner side and elastic yew softwood on the outer side, a unique combination of characteristics. Only that part of the tree where the heartwood and softwood meet was used; the rest was left as waste. It took an entire hundred-year-old yew to construct four longbows (Hageneder 2013).

Hundreds of years later in the New World, in the PNW, the alkaloid taxol in Pacific yew bark was found to be an effective breast and ovarian cancer drug, the outcome of a National Cancer Institute endeavor in the 1960s to discover natural compounds in plants with cancer-fighting properties. However, the bark of mature Pacific yew is very thin, just ⅛ inch thick (fig. 4-9b). And even though the Pacific yew is at this moment in history the most plentiful species of yew worldwide, its availability is limited, as the Pacific yew does not grow in great numbers or in stands but is scattered singly here and there in a forest.

Prior to the discovery of taxol in the bark, lumber companies considered the Pacific yew worthless, a trash tree to be removed ahead of clear-cutting, tossed on a slash pile like so much garbage and burned. After the discovery, as it was in the Old World so it was in the New—demand outstripped supply—only this time it took decades instead of centuries to deplete reserves. This time the math was even worse: the bark of six 100-year-old yews is needed to treat one cancer patient (Kolata 1991). Millions of Pacific yews had been harvested by the time conservationists brought enough awareness to the issue to slow the harvest and pharmaceutical companies felt enough pressure to develop other options. Part of the problem is that taxol is a complex insoluble molecule that has proven difficult to synthesize.

Pharmaceutical companies eventually developed a process for creating a partially synthetic taxol and have also developed methods for extracting taxol from renewable yew foliage instead of irreplaceable yew bark. However, the bark has a much higher concentration than the foliage; pharmaceutical companies therefore remain keen on harvesting bark and have shifted their focus to yew species from forests in Asia, which, while beneficial to the Pacific yew, has been detrimental to the other yew species threatened as a result of this and other pressures.

Cephalotaxus: The Plum Yew Genus
Taxaceae: Yew Family
Needles Wrap Twig and Fleshy Cones

The plum yew genus (*Cephalotaxus*) has approximately eight shrub and small tree species, all native to Asia and all of which are endangered or threatened in the wild. (Some taxonomists give the genus the rank of family, Cephalotaxaceae). Like the yew genus, botanists consider it taxonomically difficult, because characteristics of most species, such as needle length and stomata color, are not distinct and exhibit a great deal of overlap (Lang et al. 2013).

FOLIAGE

The plum yew identification problem is solved in the PNW by the fact that horticulturally one typically sees only cultivars of the Japanese plum yew (*C. harringtonii*), native to Japan. (Note: Many sources cite this species as *C. harringtonia*.) In the wild the species can be prostrate, erect, or a small tree. As with the yews, plum yew cultivars are never proper trees, available either as upright shrubs, shrubs wider than tall, or prostrate ground covers. The needles are similar to yews, though they are a darker green and noticeably longer (up to two inches) (figs. 4-10a,b).

Fig. 4-10a: Upper side of foliage

Fig. 4-10b: Under side of foliage

FEMALE SEED CONES

Plum yew cones have the same basic anatomy as those of yews but are much larger, and most notably, the aril completely encloses the seed, lacking an opening at the top. When unripe, they resemble large green olives (fig. 4-11a). When ripe they look like small red plums or large red globular grapes (fig. 4-11b) and shrivel to a dark speckled pink. Unfortunately, the cultivars aren't known for setting cones.

Fig. 4-11a: Ripening cones of Japanese plum yew   Fig. 4-11b: Ripe cones of Japanese plum yew

MALE POLLEN CONES

The male pollen cones are similar across the *Cephalotaxus* genus; plum yew pollen cones resemble yew pollen cones but are larger, more bumpy, and tinged in red before pollen release (fig. 4-12). They grow in symmetrical pairs out of the leaf axils on long stalks and are so unusual looking the genus is named after them: *cephalo* means head—in this case, tiny heads of cauliflower. It may be the only conifer genus in the world named after pollen cones.

BUDS

Plum yew buds are tawny-green and large enough to differentiate plum yews from yews, which have tiny buds.

BARK

Plum yew bark is similar to yew bark, very red and flaky (fig. 4-13), though one is unlikely to notice bark in densely foliated cultivars. These cultivars can be useful garden plants, as they are tolerant of deep shade and moist soil. The species is a forest understory plant and, as such, does well in full shade, though they'll also grow in partial sun. Like yews, they can tolerate abusive amounts of pruning, even resprouting from bare and damaged wood.

Male Pollen Cones

Bark

Fig. 4-12: Pollen cones of Chinese plum yew (*C. fortunei*)

Fig. 4-13: Bark of Chinese plum yew

Torreya: The Stinking-Cedar Genus
Taxaceae: Yew Family
Needles Wrap Twig and Fleshy Cones

Two of the six species in the stinking-cedar genus (*Torreya*) are native to the United States. One is occasionally seen in the residential or commercial landscape: the California nutmeg (*T. californica*), endemic to protected moist areas of the Coast Range of California and Sierra Nevada foothills. Florida torreya (*T. taxifolia*) is a rare endemic and endangered species found along a stretch of the Apalachicola River in Florida and Georgia where it grows among the Florida yew (*T. floridana*), another rare yew family species. The other four species are native to China and Japan. The common genus name refers to the foul odor of crushed foliage.

Stinking-cedar needles are long with very sharp tips and two thin bright stomatal bands on the underside. The cones are similar to those of the plum yew, only larger. Refer to the ID charts for images of the California nutmeg.

Taxaceae Yew Family

Foliage: Needles wrap twig	Cones: Fleshy	Chart 1 of 4

Taxus Yew genus **Cones: Red arils**

Foliage

T. brevifolia PNW NATIVE
Pacific yew

Needles to ¾"–1" (l), usually in one plane, with pointy tips and raised **midribs halfway to top**; all *Taxus* species: 2 wide stomatal bands below
NOTE: No cultivars

Cones and Buds

Young aril and green seed exposed

All *Taxus* species: open, red, ripe aril with 1 seed inside

All *Taxus* species: tiny buds

Form

Small understory forest tree with an undistinguished form; can be shrubby and multistemmed or single-trunked; not large in number and usually not found in stands but scattered singly in a forest; not fire-tolerant; can become large given enough time in forests with infrequent fires; oldish single-trunked specimen shown

Bark

Young bark flaky, bright red and purple; older bark tawny-brown and stringy

Other

Grows in moist, dark shade and from bare wood; Z4–5

Taxaceae   Yew Family

Foliage: Needles wrap twig	Cones: fleshy	Chart 2 of 4

Taxus	Yew genus	Cones: Red arils

T. baccata	English yew	Native to Europe, N. Africa, and Asia
T. cuspidata	Japanese yew	Native to Japan and Russia
T. × media	Hybrid of *T. baccata* and *T. cuspidata*	

Cannot differentiate among these 3 yews by foliage, cones, or form

Species characteristics

All 3: arched needles ¾"–1½" (l) with pointy tips and **raised midribs from base all the way to the tip**; pollen cones in pairs on the underside
NOTE: Typically only cultivars planted

Cultivars (10-year sizes given)

Wider than tall

The needles of cultivars with upright or semi-upright forms encircle the stem

T. c. 'Aurescens'   4' x 5'

Taller than wide

T. b. 'Irish yew' 6' x 4'   *T. b.* 'Standishii' 5' x 1'   Foliage encircles stem

Prostrate

Orientation of the foliage of prostrate cultivars same as the species; it does not encircle the twig

T. b. 'Repens' 2½' x 1'

Other

All have buds under the bark and can be pruned into the wood; *T. baccata*, Z6; *T. cuspidata* and hybrid, Z4

Taxaceae   Yew Family

Chart 3 of 4

	Foliage: Needles wrap twig	Cones: Fleshy	
	Torreya Stinking-cedar genus	Cones: Fruit-like	
	T. californica California nutmeg	Endemic to CA **NOTE: Very few cultivars**	
Foliage
2 bright narrow stomatal bands below
To 2¼" (l), **glossy upper side**; wide raised midrib
Very sharp tips painful to touch
Cones
Streaky green female cones to 1"–1½" (l), sessile
Emerging pollen cones in spring	
Form and Buds			To 60'–70' tall; dark reddish-brown buds with delineated scales; native to moist and protected areas of CA Coast Range and Sierra Nevada foothills
Bark			Tawny-brown bark; prominent, mounding branch collars
Other	Uncommon in residential and commercial landscapes; Z7		

Taxaceae   Yew Family

Foliage: Needles wrap twig	Cones: Fleshy	Chart 4 of 4
Cephalotaxus Plum yew genus	Cones: Plum-like	

C. harringtonii (aka *C. harringtonia*) Japanese plum yew	Native to Japan, Korea, and Taiwan **NOTE: Typically only cultivars planted**

<table>
<tr><td rowspan="2">Species characteristics</td><td colspan="3"></td></tr>
<tr><td>To 1½″–2″ (l), upper side grooved, pointy tips</td><td>Wide pale stomatal bands below</td><td>Tawny-green buds</td></tr>
</table>

Cultivars (ten-year sizes given)

Wider than tall		The foliage of wide shrubs varies; sometimes it encircles the stem and sometimes it's the same as the species 'Duke Gardens' 4′ x 6′
Taller than wide		The needles of cultivars with upright or semi-upright forms encircle the stem 'Fastigiata' 10′ x 5′
Prostrate		Orientation of the foliage of prostrate cultivars same as the species; it does not encircle the twig 'Prostrata' 4′ x 8′
Other	Tolerates damper soil and deeper shade than *Taxus* species; does well in part sun; can be sheared; Z5–6	

CHAPTER 5
Sciadopityaceae: The Japanese Umbrella-Pine Family
Thick Rubbery Needles in Whorls

The Japanese umbrella-pine family has one genus and one species, the Japanese umbrella-pine (*Sciadopitys verticillata*) (fig. 5-1), making both the family and the genus monotypic. Formerly in the baldcypress family (Taxodiaceae), it was the sole species not moved into the cypress family. DNA testing showed the Japanese umbrella-pine to be unique enough to warrant a family of its own. The genus dates back to the Jurassic and was once widespread throughout North America, Europe, and Asia, but is now limited to Japan,

Fig. 5-1: Young 'Sternschnuppe'

where it grows among Hinoki-cypress (*Chamaecyparis obtusa*) and Japanese white pine (*Pinus parviflora*).

FOLIAGE

The Japanese umbrella-pine's thick rubbery whorls of linear foliage (figs. 5-2a–c) make it a showpiece in the landscape. Each spoke of foliage, notched at the tip, is actually a flattened stem with a double vascular system, something it shares with the hard pines (*Pinus* subgenus), initially leading botanists to think the whorls were composed of fused double leaves (Farjon 2005). Both sides of the needles are bisected in the long direction by distinct furrows. Highly reduced nonphotosynthetic triangular leaves circle the base of the whorl.

The bright cinnamon-red stems (fig. 5-2d) are revealed intermittently among the shamrock-green foliage. Cuttings are long-lasting and stunning in an ikebana arrangement with a single fern frond or a flowering magnolia

Fig. 5-2a: Foliage of the species

Fig. 5-2b: 'Sternschnuppe' foliage

Fig. 5-2c: 'Sternschnuppe' foliage

Fig. 5-2d: Cinnamon-red stems

stem; the shorter, thicker and denser foliage of many cultivars is superior to that of the species.

The species, hardy to USDA zone 5, is uncommon, but pricey cultivars are becoming more available. Make sure to protect it in winter as the branches break easily under snow loads.

FEMALE SEED CONES

The two- to four-inch woody female seed cones of Japanese umbrella-pine mature over two growing seasons (fig. 5-3). Female and male cones appear on the same tree.

Female Seed Cones   **Male Pollen Cones**

Fig. 5-3: Mature female seed cone (species)   Fig. 5-4a: Maturing pollen cones   Fig. 5-4b: Fallen cluster of mature pollen cones

MALE POLLEN CONES

Fused clusters of Japanese umbrella-pine pollen cones form in the centers of the whorls in winter (fig. 5-4a) and drop as a unit after pollen release (fig. 5-4b).

CHAPTER 6

Araucariaceae: The Monkey Puzzle Family

Introduction to the Monkey Puzzle Family

The approximately thirty-seven species of the monkey puzzle family, spread across three genera, are found mostly in the Southern Hemisphere. The nineteen species in the monkey puzzle genus (*Araucaria*) include the Norfolk-Island-pine (*A. heterophylla*), a popular houseplant, and the monkey puzzle tree (*A. araucana*), the only species in this family that is typically seen ornamentally in the PNW. The seventeen species of the kauri genus (*Agathis*) include the kauri tree (*A. australis*) of New Zealand, a magnificent long-lived conifer reminiscent of a coast redwood or giant sequoia. Species in the kauri genus are not seen ornamentally. The monotypic genus *Wollemia* was created when the Wollemi-pine (*W. nobilis*) was discovered in Australia in 1994.

Araucaria: The Monkey Puzzle Genus
Araucariaceae: The Monkey Puzzle Family
Thick Sharp Triangular Leaves*

The approximately nineteen species of the monkey puzzle genus (*Araucaria*) are spread among South America, Australia, New Caledonia, and New Guinea, with the majority (thirteen) endemic to New Caledonia, an archipelago in the South West Pacific that is the center of diversity for the genus (Farjon and Filer 2013). But only the monkey puzzle tree (*A. araucana*), one of two species in the genus that is native to South America (Chile and Argentina), is typically seen horticulturally in the PNW. The foliage reference to thick sharp triangular leaves describes the foliage of the monkey puzzle tree

Fig. 6-1: Magnificent male monkey puzzle specimen at Cornell Farm Nursery

only (fig. 6-1); other species in the genus bear other types of foliage.* The monkey puzzle tree is hardy to USDA zone 7.

FOLIAGE AND FORM

Up to 2¼ inches long and 1¼ inches wide, the rigid and spiky triangular leaves of the monkey puzzle tree look like military-grade or weaponized awls (figs. 6-2a,b), resembling the defensive scales of an iguana more than they do leaves. Botanists have speculated on the advantages armor-like foliage affords the tree. Given that the genus dates back to the Triassic, one botanist suggests the foliage evolved to be inedible to dinosaurs, and another that the form of the tree and the foliage mimic the look of a dinosaur, with the effect of scaring off herbivores.

In its native habitat, the tree's resistance to low-intensity fires is an adaptation to volcanic eruptions, as is its ability to move in as a pioneer species afterward onto volcanic soil (Farjon 2010). Given enough time, the beautifully rounded crowns eventually become flat-topped. It's a tree that requires patience, taking a number of years to outgrow its open spindly youth and develop the architectural form it is known for. Although the monkey puzzle tree is a novelty species and somewhat uncommon, its usual appearance, adapted to a different Earth, makes the experience memorable.

Fig. 6-2a: Branch

Fig. 6-2b: Spiky triangular foliage

FEMALE SEED CONES

Maturing over two growing seasons, the golden orb-like female monkey puzzle cones age to a caramel-brown (figs. 6-3a,b) and disintegrate at maturity. The six- to eight-inch upright cones grow singly at the ends of short upturned branches high in the tree, as if on display.

MALE POLLEN CONES

The equally golden three- to six-inch male monkey puzzle pollen cones, which also age to brown and disintegrate at maturity, form in clusters at the branch ends (fig. 6-4) lower on the tree, where you can reach them.

Female Seed Cones   **Male Pollen Cones**

Fig. 6-3a: Ripening female cones   Fig. 6-3b: Mature female cones   Fig. 6-4: Ripening pollen cones

Wollemia nobilis: The Wollemi-Pine
Araucariaceae: The Monkey Puzzle Family

The discovery of the Wollemi-pine (fig. 6-5), and the process botanists went through to identify it, is a story that deserves retelling and a fitting story to end with, as the botanists went through the same process anyone goes through in identifying an unfamiliar conifer species.

In 1994, a young man backpacking in a remote area of Wollemi National Park in Australia stumbled on a group of trees tucked in a narrow side canyon that he suspected were unusual; he knew enough to grab a foliage sample (fig. 6-6) and toss it in his backpack, where it remained for a few days until he returned to civilization. The degraded plant sample was passed from his father, who was knowledgeable about plants, to a naturalist, to a botanist, and then to another botanist. None had seen anything like it, but two early guesses were that it was a fern, perhaps an extraordinarily large tree fern, or a plum yew (*Cephalotaxus*). After a second trip to the remote trees yielded male pollen cones, botanists knew it to be a member of the monkey puzzle family. They

Fig. 6-5: Young Wollemi-pine with mature pollen cones at the branch ends

Fig. 6-6: Wollemi-pine foliage

considered the possibility it was a weed, that somehow long ago, seeds had been transported inadvertently to the area (Woodford 2005).

303

But female cones, which would be needed to settle the issue once and for all, had to be harvested aerially. The trees are often multistemmed and coppice at the top, right where the cones form (Peakall et al. 2003), making the trees too unstable to climb. Imagine, if you will, a helicopter hovering a few feet above a stand of thin trees deep in a tight canyon, and those trees churning wildly in the downward thrust of the blades, while a park ranger, dangling from the helicopter and swaying ungovernably, reaches down and manages, after a number of awkward futile swipes, to get his hand around a female cone and to yank it out of the tree—without dropping it (Woodford 2005).

But it was worth it. A quick inspection of the cone revealed the trees were at the very least a new species. Dissection of the cone revealed the trees were a new genus—a monumental discovery that made headlines around the world. The new genus was named after the park in which the conifer was discovered and the species after the discoverer, David Noble, the observant backpacker: *Wollemia nobilis*.

DNA analysis of twenty-six of the fewer than one hundred adult trees in existence in the wild, as well as of seedlings raised from collected seed, found them to be virtually genetically identical (Peakall et al. 2003). So, there has been a push to get this tree into arboreta and botanical gardens around the world, as its continued existence in the wild is precarious—any number of events, like a fire or an introduced pathogen, could snuff the species out. As of this writing, one can visit specimens at the Hoyt Arboretum in Portland and the Washington Park Arboretum in Seattle.

There is also a push to get the Wollemi-pine into the horticultural trade, but it is still difficult to find in the PNW without spending a small fortune. Hardy to USDA zones 8–9, it is known to be easy to grow, even adapting well to life as an indoor potted plant, as long as it's not overwatered and sees a week or two outside in summer. The Wollemi-pine is an up-and-coming horticultural species and should in time become more available.

Glossary

Abscission is the dropping of a leaf, flower, or fruit.

The **abscission layer** forms between the plant part preparing to be shed and the twig or branch the plant part is separating from.

Anemochory refers to seeds dispersed by air.

Angiosperms are flowering plants; all have seeds enclosed within ovaries.

Awl-shaped foliage is triangular and pointed, as in a number of genera in the cypress family.

Bloom. See stomatal bloom.

Bole is the trunk of a tree.

A **bract** is a reduced leaf that is part of a female seed cone.

Chionophiles are species with adaptations for winter conditions.

Chlorophyll is a pigment responsible for the green color in plants and is found in the chloroplasts.

Chloroplasts are organs in the leaves, in which photosynthesis occurs.

Cladoptosis is the seasonal shedding of twigs as opposed to individual leaves.

Conduplicate describes scale-like foliage in the cypress family that is flattened and folded in the long direction.

Cotyledons are the part of a plant seed that contains food to fuel growth until the plant can begin to photosynthesize.

Cultivars have been selected from wild plants, or other cultivars, for desirable traits, propagated and raised under controlled conditions.

Decurrent leaf bases extend down along the stem.

A **dioecious** species has female seed cones and male pollen cones on separate plants.

An **endemic** species is native to a restricted area and nowhere else.

Epicotyl germination refers to how seeds in conifers germinate above ground, as opposed to hypocotyl germination, which refers to how seeds in flowering plants germinate below ground.

Exserted bracts are seen in the mature seed cones of some species in the pine family; bracts are called exserted when they are longer than the woody scales and visible.

A **gall** is an abnormal growth on a plant caused by a pathogen, such as an insect or a fungus.

Genera is the plural of genus.

Gymnosperms are plant species with seeds that are not enclosed within ovaries; these include conifers, ginkgos, and cycads.

Hydrochory refers to seeds dispersed by water.

A **leaf scar** is the mark left behind on the twig after a needle drops. In this book, only Douglas-fir and true fir needles leave leaf scars.

A **monoecious** species has female seed cones and male pollen cones on the same plant.

A **monotypic** genus has one species. A **monotypic** family has one genus.

Nymph is the immature stage of insects that go through incomplete metamorphosis, such as aphids and adelgids. Larva is the immature stage of insects that go through complete metamorphosis, such as butterflies.

An **ovule** is an unfertilized egg.

Paleo is a prefix that means prehistoric.

Pectinate leaves spread sideways, more or less in a flat plane on both sides of the twig.

Peltate cones are shaped like soccer balls, as seen in a number of species in the cypress family.

Phloem is vascular tissue that delivers glucose produced in the leaves to all parts of the plant.

Photosynthesis is the chemical process by which a plant produces glucose from water, carbon dioxide, and light.

Phylloclades are leaf-like branches. In the genus *Phyllocladus,* true leaves are rudimentary, and branches are strongly flattened and function as leaves.

Proteins are complex molecules with countless critical functions. They are composed of amino acids and are a large component of the cell wall.

Recurved scales curl back on themselves.

Refugia (singular, refugium) are places species fell back to during the ice ages of the Pleistocene until conditions improved.

Resin blisters are bulgy areas on bark that are full of resin; they are seen on the young bark of true firs, Douglas-firs, and pines.

Serotinous seed cones open in response to fire.

A **sessile** leaf, flower, or cone attaches directly to the branch without a stalk.

Shoot dimorphism is when different parts of a branch grow at two vastly different rates.

A **spur shoot** is a stalk that raises a group of needles or a cone above the branch, as in true cedars and larches.

Stomata (singular, stoma) are openings in the leaves that allow for gas exchange. They are depressed somewhat into the leaf surface and appear a lighter color than the leaf.

Stomatal bands are rows of stomata clustered tightly together.

Stomatal bloom is the waxy coating around the stomatal openings that reflect light and reduce water loss.

Taxonomy is a classification system in which species are organized and ranked according to shared characteristics.

Transpiration is water loss as vapor through the stomata.

The **vascular cambium** consists of the xylem and phloem, the actively growing part of the tree just beneath the bark.

A **witches'-broom** is stunted and congested abnormal plant growth caused by a pathogen, parasitic plant, or genetic mutation.

Xylem is vascular tissue that moves water from the roots to all parts of the plant.

Zoochory refers to seeds dispersed by animals.

References

Amils, R., C. Ellis-Evans, and H. Hinghofer-Szalkay, eds. 2007. *Life in Extreme Environments*. Dordrecht: Springer.

Anderson, R. S. 1994. *Paleohistory of a Giant Sequoia Grove: The Record from Log Meadow, Sequoia National Park*. USDA Forest Service General Technical Report PSW-151. Washington, DC: USDA.

Armitage, J. 2011. "The Fertility of Leyland Cypress." *Horticultural Science*, December, 254–256.

Arno, F. S. 1990. "*Larix lyallii* Parl. Alpine Larch." In *Silvics of North America*, vol. 1, *Conifers*, technical coordinators R. M. Burns and B. H. Honkala. Washington, DC: USDA Forest Service.

Arno, F. S., and R. P. Hammerly. 1984. *Timberline: Mountain and Arctic Forest Frontiers*. Seattle: Mountaineers Books.

Arno, F. S., and R. P. Hammerly. 2007. *Northwest Trees: Anniversary Edition*. 2nd ed. Seattle: Mountaineers Books.

Auders, A. G., and D. P. Spicer. 2012. *Royal Horticultural Society Encyclopedia of Conifers*. Vols. 1 and 2. Nicosia, Cyprus: Kingsblue.

Axelrod, D. I. 1959. "Late Cenozoic Evolution of the Sierran Bigtree Forest." *Evolution* 13:9–23.

Balch, R. E. 1932. "The 'Gout Disease' of Balsam Fir." *Forestry Chronicle* 8 (1): 46–51.

Barbour, M., S. Lydon, M. Borchert, M. Popper, V. Whitworth, and J. Evarts. 2001. *Coast Redwood: A Natural and Cultural History*. Los Olivos, CA: Cachuma Press.

Basinger, J. F., D. R. Greenwood, and T. Sweda. 1994. "Early Tertiary Vegetation of Arctic Canada and Its Relevance to Paleoclimatic Interpretation." In *Cenozoic Plants and Climates of the Arctic*, NATO ASI Series vol. 27, edited by M. C. Boulter and H. C. Fisher, 175–198. Berlin: Springer-Verlag.

Berendse, F., and M. Scheffer. 2009. "The Angiosperm Radiation Revisited, an Ecological Explanation for Darwin's 'Abominable Mystery.'" *Ecology Letters* 12:865–872.

Bevan-Jones, R. 2017. *The Ancient Yew: A History of* Taxus baccata. 2nd ed. Oxford: Oxbow Books.

Bever, D. N. 1981. *Northwest Conifers: A Photographic Key*. Portland, OR: Binford and Mort.

Bloom, A. 2002. *Gardening with Conifer*s. Buffalo, NY: Firefly Books.

Bredow, M., and V. K. Walker. 2017. "Ice-Binding Proteins in Plants." *Frontiers in Plant Science* 8 (2153).

Briand, C. H. 2000. "Cypress Knees: An Enduring Enigma." *Arnoldia* 60 (4): 19–25.

Bureau of Land Management and US Forest Service. 2003. *A Range-Wide Assessment of Port-Orford-Cedar* (Chamaecyparis lawsoniana) *on Federal Lands*. Portland, OR: BLM and USFS.

Chabot, B. F., and D. J. Hicks. 1982. "The Ecology of Leaf Life Spans." *Annual Review of Ecology and Systematics* 13:229–259.

Cheddadi, R., A. Henrot, L. François, F. Boyer, M. Bush, M. Carré, E. Coissac, et al. 2017. "Microrefugia, Climate Change, and Conservation of *Cedrus atlantica* in the Rif Mountains, Morocco." *Frontiers in Ecology and Evolution* 5 (114): 1–15.

Coffey, K., C. W. Benkman, and B. G. Milligan. 1999. "The Adaptive Significance of Spines on Pine Cones." *Ecology* 80 (4): 1221–1229.

Crepet, W. L., and K. J. Niklas. 2009. "Darwin's Second 'Abominable Mystery': Why Are There So Many Angiosperm Species?" *American Journal of Botany* 96 (1): 366–381.

D'Auria, A., M. Teobaldelli, and G. Di Pasquale. 2020. "The Late Holocene History of Cypress (*Cupressus sempervirens* L.) in the Italian Peninsula: New Perspectives from Archaeobotanical Data." *The Holocene* 30 (2): 210–217.

Dirr, M. A. 1997. *Dirr's Hardy Trees and Shrubs: An Illustrated Encyclopedia*. Portland, OR: Timber Press.

Dirr, M. A., and K. S. Warren. 2019. *The Tree Book: Superior Selections for Landscapes, Streetscapes, and Gardens*. Portland, OR: Timber Press.

Dunsworth, G. B. 1998. "Problems and Research Needs for *Chamaecyparis nootkatensis* Forest Management in Coastal British Columbia." In *Coastally Restricted Species*, edited by A. D. Laderman. Oxford: Oxford University Press.

Durzan, D. J. 2009. "Arginine, Scurvy and Cartier's 'Tree of Life.'" *Journal of Ethnobiology and Ethnomedicine* 5 (5).

Eckenwalder, J. E. 1976. "Re-evaluation of Cupressaceae and Taxodiaceae: A Proposed Merger." *Madroño* 23 (5): 237–256.

Ellison, A. M., D. A. Orwig, M. C. Fitzpatrick, and E. L Preisser. 2018. "The Past, Present, and Future of the Hemlock Woolly Adelgid (*Adelges tsugae*) and Its Ecological Interactions with Eastern Hemlock (*Tsuga canadensis*) Forests." *Insects* 9 (4): 172–189.

Endoh, K., J. Kasuga, K. Arakawa, T. Ito, and S. Fujikawa. 2009. "Cryo-scanning Electron Microscopic Study on Freezing Behaviors of Tissue Cells in Dormant Buds of Larch (*Larix kaempferi*)." *Cryobiology* 59:214–222.

Equiza, M. A., M. E. Day, and R. Jagels. 2005. "Physiological Responses of Three Deciduous Conifers (*Metasequoia glyptostroboides, Taxodium distichum* and *Larix laricina*) to Continuous Light: Adaptive Implications for the Early Tertiary Polar Summer." *Tree Physiology* 26:353–364.

Farjon, A. 1990. *Pinaceae: Drawings and Descriptions of the Genera: Abies, Cedrus, Pseudolarix, Keteleeria, Nothotsuga, Tsuga, Cathaya, Pseudotsuga, Larix and Picea*. Regnum Vegetabile 121. Königstein, Germany: Koeltz Scientific Books.

Farjon, A. 1996. "Biodiversity of *Pinus* (Pinaceae) in Mexico: Speciation and Paleo-endemism." *Botanical Journal of the Linnean Society* 121:365–384.

Farjon, A. 1999. "*Cryptomeria japonica* (Cupressaceae)." *Curtis's Botanical Magazine* 16 (3): 212–228.

Farjon, A. 2005a. *A Monograph of Cupressaceae and Sciadopitys*. Surry, UK: Royal Botanic Gardens, Kew.

Farjon, A. 2005b. *Pines: Drawings and Descriptions of the Genus Pinus*. 2nd ed. Leiden: Brill.

Farjon, A. 2008. *A Natural History of Conifers*. Portland, OR: Timber Press.

Farjon, A. 2010. *A Handbook of the World's Conifers*. Vols. 1 and 2. Leiden: Brill.

Farjon, A., and D. Filer. 2013. *An Atlas of the World's Conifers: An Analysis of Their Distribution, Biogeography, Diversity and Conservation Status*. Leiden: Brill.

Flora of North America Editorial Committee, eds. 1993. *Flora of North America*, vol. 2, *Pteridophytes and Gymnosperms*. New York: Oxford University Press.

Fordham, A. J. 1967. "Dwarf Conifers from Witches'-Brooms." *Arnoldia* 27 (4/5): 29–50.

Franklin, J. F. 1961. *A Guide to Seedling Identification for 25 Conifers of the Pacific Northwest*. Washington, DC: USDA Forest Service.

Gavin, D. G., M. C. Fitzpatrick, P. F. Gugger, K. D. Heath, F. Rodriguez-Sanchez, S. Z. Dobrowski, et al. 2014. "Climate Refugia: Joint Inference from Fossil Records, Species Distribution Models and Phylogeography." *New Phytologist* 204 (1): 37–54.

Givnish, T. J. 2002. "Adaptive Significance of Evergreen vs. Deciduous Leaves: Solving the Triple Paradox." *Silva Fennica* 36 (3): 703–743.

Goheen, E. M., and E. A. Willhite. 2006. *Field Guide to the Common Diseases and Insect Pests of Oregon and Washington Conifers*. Portland, OR: USDA Forest Service, PNW Region.

Gower, S. T., and J. H. Richards. 1990. "Larches: Deciduous Conifers in an Evergreen World." *BioScience* 40 (11): 818–826.

Graham, R. T. 1990. "*Pinus monticola* Dougl. ex D. Don Western White Pine." In *Silvics of North America*, vol. 1, *Conifers*, technical coordinators R. M. Burns and B. H. Honkala. Washington, DC: USDA Forest Service.

Hageneder, F. 2013. *Yew*. London: Reaktion Books.

Hartzell, H., Jr. 1991. *The Yew Tree: A Thousand Whispers, Biography of a Species*. Eugene, OR: Hulogosi.

Harvey, H. T., H. S. Shellhammer, and R. E. Stecker. 1980. *Giant Sequoia Ecology: Fire and Reproduction*. Scientific Monograph Series No. 12. Washington, DC: US Department of the Interior.

Hawksworth, F. G., and D. Wiens. 1996. *Dwarf Mistletoes: Biology, Pathology, and Systematics*. Agricultural Handbook 709. Washington, DC: USDA Forest Service.

Howe, R. W., A. T. Wolf, and G. A. Fewless. 2016. "Part 3: Biota of Wisconsin's Niagara Escarpment." *Geoscience Wisconsin* 22:1–10.

Hunting, P. 2002. "Isaac Rand and the Apothecaries' Physic Garden at Chelsea." *Garden History* 30 (1): 1–23.

Isah, T. 2015. "Natural Sources of Taxol." *British Journal of Pharmaceutical Research* 6 (4): 214–227.

Iwamoto, J. 2002. "The Development of Japanese Forestry." In *Forestry and the Forest Industry of Japan*, edited by Y. Iwai. Vancouver: University of British Columbia Press.

Jackson, B. A., and W. Dallimore. 1926. "New Hybrid Conifer." *Bulletin of Miscellaneous Information* 3:113–115.

Jarzabek M., P. M. Pukacki, and K. Nuc. 2009. "Cold-Regulated Proteins with Potent Antifreeze and Cryoprotective Activities in Spruces (*Picea* spp.)." *Cryobiology* 58 (3): 268–274.

Jensen, C. E. 2010. *Trees to Know in Oregon*. Corvallis: Oregon State University Extension Service.

Kasuga, J., N. Takata, K. Yamane, K. Kuroda, K. Arakawa, and S. Fujikawa. 2007. "Larch (*Larix kaempferi*) Xylem Parenchyma Cells Respond to Subfreezing Temperature by Deep Supercooling." *CryoLetters* 28 (2): 77–81.

Kauffmann, M. E. 2013. *Conifers of the Pacific Slope: A Field Guide to the Conifers of California, Oregon, and Washington*. Kneeland, CA: Backcountry Press.

Keeley, J. E. 2012. "Ecology and Evolution of Pine Life Histories." *Annals of Forest Science* 69:445–453.

Kelly, P. E., and D. W. Larson. 2007. *The Last Stand: A Journey through the Ancient Cliff-Face Forest of the Niagara Escarpment*. Toronto: Natural Heritage Books.

Keppel, G., G. Ottaviani, S. Harrison, G. W. Wardell-Johnson, M. Marcantonio, and L. Mucina. 2018. "Towards an Eco-evolutionary Understanding of Endemism Hotspots and Refugia." *Annals of Botany* 122:927–934.

Kimura, M. K., K. Uchiyama, K. Nakao, Y. Moriguchi, L. S. Jose-Maldia, and Y. Tsumura. 2014. "Evidence for Cryptic Northern Refugia in the Last Glacial Period in *Cryptomeria japonica*." *Annals of Botany* 114:1687–1700.

Kolata, G. 1991. "Tree Yields a Cancer Treatment, but Ecological Costs May Be High." *New York Times*, May 23.

Kolotelo, D. 1997. *Anatomy and Morphology of Conifer Tree Seed*. Forest Nursery Technical Series 1.1. British Columbia: Ministry of Forests, Nursery and Seed Operations Branch.

Kuprian, E., C. Munkler, A. Resnyak, S. Zimmerman, T. D. Tuong, N. Gierlinger, T. Muller, D. P. Livingston, and G. Neuner. 2017. "Complex Bud Architecture and Cell-specific Chemical Patterns Enable Supercooling of *Picea abies* Bud Primordia." *Plant, Cell and Environment* 40 (12): 3101–3112.

Kuroda, K., J. Kasuga, K. Arakawa, and S. Fujikawa. 2003. "Xylem Ray Parenchyma Cells in Boreal Hardwood Species Respond to Subfreezing Temperatures by Deep Supercooling That Is Accompanied by Incomplete Desiccation." *Plant Physiology* 131 (2): 736–744.

Laderman, A. D., ed. 1998. *Coastally Restricted Species*. Oxford: Oxford University Press.

Lang, X. D., J. R. Su, S. G. Lu, and Z. J. Zhang. 2013. "A Taxonomic Revision of the Genus *Cephalotaxus* (Taxaceae)." *Phytotaxa* 84 (1): 1–24.

Lanner, R. M. 1981. *The Pinon Pine: A Natural and Cultural History*. Reno: University of Nevada Press.

Lanner, R. M. 1996. *Made for Each Other: A Symbiosis of Birds and Pines*. Oxford: Oxford University Press.

Lanner, R. M. 1999. *Conifers of California*. Los Olivos, CA: Cachuma Press.

Lanner, R. M. 2007. *The Bristlecone Book: A Natural History of the World's Oldest Trees*. Missoula, MT: Mountain Press.

Ledig, F. T., P. D. Hodgskiss, and D. R. Johnson. 2005. "Genetic Diversity, Genetic Structure, and Mating System of Brewer Spruce (Pinaceae), a Relict of the Arcto-Tertiary Forest." *American Journal of Botany* 92 (12): 1975–1986.

Le Duc, A., R. P. Adams, and M. Zhong. 1999. "Using Random Amplification of Polymorphic DNA for a Taxonomic Reevaluation of Pfitzer Junipers." *HortScience* 34 (6): 1123–1125.

LePage, B. A., H. Yang, and M. Matsumoto. 2005. "The Evolution and Biogeographic History of *Metasequoia*." In *The Geobiology and Ecology of Metasequoia*, edited by B. A. LePage, C. J. Williams, and H. Yang. Dordrecht: Springer.

Leslie, A. B., J. M. Beaulieu, P. R. Crane, P. Knopf, and M. J. Donoghue. 2015. "Integration and Macroevolutionary Patterns in the Pollination Biology of Conifers." *Evolution* 69 (6): 1573–1583.

Limbu, S., M. A. Keena, and M. C. Whitmore. 2018. "Hemlock Woolly Adelgid (Hemiptera: Adelgidae): A Non-Native Pest of Hemlocks in Eastern North America." *Journal of Integrated Pest Management* 9 (1) 27: 1–16.

Lindow, S. E. 1983. "The Role of Bacterial Ice Nucleation in Frost Injury to Plants." *Annual Review of Phytopathology* 21:363–384.

Little, E. L., Jr. 1971. *Atlas of United States Trees*, vol. 1, *Conifers and Important Hardwoods*. Washington, DC: US Department of Agriculture.

Lucjaz, J. A. 2016. "Part I: Geology of the Niagara Escarpment in Wisconsin." *Geoscience Wisconsin* 22:1–34.

Luoma, J. R. 2006. *The Hidden Forest*. Corvallis: Oregon State University Press.

Ma, J. 2002. "The History of the Discovery and Initial Seed Dissemination of *Metasequoia glyptostroboides*, a 'Living Fossil.'" *Aliso: A Journal of Systematic and Evolutionary Botany* 21 (2): 65–75.

McIver, E. E., and J. F. Basinger. 1999. "Early Tertiary Floral Evolution in the Canadian High Arctic." *Annals of the Missouri Botanical Garden* 86 (2): 523–545.

McKechnie, A. 2010. "A Gut Feeling: Feeding and Digestion in Birds." *Africa: Birds and Birding* 15 (2): 47–51.

Millar, C. I. 1998. "Early Evolution of Pines." In *Ecology and Biogeography of* Pinus, edited by D. M. Richardson. Cambridge, UK: Cambridge University Press.

Miller R. F., J. D. Bates, T. J. Svejcar, F. B. Pierson, and L. E. Eddleman. 2005. *Biology, Ecology and Management of Western Juniper*. Technical Bulletin 152. Corvallis: Oregon State University Press.

Mitchell, R. G., and P. E. Buffam. 2001. "Patterns of Long-Term Balsam Woolly Adelgid Infestations and Effects in Oregon and Washington." *Western Journal of Applied Forestry* 16 (3): 121–126.

Moerman, D. E. 1998. *Native American Ethnobotany*. Portland, OR: Timber Press.

Moriguchi, N., K. Uchiyama, R. Miyagi, E. Moritsuka, A. Takahashi, K. Tamura, Y. Tsumura, et al. 2019. "Inferring the Demographic History of Japanese Cedar, *Cryptomeria japonica*, Using Amplicon Sequencing." *Heredity* 123:371–383.

Mugnaini, S., M. Nepi, M. Guarnieri, B. Piotto, and E. Pacini. 2007. "Pollination Drop in *Juniperus communis*: Response to Deposited Material." *Annals of Botany* 100 (7): 1475–1481.

Napier, J. D., M. C. Fernandez, G. de Lafontaine, and F. S. Hu. 2020. "Ice-Age Persistence and Genetic Isolation of the Disjunct Distribution of Larch in Alaska." *Ecology and Evolution* 10:1692–1702.

Neuner, G. 2014. "Frost Resistance in Alpine Woody Plants." *Frontiers in Plant Science* 5 (654).

Oakes, L. E. 2018. *In Search of the Canary Tree: The Story of a Scientist, a Cypress and a Changing World*. New York: Hachette.

Office of the Deputy Prime Minister. 2005. *Hedge Height and Light Loss.*
London: Queen's Printer and Controller of Her Majesty's Stationery.

Ouden, P., and B. K. Boom. 1965. *Manual of Cultivated Conifers: Hardy in the Cold- and Warm-Temperate Zone.* 3rd ed. The Hague: Martinus Nijhoff.

Owens, J. N. 2008. *Extension Note, 08: The Reproductive Biology of Western Larch.* Forest Genetics Council of British Columbia.

Payton, G. 2010. "Conserving the Dawn Redwood: The Ex Situ Collection at the Dawes Arboretum." *Arnoldia* 68 (1): 26–33.

Peakall, R., D. Ebert, L. J. Scott, P. F. Meagher, and C. A. Offord. 2003. "Comparative Genetic Study Confirms Exceptionally Low Genetic Variation in the Ancient and Endangered Relictual Conifer, *Wollemia nobilis* (Araucariaceae)." *Molecular Ecology* 12 (9): 2331–2343.

Peattie, D. C. 1966. *A Natural History of Trees of Eastern and Central North America.* 2nd ed. New York: Bonanza Books.

Peattie, D. C. 1991. *A Natural History of Western Trees.* Boston: Houghton-Mifflin.

Pielou, E. C. 2011. *The World of Northern Evergreens.* 2nd ed. Ithaca, NY: Comstock.

Powers, R. F., and W. W. Oliver. 1990. "*Libocedrus decurrens* Torr. Incense-Cedar." In *Silvics of North America*, vol. 1, *Conifers*, technical coordinators R. M. Burns and B. H. Honkala. Washington, DC: USDA Forest Service.

Preston, R. 2008. *The Wild Trees.* New York: Random House.

Ragenovich, I. R., and R. G. Mitchell. 2006. *Balsam Woolly Adelgid.* Forest Insect and Disease Leaflet 118. Washington, DC: US Department of Agriculture.

Renner, S. S. 1992. "Seed Dispersal." In *Progress in Botany 53*, edited by H. D. Behnke, K. Esser, K. Kubitzki, M. Runge, and H. Ziegler. Berlin: Springer-Verlag.

Richardson, D. M., ed. 1998. *Ecology and Biogeography of Pinus.* Cambridge, UK: Cambridge University Press.

Roy, D. F. 1966. *Silvical Characteristics of Redwood* (Sequoia sempervirens [D. Don] Endl.). US Forest Service Research Paper PSW-28. Berkeley: Pacific SW Forest and Range Experimental Station.

Sakai, A., and W. Larcher. 1987. *Frost Survival of Plants: Responses and Adaptation to Freezing Stress.* Berlin: Springer-Verlag.

San-Miguel-Ayanz, J., D. de Rigo, G. Caudullo, T. Houston Durrant, and

A. Mauri, eds. 2016. *European Atlas of Forest Tree Species*. Luxembourg: Publication Office of the European Union.

Sax, K. 1958. "The Juvenile Characters of Trees and Shrubs." *Arnoldia* 18 (1): 1–6.

Sillett, S. C., and R. Van Pelt. 2000. "A Redwood Tree Whose Crown Is a Forest Canopy." *Northwest Science* 74 (1): 34–43.

Skeesick, D. G. 1991. "Blue River Reservoir Ecosystem Restoration." In *Warm Water Fisheries 3*. USDA Forest Service General Technical Report RM-207:149–154.

Sniezko, R. A., J. Hamlin, and E. M. Hansen. 2012. "Operational Program to Develop *Phytophthora lateralis*-Resistant Populations of Port-Orford-Cedar (*Chamaecyparis lawsoniana*)." *Proceedings of the 4th International Workshop on Genetics of Host-Parasite Interactions in Forestry: Disease and Insect-Resistance in Forest Trees*, 65–79.

Spickler, J. C., S. C. Sillett, S. B. Marks, and H. H. Welsh Jr. 2006. "Evidence of a New Niche for a North American Salamander: *Aneides vagrans* Residing in the Canopy of Old-Growth Redwood Forest." *Herpetological Conservation and Biology* 1 (1): 16–27.

Spiecker, H., M. Lindner, and J. Schuler, eds. 2019. *Douglas-Fir: An Option for Europe*. Joensuu, Finland: European Forest Institute.

Spongberg, S. A. 1990. *A Reunion of Trees: The Discovery of Exotic Plants and Their Introduction into North American and European Landscapes*. Cambridge, MA: Harvard University Press.

Sprugel, D. G. 1989. "The Relationship of Evergreenness, Crown Architecture, and Leaf Size." *American Naturalist* 133 (4): 465–479.

Stevenson, R. A., D. Evangelista, and C. V. Looy. 2015. "When Conifers Took Flight: A Biomechanical Evaluation of an Imperfect Evolutionary Takeoff." *Paleobiology* 41 (2): 205–225.

Swetnam, T. W., C. H. Baisan, A. C. Caprio, P. M. Brown, R. Touchan, R. S. Anderson, and D. J. Hallett. 2009. "Multi-millennial Fire History of the Giant Forest, Sequoia National Park, California, USA." *Fire Ecology* 5 (3): 120–150.

Tomlinson, P. B., and T. Takaso. 2002. "Seed Cone Structure in Conifers in Relation to Development and Pollination: A Biological Approach." *Canadian Journal of Botany* 80 (12): 1250–1273.

Tripp, K. E. 1995. "*Cephalotaxus*: The Plum Yews." *Arnoldia* 55 (1): 25–39.

Tsukada, M. 1982. "*Cryptomeria japonica*: Glacial Refugia and Late-Glacial and Postglacial Migration." *Ecology* 63 (4): 1091–1105.

Tsumura, Y., K. Uchiyama, Y. Moriguchi, M. K. Kimura, S. Ueno, and T. Ujino-Ihara. 2014. "Genetic Differentiation and Evolutionary Adaptation in *Cryptomeria japonica*." *G3: Genes, Genomes, Genetics* 4:2389–2402.

Van Pelt, R. 1996. *Champion Trees of Washington State.* Seattle: University of Washington Press.

Van Pelt, R. 2001. *Forest Giants of the Pacific Coast.* Seattle: University of Washington Press.

Van Pelt, R. 2007. *Identifying Mature and Old Forests in Western Washington.* Olympia: Washington State Department of Natural Resources.

Walsh, C., and J. O. Dawson. 2014. "Variation in Buttressing Form and Stem Volume Ratio of Baldcypress Trees." *Transactions of the Illinois State Academy of Science* 107:5–11.

Wang, W. P., C. Y. Hwang, T. P. Lin, and S. Y. Hwang. 2003. "Historical Biogeography and Phylogenetic Relationships of the Genus *Chamaecyparis* (Cupressaceae) Inferred from Chloroplast DNA Polymorphism." *Plant Systematics and Evolution* 241:13–28.

Warren, R., and E. W. Johnson. 1988. "A Guide to the Firs (*Abies* spp.) of the Arnold Arboretum." *Arnoldia* 48 (1): 2–48.

Weatherspoon, C. P. 1990. "*Sequoiadendron giganteum* (Lindl.) Bucholz Giant Sequoia." In *Silvics of North America*, vol. 1, *Conifers*, technical coordinators R. M. Burns and B. H. Honkala. Washington, DC: USDA Forest Service.

Wilhite, L. P., and J. R. Toliver. 1990. "*Taxodium distichum* (L.) Rich. Baldcypress." In *Silvics of North America*, vol. 1, *Conifers*, technical coordinators R. M. Burns and B. H. Honkala. Washington, DC: USDA Forest Service.

Williams, C. G. 2009. *Conifer Reproductive Biology.* London: Springer.

Woodford, J. 2005. *The Wollemi Pine.* Melbourne: Text Publishing.

Wulf, Andrea. 2010. *The Brother Gardeners: Botany, Empire and the Birth of an Obsession.* New York: Random House.

Yasue, M., K. Ogiyama, S. Suto, H. Tsukahara, F. Miyahara, and K. Ohba. 1987. "Geographical Differentiation of Natural *Cryptomeria* Stands Analyzed by Diterpene Hydrocarbon Constituents of Individual Trees." *Journal of the Japanese Forestry Society* 69 (4): 152–156.

Yazawa, T. 1979. "Monsoons and Japanese Life." *GeoJournal* 3:153–160.

Index

S

Sargent's juniper. See *Juniperus chinensis* var. *sargentii*

savin juniper. See *Juniperus sabina*

sawara-cypress. See *Chamaecyparis pisifera*

Sciadopityaceae (Japanese umbrella-pine family), 30, 37, 40, 43, 295–297

Sciadopitys (Japanese umbrella-pine genus), 30, 43

Sciadopitys verticillata (Japanese umbrella-pine), 169, 295–297

'Sternschnuppe', 295–296

Scots pine. See *Pinus sylvestris*

seaside juniper. See *Juniperus maritima*

seedlings

of deodar cedar, 26, 84–85

of Douglas-fir, 26, 149

of grand fir, 27, 73–74

of incense-cedar, 26, 175–177

of Port-Orford-cedar, 26, 188–189

of shore pine, 26

of western hemlock, 152

Sequoia (coast redwood genus), 28, 30, 43, 164, 265–269, **271**

Sequoia sempervirens (coast redwood), 168–169, 224, 265–269, **271**, 275

'Prostrata', 269

Sequoiadendron (giant sequoia genus), 28, 30, 42, 164, 224–227, **229**

Sequoiadendron giganteum (giant sequoia), 220–221, 224–227, **229**

'Pendulum', 227, **229**

Serbian spruce. See *Picea omorika*

shoot dimorphism, 47, 82, 94

shore juniper. See *Juniperus rigida* ssp. *conferta*

shore pine. See *Pinus contorta* var. *contorta*

Siberian larch. See *Larix sibirica*

Sierra lodgepole pine. See *Pinus contorta* var. *murrayana*

single-leaf pinyon pine. See *Pinus monophylla*

single-seed juniper. See *Juniperus squamata*

Sitka spruce. See *Picea sitchensis*

smooth Arizona cypress. See *Cupressus arizonica* var. *glabra*

soft pines, 122

Spanish fir. See *Abies pinsapo*

species longevity, 253

spruce genus. See *Picea*

staghorn-cedar. See *Thujopsis dolabrata*

staghorn-cedar genus. See *Thujopsis*

stinking-cedar genus. See *Torreya*

stomata

definition of, 11

in cypress family, 167–168

in pine family, 48–49

Strobus (subgenus), 115, 117, 119, 121–122

subalpine fir. See *Abies lasiocarpa*

subalpine larch. See *Larix lyallii*